Better Homes and Gardens®

Decorating the
American Home

Meredith® Books
Des Moines, Iowa

Contents

Design Principles

The building blocks of home decorating

Room by Room

Fresh ideas for every space

Better Homes and Gardens®
Decorating the American Home
Editor: Paula Marshall
Contributing Writer: Mitchell Owens
Contributing Graphic Designers: John Jensen, Chad Johnston, On-Purpos, Inc.
Copy Chief: Terri Fredrickson
Publishing Operations Manager: Karen Schirm
Senior Editor, Asset & Information Management: Phillip Morgan
Edit and Design Production Coordinator: Mary Lee Gavin
Editorial Assistant: Kaye Chabot
Book Production Managers: Pam Kvitne, Marjorie J. Schenkelberg,
    Rick von Holdt, Mark Weaver
Contributing Copy Editor: Jane Woychick
Contributing Proofreaders: Becky Etchen, Nancy Ruhling
Cover Photographer: Bill Holt
Contributing Indexer: Kathleen Poole
Contributing Illustrator: John Jensen, On-Purpos, Inc.

Meredith® Books
Executive Director, Editorial: Gregory H. Kayko
Executive Director, Design: Matt Strelecki
Managing Editor: Amy Tincher-Durik
Senior Editor/Group Manager: Vicki Leigh Ingham
Marketing Product Manager: Steve Rogers

Publisher and Editor in Chief: James D. Blume
Editorial Director: Linda Raglan Cunningham
Executive Director, Marketing: Steve Malone
Executive Director, New Business Development: Todd M. Davis
Executive Director, Sales: Ken Zagor
Director, Operations: George A. Susral
Director, Production: Douglas M. Johnston
Director, Marketing: Amy Nichols
Business Director: Jim Leonard

Vice President and General Manager: Douglas J. Guendel

Home Tours

Inspiration by the houseful

Workshops

Better Homes and Gardens® Magazine
Deputy Editor, Home Design: Oma Blaise Ford

Meredith Publishing Group
President: Jack Griffin
Executive Vice President: Bob Mate

Meredith Corporation
Chairman and Chief Executive Officer: William T. Kerr
President and Chief Operating Officer: Stephen M. Lacy

In Memoriam: E.T. Meredith III (1933–2003)

What's old is new again: The fabric on the cover of this book is from the new *Better Homes and Gardens®* Carnivale fabric collection. It's almost an exact match for the fabric featured on the cover of the 1956 edition.

Portions of this book are excerpted from the *Better Homes and Gardens® Decorating book*, 1st edtion, published in 1956, and the *Better Homes and Gardens® New Decorating Book*, 8th Edition, published in 2003

All of us at Meredith® Books are dedicated to providing you with information and ideas to enhance your home. We welcome your comments and suggestions. Write to us at: Meredith Books, Home Decorating and Design Editorial Department, 1716 Locust St., Des Moines, IA 50309-3023.

It's Déjà Vu
all over again!

The more things change, the more they stay the same. For 50 years, this book has provided the best home decorating advice.

Similarities between the very first *Better Homes and Gardens®* *Decorating Book* and the current edition are striking: While so much has changed in style, little has changed in the guiding principles you use to decorate your home. It's a déjà vu moment that happens as you look through both books. In this special edition, those timeless design principles—from selecting color to arranging furniture to using accessories—are drawn from the first edition, complete with the photos and sketches first used in 1956. Enjoy the

Colors and styles shift and combine in new ways with every new edition.

Better Homes & Gardens
DECORATING BOOK
Complete how-to help for decorating your home
432 pages, over 300 full color illustrations

new decorating book
Better Homes and Gardens.

Sleek lines, groupings that welcome, and of course comfort span the editions.

decorating lessons along with a trip down memory lane. And you might be surprised just how many elements from these "nostalgic" rooms are found in homes today.

Speaking of modern homes, the book switches gears to the 2003 edition for room-by-room examples and home tours to inspire your decorating plans for your 21st century rooms. The time-tested principles of color, furniture arrangement, and the rest come to life in contemporary spaces. And to help you make the smartest decisions, workshop information on fabrics and furnishings rounds out the book.

Enjoy Your Decorating

The introduction from the 1956 edition expressed the enduring philosophy behind the best home decorating books:

"The new Better Homes and Gardens Decoring Book *can help you plan a home that comes nearest to your hopes and means. Each chapter of the book approaches in a personal and practical way one of the many problems confronted in everyday decorating. The text speaks simply, and the illustrations say so much that you will be able to find your own solution to these problems.*

This book... has complete information to make every home functional and individual, personally satisfying, and beautiful."

We began this book with the goal of celebrating the rich tradition of 50 years and eight editions of the *Better Homes and Gardens Decorating Book*. Along the way, we were reminded how much fun decorating can and should be. We hope you're inspired by these pages. Within them, you'll find ways to add comfort, convenience and style and, perhaps, a bit more joy to your home.

The Editors

50 Years of American Decorating

by Mitchell Owens

The decorating process always starts in the same place: with a room. Even empty of furnishings, every room is filled with promise. And whether it's in the cramped confines of a high-rise apartment or the generous square footage of a suburban McMansion, that room is generally a rectangle. Each room comes equipped with at least one door and one window. Unfurnished, the room patiently waits for you to provide the elements that transform emptiness into an *environment*: fabrics and furbelows, knickknacks and sofas, carpets and clocks. Art will be hung on the walls, and flowers arranged in vases set on tables or perhaps ferns in pretty pots set near a window. Only then will that lonely room graduate from basic shelter to home; that's when it becomes your room, its function defined and your style expressed.

The basic process may be similar for every room, but as the history of interior decoration bears colorful witness, the end result for any individual space is anybody's guess. Styles have shifted from passé to popular and back again, powered by cultural whims and persuasive marketing campaigns, invigorated by potent trends.

In the past decade or so, the imperious nature of trends has greatly diminished, not only releasing us from arbitrary structure but also greatly increasing the availability of well-designed items in every style and price range. Today your rooms can embrace sleek minimalism (white walls, accessory-free tabletops, poetically spare floors) or be submerged in aristocratic elegance (dense patterns, homey clutter, moody pools of light) without fearing judgment from some domestic doyenne who, ironically, will never cross your threshold. And you can afford to create that room within a reasonable budget. To get to this point of design freedom, however, decorating started with more rigid rules and, most recently, five decades of design experimentation.

Where It All Started

As a mainstream activity, American decorating started at the beginning of the 20th century. In 1905 Elsie de Wolfe, an American actress better known for the cut of her clothes than the eloquence of her acting, launched a new career and was the first interior designer to become a household name. Her words were repeated and her designs copied across the country. Throughout the years, much of the advice given by high-end designers has had practical application for any home decorator.

In the century since, decorating one's home has become a global phenomenon, a cultural imperative. There has been no shortage of design mavens and decorating dictators to fill Ms. de Wolfe's shoes. And there's been no shortage of media coverage. Magazines offer glossy monthly glimpses inside inspirational houses around the world. Newspapers cover the subject of design on a weekly basis, reporting on the latest furniture, innovative fabrics, and must-have accessories. The quest for good design fuels do-it-yourself books, videos, cable television shows, and more recently, Internet blogs. Each of them is built on the premise that a well-loved room is an essential part of a well-lived life. Given the alternative, who's to argue?

The physical elements that create a room remain the same, though often significantly altered and much improved—and always evolving. New fabrics have been printed, new materials developed. Sofa arms morph from artfully angular to romantically rolled, depending on popular taste. Televisions slimmed down from bulky behemoths to sleek wall-hung panels. Thanks to high-tech windows that keep foul weather at bay, curtains evolved from quilt-heavy (to keep a drafty room warm) to feather-sheer (to welcome the sun).

THE 1950s

In the cliché of American men and women navigating the suburbs of America in the 1950s, the home was the centerpiece of a brave new postwar world, as peaceful as it was prosperous. In that scenario, the average home was aesthetically bland, a residential equivalent of a gray flannel suit. If the family homes depicted on shows such as *Leave It to Beaver* or *The Adventures of Ozzie And Harriet* were accurate, America's ideal home was outfitted with maple bedroom suites, picture windows framed with frilled organdy curtains, and a kitchen table tucked into a breakfast nook.

But that's the problem with clichés—they only tell one side of a story, and even home decorating is multifaceted. Far from being the seamless landscape depicted on television, America in the 1950s was as varied on the home front as always: People had individual tastes and budgets.

One thing many Americans wanted in the postwar years was modernity. The styles popular before World War II represented the past. GIs returning to big cities and small towns were seeking a fresh start in a world of sparkling surfaces they could buy with their steady paychecks. Their optimism was reflected in the products: Stoves and refrigerators had as much chrome as the tail-finned car in the driveway. They subscribed to magazines that promoted a break with the aesthetic past and set up revolving charge accounts at furniture stores with product lines and displays promising a bright future. Those stores featured unexpected pairings of sleek modern furniture with antiques or reproductions and redefined interior decoration as a popular pursuit achievable in any home by anyone with a sense of adventure.

By the mid-1950s, the ideal American home was no longer a Cape Cod cottage with a white picket fence. Instead, suburbs were becoming residential paradises of ranch houses and split-levels. Big picture windows and sunny expanses of sliding glass doors were influenced by California's famous modernist Case Study houses. Free-form swimming pools and undulating gardens reflected the revolutionary work of the landscape architect Thomas Church. Style indoors was dominated by futuristic design characterized by low-slung sofas, hi-fi cabinets, and wall clocks shaped like supernova starbursts.

Modern, however, was not just sleek and space-age. Beyond the bent-plywood populism, wasp-waisted white Saarinen tables, and boomerang silhouettes, many forward-thinking homeowners were making room for side chairs that looked suspiciously like potato chips with chrome-plated metal legs and hanging curtains made of colorful handwoven fabrics with earthy, almost primitive textures. A scholar could call the 1950s "the decade

From the 1950s on, the appreciation of the globe as a grab bag of decorative inspiration grew. Rather than aping French, English, or Italian period interiors, a hallmark of American interior design in the early 20th century, smart young homeowners opened their eyes. They appreciated the mixmaster chic and air of well-traveled worldliness that a varied decor could provide. Billy Baldwin, one of the most important American decorators of the postwar period, declared, "A mixture of styles and periods and nationalities is what we want today. All rooms should be contemporary, a mixture of the antique and the modern." The home you love should reflect the rich heritage of the multifaceted world you live in.

of the parabola," but notable pockets of resistance echoed style preferences to come. Some people in the neighborhood were exploring less radical, though equally popular, avenues of interior decoration, many of them rooted firmly in the past.

There was a strong contingent of American homeowners in the 1950s who subscribed to an aspirational country-club look that included plaid-covered wing chairs, wallpaper patterned with thoroughbred horses endlessly leaping over white wood fences, and fieldstone fireplaces with shining brass tools. (The sprawling house known as Upson Downs in the high-design movie *Auntie Mame* was a prime example of this faux estate look.) Brand-new furniture adapted from Colonial American models, from Windsor chairs to Chippendale-style coffee tables, reflected slower, presumably more wholesome days, allowing a new generation of Americans to greet the future while maintaining a connection with the country's roots. This was their antidote to the functional modernity of Scandinavian-style design of the modernist movement.

Fashionable homeowners of the era who maintained a more international frame of mind—including a newlywed named Jacqueline Kennedy, who had set up housekeeping in a 19th-century brick townhouse in Washington, D. C.—found their comfort amid the timeless elegance of the neoclassic French styles popular during the reigns of Louis XV and Louis XVI, a taste that continues unabatedly popular to the present day.

Two centuries and a more technologically advanced world later, however, the traditional aristocratic shapes of the ancien régime often were being upholstered in sassy patterned fabrics that gave the venerable silhouettes a spirit of fresh-faced optimism. It was a typically American take on historical decoration, where veneration made way for reinvention.

THE 1960s That sense of ease combined with refinement became stronger in the 1960s, a decade of increasingly cheerful, clean-lined rooms where antiques shook off their antiquarian airs. They sat in the company of glossy white woodwork and wall-to-wall carpets woven with colorful geometric patterns. Crisp printed cotton fabrics overtook artisanal weaves in the popularity sweepstakes, and the lush colors pioneered a decade earlier became clearer, stronger, more intense. These colors and patterns were inspired by the graphic paintings of European artists such as Henri Matisse. Even rooms with a historicist spirit became brighter and bolder, thanks to the brilliantly colored interiors such as the restored Red Room at the White House arguably the most famous room of the decade and one whose startlingly intense color scheme quickly trickled down into mainstream America.

Following the example of interior design magazines, trend-conscious American homeowners began to keep tabletop accessories to an eloquent minimum. And they thought nothing of hanging an elaborately framed antique painting above a modern lacquered Parsons console table. They became enthusiastic devotees of a gospel of domestic style that was composed of equal parts ease and orderliness, luxury and humbleness, fantasy and common sense.

Sister Parish, the New York interior decorator who created private rooms for President John F. Kennedy and his young family at the White House, once claimed that "All decoration is about memories." That statement wasn't just sentimental twaddle. What the undisputed grande dame of American decorating meant was simple. All rooms have influences—some superficial, others deep—and the more personal those layers, the more spiritually fulfilling the space. Those echoes deepen the character of any decorating scheme, making every space you inhabit truly, unmistakably yours.

As a movement, it could have been christened Practical Posh. Inexpensive denim or cotton duck upholstery, perfectly tailored, became more highly prized than costly French silks. Rough-woven wicker trays began showing up on 18th-century French desks, appreciated as much for their low cost as for the unexpected way the humble material gave its stately ancien regime partner a youthful kick in the aesthetic pants. Fabrics long defined as precious, such as silk velvet, were revived through reverse-chic uses, such as upholstery on a simple banquette. A development that became known as the *tablescape* became de rigueur as creative homeowners combined similarly colored objects—a bowl, a tile, a vase of fresh flowers, a chunk of marble—into artful still lifes ensconced on side tables.

The 1960s' obvious charms were fresh colors, modern art, crisp upholstery, and period furniture, such as a folding Chinese screen or a Louis XVI armchair, utilized as sensuous and occasionally surprising accents. These quickly were adopted by homeowners eager to live in rooms that spoke of the present without being too coldly, cruelly modern. Patchwork quilts and rag rugs became popular again, although

Color is fun and easy to use

Contrasting colors emphasize

Make the most of handsome architectural features, point up the beauty of a prized chair or sofa, or create an exciting focal point of interest in your room. Colors that contrast boldly and sharply with background will make these features stand out, draw attention to them

Closely blended colors conceal

Want to hide an ugly radiator—or a monstrosity of a fireplace mantel—or the bulky lines of an awkward-looking but comfortable chair? Color them to blend with the wall behind, and they will be hardly noticeable. They will seem to melt out of sight before your eyes

Pale colors recede

The eye accepts pale colors without shock. These tones do not stop the eye, but let it seemingly look past and through. So use pastels and pale tints to make a room look larger. If ceilings are too low, white or light tones will give the room an impression of extra height

Bold colors advance

Bright, strong colors *do* stop the eye, give a feeling of coming toward you. They are good to use on extremely high ceilings, to bring them down into proportion with the furniture. Or square a long and narrow room by painting the end walls a brighter, bolder color

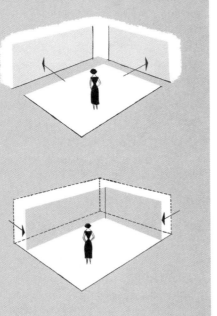

reinterpreted in fresh color combinations such as lime green, chalk white, and cobalt blue. Golden oak furniture of the early 1900s, once despised as the poor man's mahogany, found a new generation of admirers, who coated the dramatically grained wood with shining

white paint. The simple but luxurious look that dominated high-end interiors was modern living at one of its finest moments: not too traditional, not too modern, but obviously, enthusiastically contemporary.

THE 1970s By the late 1960s and into the early 1970s, however, that crisp vocabulary began to be infiltrated by a potent streak of Bohemia. It was, after all, the Age of Aquarius, and the counterculture vibe penetrated decor. Previously outmoded Victorian houses suddenly became desirable among a granola set of postgraduates (and more than a few academics) who were eager to distance themselves from what they saw as the sterile perfection of the past. Porches and parlors were graced with hanging macramé plant hangers, beds covered with inexpensive cotton spreads printed with swirling paisley patterns, and extravagant rattan chairs tucked into those plant-filled corners. The exotic early-20th-century style known as Art Nouveau had a revival at this time as well, its sinuous silhouettes and vaguely predatory undertones an appropriate embodiment of youthful rebellion. It was the decorating equivalent of going to India and finding self-enlightenment among gurus and ashrams. And far cheaper to acquire.

As the 1970s progressed, however, hipper design movements began to bubble. Italian modernism—characterized by graphic furniture made of acrylic or plastic laminate, shining chrome accents, built-in storage, and the occasional surprise accent of a 19th-century table or a Baroque mirror—was one of the leading looks of the day.

Postmodernism also made its way into the mix with witty furnishings that were often cartoon takes on classical styles. The rise of the discotheque in America sparked equally dramatic backgrounds—living rooms lined with Mylar wallpaper, modern art, and Art Deco furniture coated in shimmering layers of lacquer. Even the sedate of style, however, could get a similar dose of urbane glamour with reflective wallpaper in their bathrooms and paving their entrance halls with polished squares of travertine. The 1970s was a decade of feverish experimentation and pendulum-swing styles, an era when all-white rooms vied with spaces crammed with Victorian-style nostalgic collisions of pattern, texture, and color.

desirables were slipcovers, gilded sconces, Georgian armchairs, Persian and Turkish carpets, and gilt-framed portraits that looked like heirlooms but most likely were not. Most, if not all, was quiet on the western decorating front.

Although industrial-style chic and postmodernism both continued to be popular in certain circles, especially in urban areas, the 1980s was inarguably the decade of the historical revival. And that meant preferably the century-spanning jumble of furnishings associated with English country mansions, although Anglo-American country—a tidier, more manicured, homegrown version of the style that was practiced on the other side of the Atlantic—would do in a pinch. It was a look that spoke of solidity, continuity, luxury with comfort, old-fashioned values. This Anglophile movement also marked a subtle but important shift in American taste.

For hundreds of years, the typical American homeowner venerated perfect, immaculate surfaces, whether a painted door or a japanned cabinet. But with the influence of English design on American homes in the 1980s, that pursuit of perfection gave way to an admiration for the worn and distressed, for furniture and accessories suffused with the patina of history. It was the beginning of the admiration for the perfection of imperfection.

THE 1980s Some sort of aesthetic correction happened in the 1980s, signaling a last-call for disco drama. The lights came up, and reality set in. It was a highly refined but equally artificial sense of reality, however, where the stage-set drama of the 1970s met the undercurrent of historicism, long a part of American interior design but recently not on the forefront. America may have cast off the British crown in 1776 in pursuit of a classless society, but little more than 200 years later, an antiques-laden decor that spoke of British country houses, generations of clan stability, and aristocratic bloodlines was suddenly the most desirable of environments.

In seeming reaction to the country's bicentennial celebrations in 1976, as well as to the restoration of Gracie Mansion in New York City and Blair House in Washington, D. C.—not to mention the world-riveting nuptials of the Prince of Wales and Lady Diana Spencer, a bride with American ancestry—it seemed that almost overnight, polished chrome was out, and glazed chintz was in. Also in the list of decorating

THE 1990s TO TODAY The foreign influence on American decorating only deepened in the 1990s. Thanks to the rise of interest in French and particularly Italian cuisine, American kitchens began to sport hand-carved wood cabinets and stone countertops that gave the impression that the owners had spent their formative years deep in the Tuscan countryside, probably in a romantic

Decoratively speaking, there's no reason to meticulously dot every *i* and cross every *t*. Approach the decoration of a room slowly and easily. While it can be difficult to know when to stop adding another fringed cushion to the sofa or another hurricane lantern to the mantel, think twice before over-egging the pudding. "I like a nice, undercooked look," said Mark Hampton, the great American decorator whose Anglo-American country house interiors dominated the 1980s. For him, a fussy, overly detailed space was the definition of stodgy. And that's a fate that no room, modern or traditional, deserves.

villa or farmhouse. Swedish neoclassicism—the humble cousin of 18th-century French palace decor—made small but significant inroads as well, encouraging American homeowners to appreciate blue and white color schemes and discover new charm in painted furniture. It was a lighter, less complicated alternative to the still-desirable English country look, and more attractive to a younger generation whose lifestyles had become even more casual than their parents'.

Today, just a decade later, America's domestic landscape has been turned upside down yet again. Part of this revolution is due to technological achievements, including the Internet, which connects us to the world more intensely than at any other time in our country's history. Fashion influences interior design more quickly than in the past, too, which means that trends and fashions trickle down to the average homeowner with head-spinning velocity. Best of all, however, American consumers have had their eyes opened to the personal style possible in interior design. They understand that it is possible to like modern art, French provincial chairs, and Venetian chandeliers. And that they can combine them into a satisfying interior that looks nothing like their neighbors' houses. If there is a lesson to be learned so early in this new century, it is that personal style is within everyone's reach.

The so-called lady decorators who pioneered the decorating profession, like Ms. de Wolfe and her white-gloved followers, left America with a legacy of well-mannered rooms decorated for proper people with presumably deep pockets—if the blue-chip living rooms featured in the era's magazines were any indication.

The younger generation of decorators and designers who swept in to take their place, on the other hand, appreciated the lessons of their elders but also were determined to create fresh, comfortable rooms that reflected the contemporary world without entirely eschewing the past. For them, it was not enough that a house reflect real or perceived social status; that was the old-fashioned way of decorating rooms as symbols of financial success. Then as now, however, most homeowners just wanted good ideas, lots of them, and the more accessible, the better.

Since its inaugural appearance in 1956, the *Better Homes & Gardens Decorating Book* has been just that: a dependable primer for homeowners looking for up-to-date style combined with commonsense comforts that are achievable. Fifty years later, it's still here to help you create the home you're dreaming about. And the comfort you deserve.

CHAPTER 1

Decorate for

This thoroughly modern midcentury living room would have been the pride and joy of any 1956 homeowner. While styles may change, decorating today should bring the same pride.

the way you live

Truer words were never spoken. Your home should feel welcoming every time you walk through the door, whether you've been gone an hour or a week. You should be comfortable in every room and with every decorating decision. Your house should have a unique personality reflected throughout.

Fifty years ago, the editors of the original *Better Homes and Gardens Decorating Book* understood this bedrock principle of home decorating. Here, from their introduction letter, is what you can expect to get from this book:

"Your home should have more than a pleasant appearance. It should have a pleasant feeling, too... a feeling of welcome, of family warmth, of comfort and convenience. Once you understand the nature of color, space, and design stressed in this book, your home will reflect good planning and radiate a personality only you can give it."

Family-Style Decorating

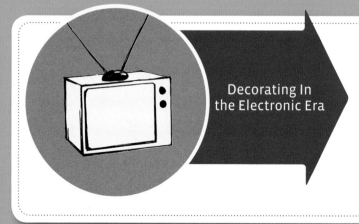

Demographically speaking, there has been quite a shift in what constitutes a household from 1956 to today. The *Leave It to Beaver* household, never as pervasive as presented, now accounts for a small fraction of American households. But many of today's family configurations need the same functional spaces required of that "average" mid-century house. The short list includes a relaxing area to escape from the outside world, a place to engage in hobbies or other activities, a spot for taking care of business (at least of the household variety), and plenty of space for children's activities.

Successful decorating is the art of creating convenience and function in stylish spaces. So start your decorating plan with an overview of household activities: Note what everyone in your home requires of their individual spaces and of communal spaces. Consider how those needs can be accommodated as you decorate.

Junior wants a wide-open space to play and gay colors

Decorating In the Electronic Era

In the 1950s, proper placement of the hi-fi and a modest-size television set in one room was the extent of accommodating home electronics. *How quaint is that!*

Today almost every room requires a nod to electronics—from a baby monitor in the nursery to a water-tolerant TV in the bathroom.

Consider placement and power needs up front or you'll surely be struggling with power cords or squeezing in a screen later.

The original editors knew that new technology TV was here to stay. See pages 70-71 for more of their sage advice.

Mother wants a beautiful home to express her personality

Father needs a quiet spot to rest after a tough work day

The family roles described here are more than a little narrow and dated, but expressing personal style, creating a respite from the world, and giving kids room to play are still important.

Modern

Traditional

Modern or Traditional?

Funny how the rooms called modern or contemporary in the original edition are called "retro" today. Some of those furnishings even have been elevated to "classic"—a term once strictly reserved for traditional pieces.

Style lines have blurred and blended significantly since the mid-1950s. You can now find the formerly fusty, French-inspired Louis-the-whatever chairs available in über-modern polycarbonate. Such changes provide a lovely way to add traditional style pieces to contemporary spaces, or vice versa.

Unless every item in a room was bought together right off the showroom floor, chances are the room is not one style. So whatever your style preference, think of it as a guideline. As you shop, you are going to see a lot of things you like but that won't work in your rooms. Use your style preference as the anchor for all your choices: Will this (chair, color, lamp, rug, et cetera) fit in with the other pieces?

Traditional

Wing chairs express an affinity for the charms of comfortable Colonial and traditional style.

It's a Big
Style World
After All

1956 predates the "mass market retailer" and the explosion of styles available everywhere. Stating the obvious, you couldn't enter such a store and purchase home furnishings in African Bazaar or even French Country styles. So the original edition focused on the modern and traditional styles readily available at department and furniture stores of the day.

Fast-forward to today: Choice is good, but so many styles can be overwhelming.

Ease anxiety by adding fresh influences sparingly at first. The styles may not be perfectly harmonious. Good design, however, does pretty much go with good design: After all, the classic upright piano and Rick's white tuxedo jacket fit in perfectly well against the exotic Moroccan backdrop of Casablanca.

Pastel colors and lots of ruffles, often in floral prints, set the sentimental tone for a pretty cottage room.

Clean lines with a minimum of ornamentation are the marks of modern furniture. Lots of color and curves add interest to the style.

Modern

19

Informal

Formal or Informal

Please pardon the presumption, but the formal/informal distinction crosses into lifestyle as much as decorating style. It relates to how you live in your house. Formal decorating is for people who like straightforward room composition, everything neatly placed in their rooms. Informal is for the rest of us.

The term "formal" often conjures up the image of rigid adherence to placement, used in rooms that were pretty much untouchable and most often decorated in very traditional styles. Perhaps a more realistic approach for the present day is to think of decorating on a scale of informal style. A state of orderly informality is an achievable goal, whereas creating a formal room and keeping it formal is about as likely as a visit from aliens.

If you still yearn to create rooms with formal appeal, consider the minimalist approach. Minimize the amount of stuff in a room; whether you choose traditional or modern keep it all high-caliber—then any room can be both formal and low-maintenance.

"A formal home reflects an orderly way of life." Today this thinking applies as much to modern style as it does to traditional; it's all about how you live in your rooms.

An Orderly Fashion

If you desire a more formal room, one way to achieve the look is to buy the major pieces at the same time, even if you buy them from different places.

Look at the two rooms on this page. Although the major pieces in the "Formal" room have some variation, there's a lot of similarity in them. In the "Informal" room, the pieces look as though they've been accumulated over time. Even with a decorating plan in hand, when you buy over time your perspective will shift enough to affect your choices. What's available changes too. Buying everything at once gives you the consistency desired in formal rooms.

Formal

Informal

Material World

Maintenance was a key defining factor in the formal/informal distinction: Anything easy-clean was informal; anything that needed more care was formal. And designs for furniture pretty much matched: Plain laminate tables with vinyl-seat chairs were for informal kitchen meals, and carved oak "sets" were for formal meals in the dining room.

Manufacturers got wise and now make many furnishings that stand up to the aggressive wear-and-tear of daily life with the look of expensive untouchables. Laminate wood flooring and stain-resistant fabrics are only two examples.

Today you'll find almost indestructible surfaces on every style of furniture and you can create an easy-to-maintain room in just about any style.

Mixing It Up

Even though people nowadays often don't follow a particular style (one of the buzzwords in home decorating styles is *eclectic*), really mixing up styles is sometimes thought of as akin to decorating calculus: You practically need a doctorate in decor to figure out how to get it right.

If re-creating the feel of a well-blended room you've seen seems about as doable as dancing like Fred and Ginger, relax; the secrets are not nearly so complicated. Think more *Dancing with the Stars*—a couple of lessons to learn the basics and you're on your way.

First establish a basic color scheme for the room. Choose items of most any style that are in the hues of your color palette or complementing neutrals. In this room, for example, lots of warm wood and neutral tones make the red and blue accessories pop. And the two main seating pieces, sofa and lounge chair, are in similar colors and situated across from each other to visually anchor the room.

The key: Know your comfort level with mixing styles. To prevent a style mishmash, make one style dominant and add only a few things in other styles. Spread outré items around the room so you're not creating little style shrines.

Remember, the eye you're working to please is your own.

Look at only the furniture in this room (for a moment, ignore the accessories) and this room could be 21st century. OK, maybe that coffee table really ought to go...

Even if it isn't *Antiques Roadshow*-worthy, your family items and travel treasures should find a place in your decorating plan. Those things make you smile or give you a warm feeling every day, making your home unlike anyone else's. So style be darned! Find a place for Aunt Matilda's crewelwork, the battered table that every child for three generations has used for doing homework, and that carved plaque your husband found in Mexico. Remember: You don't have to put it in the middle of the living room and you don't have to design a whole room around it—But if you do put it in plain sight, just think of all the conversations it will start!

Snappy yellows, crisp whites, and solid blacks give this room a sharp look. So while the styles have changed, the appeal of a good color combination lives on.

CHAPTER 2

Color

The hues of style come and go, but the challenge of finding just the right colors is an eternal issue for home decorators. The original edition of the *Better Homes and Gardens New Decorating Book* bears out the point: Nearly 100 pages in two chapters are devoted to the topic. Here's some timeless advice on the basics of color in the context of decorating.

Facts About Color

Designers like to say color can add a visual tension that makes a room interesting. But the tension really can peak long before color is chosen—when you're standing in front of a wall of paint chips, a rack of upholstery swatches, or a table stacked with wallpaper sample books. Breathe deeply, and begin with the basics. With an understanding of color essentials, you'll not only be confident when selecting colors, you'll be mixing swatches up in no time.

Just about every big decorating book shows the color wheel; it's a good way to become familiar with colors and their relationships. The definition between colors and the rings of intensity on this old-fashioned color wheel make it easy to see the change between hue and the effect of saturation (from pale to deep) within a color. Try creating a few basic color palettes to see whether you like the outcome. Start with one color in several shades, then try three different colors, and finally step out into the wide world of options.

How deep you want to go into color mixing, blending, and theory is a personal choice. The key is to learn what you need to create a room that pleases your eye and gives the feeling you're after.

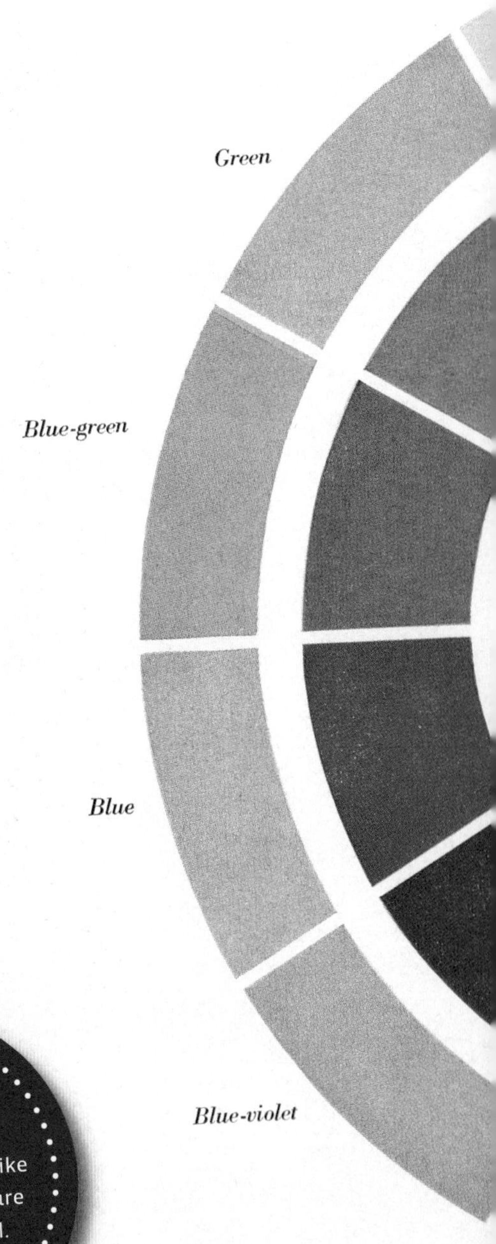

Green

Blue-green

Blue

Blue-violet

Cool
These colors are dominated by blue. Like sky and water, they are cooling and restful.

ow-green

Yellow

Yellow-orange

Basic Color Terms

- Blue, red, and yellow are the *primary* colors. These are pure colors that can't be created by mixing other colors.

- Orange, green, and violet (or purple) are *secondary* colors. They're created by mixing equal amounts of primary colors.

- All the hyphenated colors—yellow-orange, blue-green, and so on—are called *tertiary* colors. Mix a primary with its closest secondary color to get these tones.

Colors also can affect a room's sense of temperature. Red, yellow, and orange tones are called *warm* colors. Blue, violet, and green are considered *cool*. However, take a dab of color from across the wheel and you can change a color's temp: A little yellow warms up green; a drop of blue cools red.

Orange

Red-orange

Red

Violet

Red-violet

Color Rules!

The founding editors had one thing right: You only need to know a few simple rules to understand how color works; use these nine pointers to become a color expert. Color really is that straightforward, but balancing the importance of each rule can overwhelm. As you read, think about what you want color to do in a room: Shout or whisper? Blend elements together or define each piece? Use the "rules" to help you understand how color can work for you.

The first two rules refer to color intensity: It's often the strength of color that gives home decorators pause.

RULE 1: Pale Colors Recede

Light colors don't readily catch the eye, giving a sense of spaciousness to a room. Using light colors to create rooms with an open, airy feeling became especially popular with contemporary architecture. And the original editors wisely predicted, "The light look is here to stay." As with bold colors, balance is the key. All light rooms feel as though they're floating; add a few dark pieces of furniture and accessories to keep the room anchored. Textures and simple patterns are another way to add interest in a light-tone room; their subtlety isn't overwhelmed by the color.

RULE 2: **Bold Colors Advance**

Strong, saturated colors can stop the eye and make you feel as though they are coming toward you. Use them to reshape rooms or emphasize an element in a space. And think beyond solid colors. The brightly colored wallpaper here brings the wall closer, while the white wall next to it is almost unnoticeable by comparison. A yellow table like this is another way to add a burst of color. The strength of these colors is in their contrast because too much bold color can feel heavy and overwhelming.

My, How Times Have Changed

Bold colors' advancing nature has long made them taboo for small rooms and ceilings. Often bold colors were relegated to a single item or to one feature, such as a door.

Perhaps the prevalence of flat white ceilings and beige walls wrapping American rooms inspired designers to take up the cause of bold colors for ceilings and small rooms, a trend you may have noticed in magazines and decorating books.

If you're thinking of using a bold color for a large space, consider how often you'll be looking at that color every day.

An abundance of bright bold colors can almost vibrate. Uninterrupted fire-engine red, for example, could be toned down a notch and be a great choice.

Dark bold colors absorb a lot of light, making a room seem perpetually in shadow. Add extra lighting and use white lampshades to extend the available wattage. Light bold colors can reflect a lot of light; flat paint and soft lightbulbs help tame the tone.

The strong contrast between the dark walls and light furniture on this page is punctuated by the white fireplace mantel. Compare this to the smooth flow of color between the elements on the opposite page. It's the difference between drama and dreaminess.

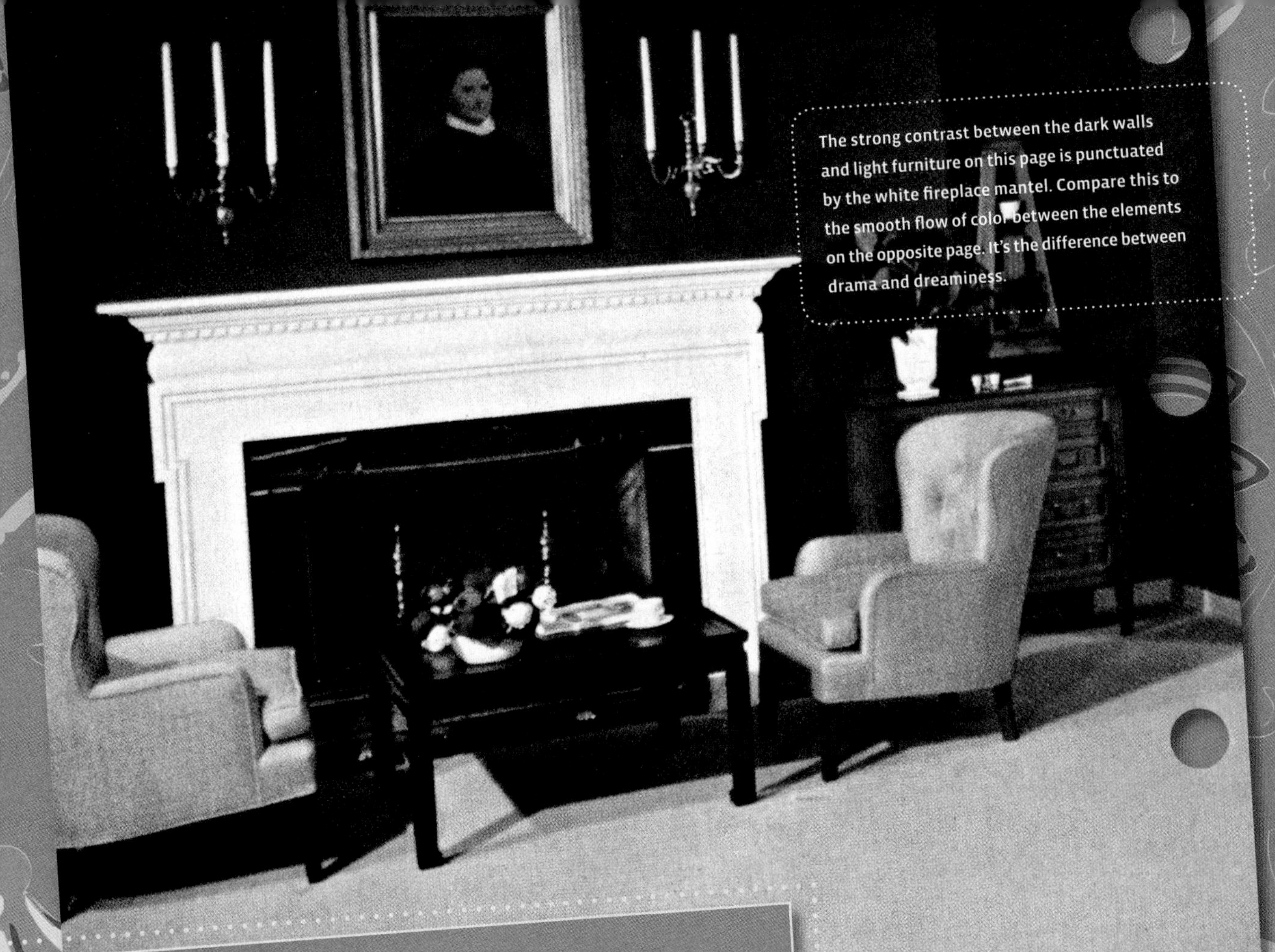

Contrast or Blend

Rules 3 and 4 constitute The Basic Theory of Color Relativity: Any single color either stands out or blends in based on the color next to it. So check out the color neighbors when evaluating a hue.

Contrast creates emphasis and drama; blending blurs the edges for a smooth look. These vintage photos show how very differently two similar hearthside spaces look when the color palettes are contrasting or blended.

Rooms with blended colors can create ease for the eyes, and blended color rooms are often done in muted tones. This is a good choice for take-me-away spaces such as adults' bedrooms and baths; think of today's spa-look spaces.

In rooms with more contrast in color, at least one color is often a saturated tone. The effect is vibrant and stimulating. Kitchens and kids' rooms are lively spaces that benefit from that spark of color and contrast.

It's a Washout

Consider color relationship for all items in a room. Deep blue rugs over pale hardwood floors, for example, grab attention. If the walls are a neutral tone, slipcover the sofa in blue and paint bookshelves blue or add deep blue artwork, vases, and other accessories. The blue waves up from the floor throughout the room.

RULE 3: Closely Blended Colors Conceal

Want to hide an ugly radiator—or a monstrosity of a fireplace mantel—or the bulky lines of an awkward-looking but comfortable chair? Color them to blend with the wall behind, and they will be hardly noticeable. They will seem to melt out of sight before your eyes

RULE 4: Contrasting Colors Emphasize

Make the most of handsome architectural features, point up the beauty of a prized chair or sofa, or create an exciting focal point of interest in your room. Colors that contrast boldly and sharply with background will make these features stand out, draw attention to them

Some Colors Are Cool, Some Are Warm

Coolness is suggested by blues and greens, the colors of water and trees. Use them in sunny rooms and on hot-weather porches. But these are also the colors of ice and snow, and will seem cold and dreary unless warmed with cheery accents and accessories.

Warmth is suggested by red, orange, yellow—the friendly colors of sunshine and glowing hearth. Sunless rooms welcome these. In concentrated form they recall the savage fury of desert sun and uncontrolled fire. Use these in small quantities, for drama.

Examine the color wheel on pages 26–27 and it's clear which colors fall on which side of the temperature scale.

All the color rules are based on the effects of color; the list simply formalizes what your eyes see and how they respond. Rule 5 on color temperature may be the most obvious; many people actually respond to a room's color, feeling warm or cool when they walk in.

Think of the colors you're drawn to and how the room will be used to select a "room temperature." Warm colors are energizing and work well in high-activity rooms. Cool colors are relaxing, making them well-suited to rooms where you might want to escape from the hubbub of daily life.

Also, like a parka in winter or a cool breeze in summer, include at least one moderating color for your room. You can achieve this shift without necessarily introducing colors from the other side of the color wheel. Greens with a hint of yellow lean toward the warmer side of the spectrum; reds with a splash of violet run cooler than the rest of the reds. Dab these colors around the room to soothe the eye.

Wood is a color

You've developed a color plan that contains all the elements of your room—paints and papers, slipcover, upholstery and drapery fabrics, carpeting. But wait—there's one important piece missing. *Wood is a color, too.*

Consider what a large part of your color areas is in wood finishes—in the living room, in larger quantities in the bedroom, and in the dining room or dining area.

You select the colors of these woods just as you choose any other color for the room. First, establish the basic plan, around the things you must keep, or with the things you intend to buy in mind. Then get down to specifics—the tones and shades to go in each place, on each piece. If the room is to be done in light tones in the background, with brighter ones for upholstery, you will probably want the contrast of dark woods in tables and in chairs.

If the basic color theme is somewhat dark, then you will probably prefer lighter woods, so that the pieces will show off against the background. If your colors are medium values, then either very dark or very light woods will contrast.

Don't try to match all the woods in one room. The effect will be much more pleasing if the finishes and the woods themselves vary a little. They should blend with each other, however, and be consistent to the basic color scheme. And don't overlook the potency of one contrasting piece to accent and underscore the others.

Wood tones are, generally speaking, shades of tan or brown with lots of warmth. But that is a broad range of color, and pieces that have been stained usually enhance a wood's natural undertones. For example, mahogany stain brings out the red tones of the wood. Opaque stains can add any color you wish to include without eliminating the wood's attractive grain pattern.

Consider wood's many tones as you decorate. If you have several pieces of wood in a room and each one is from a different species of wood, you could be surprised by what that does to your careful color scheming.

Wood is a Color

The caramel color of the wood dining set and carpet is warm and inviting. The contrasting white walls and blue upholstery give the room a cool, relaxed feeling. The room is a good example of how wood works in a space to anchor the color choices.

Here's a color rule, No. 6, that has been lost in the passage of time, but one that really ought to be stated clearly in decorating books. A poorly chosen coffee table can be the white elephant in the room no one's talking about, and a problem easily avoided. Just think of wood colors in general terms: light or dark, warm or cool.

Large Areas of Color Are More Intense

This rule, No. 7, was likely developed to warn against the dreaded Swatch Syndrome or Post-Chip Trauma. After finding the most beautiful color in the world on a paint chip, the unsuspecting homeowner drives home with gallons of High-Intensity Yellow to paint the living room—see dismayed cutout figures at *right, above*. Relationships add to the problem—sample relationships that is. Paint covers a larger proportion of the room; paint chips usually come in a 1x2 or 2x2 sample. Fabric samples are usually much larger. Put them side by side and you'll know whether they create the combination you want, but envisioning them together in a room takes imagination.

Modern technology has the cure. For the computer-savvy, there are dozens of online color sampling programs. Even if the furniture in the examples isn't even close to yours, the effect of the color on the walls should give you a pretty good sense of whether the color is a smart choice before you step up to the paint counter. Then buy a small amount of paint to test on a wall or a sample board. Yes, $2 to $10 for a mini can of paint seems pricey, but it's nothing compared to a full room of Really Wrong Red.

Bold Colors Are Friendly

Scores of books have been written on the psychology of color, so it's no surprise that even in 1956 the original editors dipped their collective paintbrush into the topic. Of course, the result was some pragmatic advice for color choice:

"Everyone has two subconscious and conflicting desires. One, to be free and unconfined; the other, to be warm and friendly and together with a group. Bright, bold colors used as accents and accessories help relate the people in a room to the room itself. Used with large areas of pale colors, both needs are satisfied."

Perhaps that's why even the most subdued color palettes are more inviting when a single bold color is introduced.

In the images *left* and *above,* the intensity of bold color choices is tempered with subtle colors. The styles of the rooms are very different, but both are dramatic.

Unequal Areas of Color Are More Pleasing

Fifties fashion helps illustrate Rule 8. Not only is the dress style unflattering on the figure on the right side, the even split of color is downright boring. The figure on the left in a full-skirted shirtwaist dress not only shows how unequal areas of color are much more visually pleasing, but the relative proportion of good color balance is revealed: The main color should cover about two-thirds of the room including part of the floor, walls, and ceiling. And it doesn't have to be solid color—look at the room *opposite*; the greens are varied and include the wallpaper pattern.

The warm wood tones and cocoa upholstery make up the core of this brown-hued room. The white fireplace and ceiling add the needed contrast. Brass tones in the light fixtures add a sparkling touch to the accessories and elements.

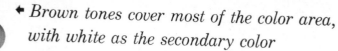

*Brown tones cover most of the color area,
with white as the secondary color*

From the beige floor to the cocoa upholstery fabric, from the warm wood finishes to the honeyed paneling, this subtle scheme is a symphony in brown. It is heightened and emphasized by the secondary color—white, in the brick fireplace wall, the ceiling, dining table top, lamps and accessories. Bright brass and vivid flowers provide the small accents

Green is dominant here, with lavender secondary

Softly feminine colors from a wallpaper set the theme in this guest-sitting room. Walls and carpeting pick up the green background, while secondary areas of couch and chair stem from the lavender motif. Notice how much convenience has been added with built-in storage and clothes closets flanking a window with a ready-made dressing table beneath it

Fear Not Color

Beginning in about 1980 and running through the 1990s, with some spillover even into today, this rule is often completely ignored. And the results can be sad, sad indeed. Often one very neutral color so completely dominates a room that it seems to swallow any other color. "Contrasting" colors are so close they disappear into the beige. Note how lively the colors are in the 1956 edition and be inspired to push your color envelope.

Select One Definite Pattern and
Repeat It – or Not...

A bold print in matching paper and fabric sets the theme here

This color scheme begins with the warm patchwork design of the hall paper and the matching living room slipcovers and draperies. Grayed-green woodwork stems from the pattern, and a brighter tone is in the carpet. Tiny blue note is picked up as the only accent color

Poetic Harmony

Getting all these rules to work together with the colors and patterns you've chosen can seem like a big puzzle. The original editors understood this dilemma, and their solution was a bit of poetry. Here's what they had to say:

"Now, let's add one more good rule for decorating your home. A little poem will help you remember the elements of most well-decorated rooms. Be sure to include something dark; something light; something dull; something bright."

Even the original editors had trouble with this one. Buried in the explanatory copy is the caveat that, yes indeed, you can use more than one pattern in a room. Pattern changes the effect of color. If, like the golfer on the *right*, you use several patterns the effect can be disconcerting. If his slacks were a solid color and his cap were the black-and-white check, the effect would still be bold but not so jarring.

Improvements in printing fabrics and wallpaper have vastly increased pattern choices. You can get a whole heap of options in one pattern grouping from one manufacturer, allowing you to create a personal mix. Start with a basic color choice, then select two or three florals in large and small patterns, and toss in a stripe or check to round out your selection.

You are now free to roam wallpaper pattern books and fabric swatches with reckless abandon. Almost . . .

Fun Fact: How Fashionable!

Current clothing styles and furniture styles often strongly relate to each other. Using fashion to guide decorating is a natural. However, as quickly as fashion fades, that may be a risky proposition. It may have been just as risky in 1956, but it makes for an amusing time capsule of images in the original edition.

CHAPTER 3

Creating

Color Schemes

Another timeless distinction in home decorating advice: Understanding basic color principles is a whole different thing than putting together a color scheme. You can flirt with color principles. However, once you've chosen a color scheme, decorating begins and you're beginning a walk down the aisle to a fully decorated room. While that's bound to make anyone a little anxious, trust your color instincts. From the vantage point of your starting hue, you'll begin to see the full view for decorating one room or your whole home.

All the colors used in this neatly decorated room are drawn from the drapery fabric. The look shows the pleasing effect of using a few coordinated colors.

When the floor covering is going to stay, like this striped tile, choose a few colors from it to use in the room. The neutrals on walls and window treatments complement the background; bright tones add a lively touch.

Sources for Color Schemes

Obvious Advice Alert! The search for life's deeper meaning may require much meditation. The search for the right color to decorate a room does not. A little organized thinking does the trick. Start by selecting your favorite colors from several sources. For example, your favorite color in nature: flowers, a favorite view, or a vacation location. Or choose an appealing hue from a pattern: wallpaper, fabric, or dinnerware. If the flooring—be it carpet, linoleum, area rug, or hardwood—is going to stay, draw a color from that palette to keep the look cohesive. Pay attention to the colors that you're drawn to and the colors in a room's unchanging elements.

Be aware that compromise may be in the air when favorite and fixed colors aren't obviously compatible. Devise a work-around for immovable bath tiles, for example, that aren't anywhere close to your favorite hue. Do a little deep color thinking to disguise or cover up a less-than-desirable color.

Find a picture you like

A large piece of artwork can dominate the room; take advantage of the colors to set the room's tone. For several pieces of artwork with different color palettes, look for shared colors to accent a neutral scheme.

The picture dominates the room, sets its color theme

Notice how the proportions of color in the room are almost exactly those of the picture, giving complete harmony between them. An alternate scheme might use rose-red carpeting and sofa, deep blue chairs, accents of bright blue, rose-pink and red

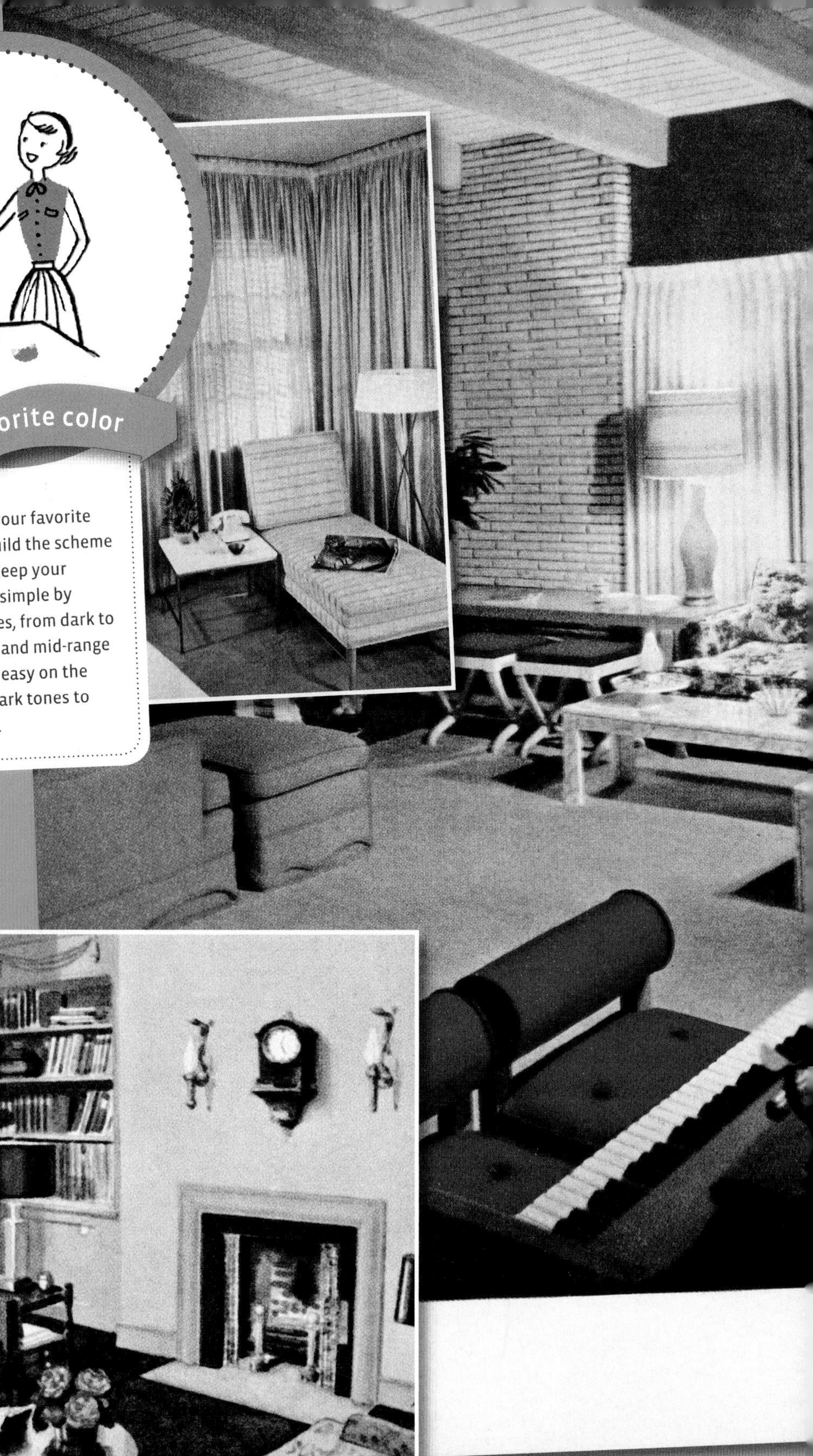

Use your favorite color

Start from your favorite tone and build the scheme around it. Keep your decorating simple by using shades, from dark to light. Light and mid-range shades are easy on the eyes; use dark tones to add punch.

Find a pattern you like

If in your decorating travels you find a wallpaper or fabric that captures your color heart, start your scheme there. This room's color started from the drapery fabric. The extra good news: Starting from a fabric that appeals is probably the easiest method: The color options are already in front of you.

Choose nature's colors

Flower gardens in full summer bloom are often an explosion of color. If you're drawn to them, the difficulty is in reducing your selection to three or four favorites. Choose one as your base color and coordinate from there.

Another option is to select colors of nature in an "off-season" such as the bright leaves of autumn or the bright greens of spring.

Create a room from a view

Another way to incorporate one of nature's color schemes is to start from a favorite view.

Begin by flipping through favorite vacation snapshots, a stack of postcards, or books from places you long to go. Draw the colors and patterns from those images to create your color scheme.

Grand images like the one *above* also help with color proportions.

Any Color Can Be Formal or Casual

While certain colors seem to be permanently paired with particular styles, color is essentially style neutral. Start your color scheming with the freedom to put any color into the look of your choosing. These two examples—naturally neutral grey and vibrant yellow—show color's true flexibility. One guiding tip: Think of the shade. If the tone of your dreams often is shown on a certain style, that may be where it looks best.

Modern

Traditional

Vibrantly versatile yellow in sunny tones and simple lines is thoroughly modern. Or use golden yellows in a pattern with a formal valance, and the look is clearly more traditional.

Gray can be contemporary

Gray is essentially a cool color, and if it is your favorite you probably like cool blues and greens, too, lots of room, and the feeling of space.

Gray is an excellent background color to expand the open-planning theme of contemporary architecture, particularly in its lighter tones. A pale gray will almost literally "push" the walls away. Used from room to room, ranging from very light to a medium value, it will give a neutral background to all the furnishings, with a little variety as well.

Gray gives sharp contrast

If you like vivid contrasts, gray is a good background choice, because it makes almost any other color more vibrant when used with it. Bright tones glow, whites and blacks are starkly brilliant against gray.

Gray can be warmed

If you want a more blended background, then warm the gray you are using with the other major color in the room. You can use blue or red, brown or yellow, your choice depending on your other colors. In the room at the right, gray walls are shaded lightly with green to soften the tone, blend it with the green of the upholstery pieces. The gray still gives contrast for brilliant flowers.

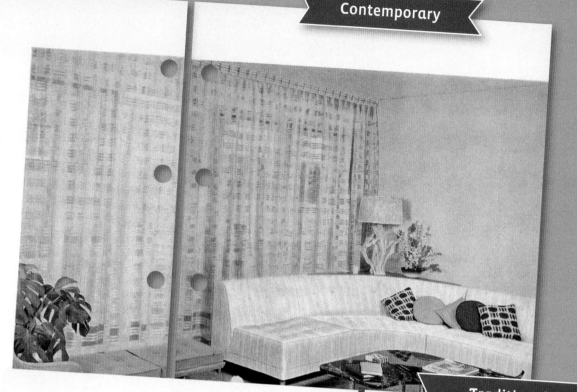

Gray can be formal

Here is the other side of the story—cool gray elegantly translated into a rich and friendly traditional setting. This color scheme started with a pair of prized antique bowls, now displayed on the mantel.

Since the room has many windows and is very light, the soft, cool gray of the patterned border on the bowls was selected as the dominant color. The drapery- and upholstery-fabric pattern has the same gray background, warmed by a golden-yellow flower, and touched with white. A soft gold is the other major upholstery color.

If the room had been very dark, the scheme could have been reversed, using sunlit gold as the dominant color, accented by the neutral gray.

Accessories keep to the yellow, gray, and white theme.

Dark, light, dull, bright

Remember the jingle of "something dark, something light, something dull, something bright"? Here, the background is dull, to absorb light, give a pleasant, restful feeling. Warm, rich mahogany and marble hearth are the "something dark." Light gold is a major color, and the vivid yellow-gold of the bowls and the flower pattern make accents in the room. The luster bright of bowls, polished andirons and woods, give us "something bright."

49

One-Color Schemes

It's OK to be single-minded in color choice. Perhaps the one-color scheme fell into disfavor at the end of the 20th century after too many builder-beige rooms. Yes, beige is a color. No, you don't want to do your entire home top-to-bottom in it even if your home is going up for sale tomorrow.

This 1956 interpretation of a one-color scheme began with a favorite color and a contingent of complementary colors and shades that flowed room to room through a house. While this approach isn't currently highly popular—people seem to be decorating rooms separately—the lessons of proportion and shade, of considering the connections between rooms and their use still are helpful.

You can plan a one-color scheme without monotony

There are two applications of one-color schemes—one is literally just that, and called monochromatic. It is confined to shades and tones of the same basic color, with bright accents used sparingly. This color plan is usually found in just one room. The other one-color scheme is the use of one basic color throughout the house in varying shades and tones, but in different amounts in each room, so that there is no sameness or tedium.

Cool blue sets the theme for this house

Blue in the floor, the rug, and the walls accounts for about 75 percent of the color in this living room. Strong pink and white divide the balance of large areas about equally. Red is the accent color

Blue, pink, white —in equal amounts

Pink shares honors with basic blue and white. Blue walls and doors in the dining room, kitchen cabinets, account for about one-third of the color. Pink kitchen wall and sweep of floor are another third. Balance is in white rug, kitchen ceiling. Bright red is again the accent—in counter tops, kitchen accessories, chair seats

The first kind of one-color scheme—the monochromatic—is particularly useful where you want a shell background for one dramatic piece. This could be a brilliant fabric in drapery or upholstery, an elegantly ornamented breakfront or chest.

It is also of great service in making small rooms seem larger, because there is never a definite break in any color line, from floor to walls to ceiling. The plan suits the contemporary open architecture, too, lets the eye range from one living area to another without interruption.

The other one-color plan is a little more complicated, but not difficult to execute, as shown on pages 102-103. Start with the color you want to live with—blue or green, pink or red, yellow, brown or gray. Since it is the basis of your color planning, you will probably want to use it in large quantities in your living room. Plan its quality there—should it be bright or dull, dark or light? Should it be on the warm side of the color wheel, or with a touch of coolness? When you have made your choice, it's always wise to start your buying with a floor covering, since you can match or blend wall colors with it easily.

Plan family rooms first

Since the rooms where all the family—and your friends—gather are really the most important, start your color planning with the living room, then the dining room and kitchen.

Using a one-color scheme

You've established the proportions of your favorite colors in the rooms where family and friends meet. Now carry them on into the other rooms in the house. In the master bedroom they can have a formal feeling, dignified, restful. In the children's rooms, select these same colors in fabrics and furnishings that are simple and easy to keep, won't show dirt or wrinkles. In the nursery, use bright accent tones for the major areas, because little children thrive under strong color—prefer it to pastels.

In the bathroom, be sure to include the color of your fixtures—white or pastels—in shower curtain, rug or wallpaper pattern.

Red replaces pink as main color in master bedroom   Just as in the living room on page 104, about 75 percent of the color here is blue, with white and red sharing the rest of the major areas. Pink replaces red as the accent in this room

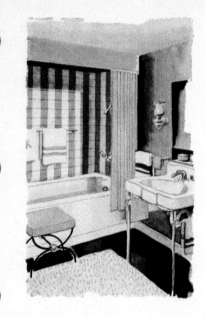

Paler shades, much white, distinguish bathroom

A bathroom is a place for make-up and shaving, needs pale colors so that light will reflect properly. The largest areas here are in white. Walls are a pale blue—the dominant color of the house—with gay pink ceiling, stool cover and towels. The same dark blue used in the living room is found in hard-surfaced floor, to provide the "something dark" every color scheme should have. Bright red accents in other rooms could be used for bottles, towels, other accessories

Television-guest room is bright but easy to keep

Here is a room sturdy enough for the family to relax in—handsome enough to be an inviting guest room. Blue is again the major color, accounting for about 75 percent of the color area. This time the darker shade is in the practical slipcover and tiered draperies, with a lighter tone on the walls.

White is the second major color, in curtains, and the scrubbable paint of the built-in back of the bed. Bright red accents the scheme, with pink at a minimum.

Floor could be random boards or a plank-patterned linoleum.

My, How Times Have Changed

Modern one-color schemes often are based on white. The crispness is appealing to those looking for clean lines—from stark contemporary to cool Zen. When the first edition of *Better Homes and Gardens Decorating Book* hit the shelves, that approach may have been a bit too radical. The book doesn't feature the all-white rooms that often grace the pages of present-day decorating books and magazines.

Not Getting Lost
in the Wood (tones)

Oddly enough, the original editors recommended brown as the best color for rooms with lots of wood. This seems to fly in the face of the advice they gave in the previous chapter. In discussing color principles, they rightfully stood on a finely carved soapbox pronouncing that wood has colors that must be honored. They urged readers to create settings that define and celebrate the warmness and interest of wood in every species and stained tone.

One might have a hard time telling the forest from the trees in this situation. Look, however, at the inviting, rich settings they offered and you'll see the distinction. Like any color, wood tones benefit from a level of contrast. So if you're working in a mono-tone color scheme that's based on warm wood tones, vary the shades enough to define the wood from windows, walls, and whatever else is in the room.

Try wood tones with brown

It isn't the colors you choose, but the way you use them, that makes a room gay or subtle, sophisticated or informal. One of the reasons for the current popularity of the brown tones is their versatility—blending with casual or formal homes.

Brown is an obvious selection for use with natural-wood paneling, both in contemporary and traditional settings. The one-color background which displays pattern and design in its furnishings, requires variety of texture and tone within the color, to avoid a monotonous feeling.

The trend toward clear, warm tones in wood for backgrounds and for furnishings extends to these same tones in paints and papers, in rugs and carpets. Subtle browns, taupes, beiges, ranging from deep chocolate to light cream, and combined with natural-wood finishes, will give you this one-color look, but one that is rich and elegant. You won't go wrong if you use the darkest tones on floor, palest on ceiling, variations of the medium values in-between.

My, How Times Have Changed

If you're lucky enough to have an antique wood carving with the patina of age, like the one featured *left*, or even a brand-new hand-carved beauty, setting it in front of a matching wood background isn't the best choice: You simply can't see the item or, therefore, enjoy it.

Silhouetting the piece against a white wall would greatly enhance its beauty. And keep heirloom-quality items away from the fireplace; the rising heat will dry out the wood.

The black rocker and red love seat help to accent the wood tones. Note, too, how the white wall emphasizes the stone hearth.

Copy a Color Scheme

There's no reason to reinvent the (color!) wheel, and no reason to agonize over color choices if you've seen the perfect color mix in a friend's home, on a magazine page, or in some other place. Even with an excellent selection of colors at hand, however, you'll still wear out a good deal of shoe leather just trying to find good matches in fabric and furnishings.

Having had, no doubt, their own experiences in attempting color re-creation, the original editors devised a practical method for dealing with the issue.

Is It Love or Rose-Colored Glasses?

If you've fallen hard for a color scheme in a magazine or book (alas, even this one), remember that you're only seeing part of the picture. Such rooms are dressed in their Sunday best—not to deceive but to maximize impact and convey ideas. You're not only seeing a room from its best angle, you're also probably not seeing the entire house and how that room relates to other rooms. So enjoy the photos, and take the time to paint a swatch and look at it in the real-life lighting in your home.

You can copy a color scheme

Everywhere you look—in your friends' homes, in the model rooms of your favorite store, in smart new offices, or a gaily re-decorated drugstore, in a fine restaurant, in the pages of magazines, pamphlets, and books—in all these places you find ideas for your own home. Sometimes it's a way of arranging a few pieces of furniture, or of hanging a picture, or an interesting window treatment that caught your eye.

Often, the idea that strikes your particular fancy is a fresh and exciting color scheme. Even though it is in a room very different from your own, you *can* copy it, and adapt it to your own family tastes.

Analyze colors

First, analyze the colors in the room. What is the one note that sets the theme? Is it the drapery fabric, the floor covering—a picture, a color, or a wallpaper pattern? List the colors you find—note that here is red and pink on a white background, with a rose-red carpet, pink walls, stark white accessories, underscored with ebony wood tones. Which of these colors is dark, which is light—which is dull, which is bright?

Analyze color proportions

Then, pay special attention to the proportions of each color used. Which cover the greatest area, which serve a moderate area, which are accents? Now you can transpose this scheme to your own home, in your own style, to suit your own tastes.

Large neutral areas accent

the brilliance of smaller

amounts of dominant pattern

Although the big, bold fabric pattern is less than 10 percent of this room's color, it is the dominating force, accentuated by the pale background shell. From its mixture of black, green, gray, white, and earth-brown, all other colors are derived. Dark and medium wood tones pick up the brown, as do the pottery lamp bases and planters. Soft gray appears in the textured walls, carpeting, solid-toned draperies which frame the view. Big pictures contain these colors, too. Growing plants pick up the green tones. A splash of brilliant golden flowers brightens the subtle scheme

Proportions & Placement

When you're taking your cue from an existing color scheme, account for the change in environment—perhaps a different room in the house, a room of a different size with different furniture. Focus on the colors and patterns, proportions and placements. Consider how the whole package will work in your home rather than slavishly copying a room. With a little creativity almost any color scheme can make the journey to become the perfect palette in your home as these vintage examples attest.

Same colors, proportions, translate into dining area

See how you can vary the basic idea. The colors are used in almost the same proportions, in the same areas. The pattern is still in the floor, but this time the bright, clear yellow is combined with the brown of the wood flooring. The coral is used for chair seats, is pulled high in the lampshade. The yellow table is against the yellow wall. White and yellow meet at the corner, interrupted only by blue-lined shelves. Black metal chairs pick up black accent

Textures vary this color interpretation

Here again, yellow and white meet dramatically at the corner, this time with crisp, sheer draperies and textured brick instead of the smoother, flat surfaces of the original. Yellow against yellow is found in the contact of floor and draperies. Pattern is still in the rug, this time in wood-brown sparked with coral. Coral is found in the spread for the couch, is raised high into the room in the Oriental design on the lamp

Pattern goes up, color areas remain the same

This time, the pattern is on the bedspread instead of the floor, but the color areas remain in about the same proportions. Yellow against yellow, yellow against white, are found in the meeting of the yellow ceiling with the yellow wall, and the white wood paneling. Bright coral hugs the floor, is repeated higher in the flower centers of the bedspread. Black appears in the chair. This crisp color scheme brightens the old furniture

Bathroom colors are inspired by same Provincial scheme

If your bathroom fixtures are white, you will want your area of brilliant pattern to feature white, too, so that one will relate to the other. Here, we've concentrated the accent pattern into one spot because the room is very small, and have carried the dominant light red onto the floor in the bath rug, onto the opposite wall with bright red and white towels. Straw-colored walls and darker hard-surfaced flooring complete a lively color scheme

Spark a drab old bedroom with this color adaptation

Bleach the old bedroom furniture down to a straw tone, paper or paint the walls and ceiling. Give texture with a white-on-white bedspread, thick scatter rugs, filmy curtains. Maybe you'd prefer the accent fabric in emerald green or bright blue instead of the original red. Here it is used to cover headboard, a slipper chair, cornice. A softer shade of the blue in the lampshades helps distribute the color throughout the room

A budget variation translates scheme into a small room

With a little imagination, you can achieve the same dramatic effects as in the room at the right. Use white sheeting or dress material for draperies, coarse-textured cloth in sand or straw tones for the sofa, honey-colored furniture, straw matting on the floor. Then splurge on a few yards of brilliantly bold fabric to accent the chairs. Be sure to include an eye-catching picture that picks up fabric colors, and use black accents

Plaid can be a tricky beast—elegant and refined in one setting, absolutely camp in another. In this dining room, the effect is fabulous. Often it's the plaid itself. Tartan plaids are handsome and elegant, a good way to ensure a rich result. In the examples, *left*, the proportion of plaid to plain is balanced to achieve the same eye-pleasing results.

Building a Color Scheme

Technology may have given the world better images to convey color concepts. But these doll house-size sets from the 1956 edition told the story of layering colors in a room to create a pleasing palette. Here is the advice of the original editors.

1

Pale colors make a small room look larger

A pale version of the grayed-green in the drapery material goes on three walls. Since the view window, or picture window, looks out on a woodland scene, that window is a soft, pale brown, with a deeper shade of the green wall appearing in the area rug.

2

One bold pattern is enough—sets the theme

The bold, wide stripes of the drapery fabric have set the color theme. The major upholstered pieces pick up two of the colors—bright blue for the sectional sofa, olive green for the pair of chairs. The wood color is light, to join with the wall tones in giving an effect of added space.

The 1-2-3 Color Plan

Good color proportions needn't be difficult to accomplish. Here's the simplest method:

1. Use neutral tones for the walls and floors.

2. Choose medium tones on sofas and chairs.

3. Reserve bright, strong colors for use on accent pieces only.

Accessories and accents finish the scheme

3 — Select Accent Colors

Keeping accent colors related to the main color theme is one way of making a small room look larger. So all accents and accessories in this room are selected from the colors in the drapery fabric. These are kept simple, and few in number. The pillows on the sofa, the chairs, and the stools are solid tones of the fabric stripes. The lampshades . . . are chosen so they match the dominant blue of the sofa.

As the Color Wheel Turns

Choosing colors based on which direction a room faces is more than a tad limiting, but the advice given in 1956 does help you understand the effect of sunlight—or lack thereof—on color. Today, the experts advise choosing and placing colors with personal appeal: If you want

NORTH: *Cool light requires warmth in color*

Colors retain their purity best of all under a north light—which is why artists always try to work in such surroundings. But this light is cool, so that you should use lots of warm tones to bring a feeling of friendliness to the room.

The large color areas—your walls, floor, and the major upholstered pieces, can be gayer and brighter than in rooms facing any other direction. Use cool colors for smaller pieces and for accessories, accents, to give necessary balance

WEST: *Afternoon sun calls for cool colors*

Even though it's in shade for part of the day, the rich reds, oranges, and yellows of the evening sky give warmth to a west room.

It's well to think of color in medium values—between the bright and the dull, the warm and the cool. For example, if your favorite color is green, be sure that there are big areas of cool green, then spark them with tones in upholstery that are on the yellow side. Keep bright accessories to a minimum, select most in neutral dark shades yellow in a south-facing room, go for it.

This information also reinforces an important point in color selection: Location and lighting affect colors. Put good-size samples of all your decorating materials in the room they'll be used; view them over several days to see the effects of different light conditions on the colors. This will help you choose the right shades and balance of colors.

EAST: *Divide colors between warm and cool*

As in the case of a west room, an eastern exposure is in shade part of the day. But the rising sun's rays are essentially cooler than those of the later day, and you will probably prefer to apportion your colors about two-thirds on the warm side, one-third cool.

If your choice is a cool green or blue, use it as pattern against a neutral background, and as accents, with largest areas in tones from sunny side of color palette. Spark with black and white.

SOUTH: *Keep colors grayed for this exposure*

The hottest, brightest light for most of the day comes from the sun moving into a south room. Here you will be flooded with the happy gaiety of summer, get most of your winter richness of yellow light.

You will probably want some brightness in your color scheme, too, but keep it to a minimum, with the largest areas in dull, absorbing, cool tones. Vary these with neutrals, and keep color combinations simple. A one-color scheme is effective in warm rooms.

Think Before You Buy

The original editors called them pretty misfits—those items bought in the heat of the moment in colors outside the scheme. Here a pink lampshade and accessories made a well-groomed room look like a mishmash. Their advice: Stick to the color plan, no matter how charming the temptations.

CHAPTER 4

Create Convenience with *Furniture*

"Please, have a seat!" If after this friendly invitation, your guests need to shimmy sideways between sofa and coffee table, or experience a mildly disconcerting posterior bump on the wall as they pull a dining chair away from the table, your furniture arrangements need some help.

Achieving placement perfection starts with a puzzle of furniture pieces and a floor plan. Get it right on paper or, perhaps, on a computer screen, first. Then the aerobic efforts of actually moving sofas, tables, chairs, and cabinets will go smoothly, and the end result will be quite user-friendly.

Arrangements

While there's always more than one way to arrange the furniture in a room, the best ways maximize use of space and ease of movement through the room.

Going with the Flow

Furniture arranging starts with understanding traffic patterns: Where do people enter the room and what are the destinations in the room? Wait a minute—Traffic? Destinations? While you're not planning a trek up Mount Everest or directing the Rose Bowl Parade, it is important to take a thoughtful look at how people move through, or should move through, every room and then arrange furniture with those patterns in mind.

As the original editors exalted, the main "rule" is comfort, and bad furniture arrangement can result in discomfort: stubbed toes, bumped shins, and the occasional Dick Van Dyke-esque flip over the footstool. All of which are easily avoidable if you thoughtfully map the path from Point A (the door or doors) to Point B (chair, desk, or sofa, for example).

Plan for rooms with fireplaces

Consider the need for open floor space in a small, square room

A square room is almost always a small room, too, which makes it even more difficult to decorate. Be careful to conserve your limited floor space—use chairside tables instead of coffee tables which would swallow up the scarce footages in the center of the room. If the traffic pattern moves across one end, arrange the furniture along the walls adjoining the fireplace wall. The arrows point up how the traffic lanes from the three entrances have been kept free from congestion

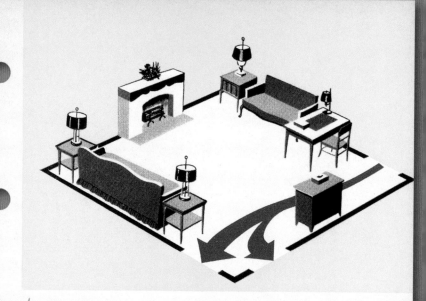

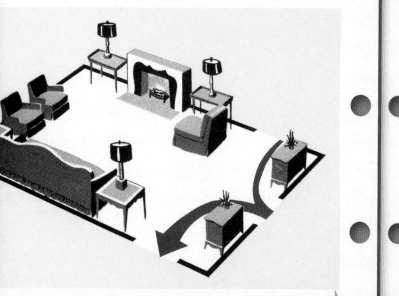

A big, rectangular room calls for separation of living areas

Conversational groupings need to be placed so that people can talk comfortably, not have to shout. In a big, rectangular room with a traffic lane through the middle, place such a grouping at one end, around the fireplace and out of the way of through-room traffic. The other end of the room may be used as a study or a letter-writing area, for a music or a hobby corner. A divider could be used here to good effect, standing across the room, separating the room into distinct areas

Plan furniture groupings to cut length of long narrow room

To avoid the bowling-alley look of a long, narrow room, arrange the furniture to cut the length. Place a chair, a desk, or a sofa at right angles to the wall, preferably backing the traffic lane and creating a "hall." Then a more intimate conversation grouping can be arranged around the fireplace in the remaining portion of the room. Here, a storage wall with built-in television would fit in one of the unused corners. The big lounge chair by the fireplace might be a swivel

Plan for rooms without fireplaces

In this rectangular room, a chair-chest grouping is focal point

A big, rectangular room will offer plenty of space for a center of interest. You can make a focal point of bookcases, a window treatment, or just an interesting grouping of pictures above the sofa. In this room, two wing chairs and a pair of chests at the end of the room act as the focal point. Hang a dramatic picture arrangement or some other grouping above the chests. Following the traffic arrow, you move smoothly past the desk and chairs without disturbing conversation

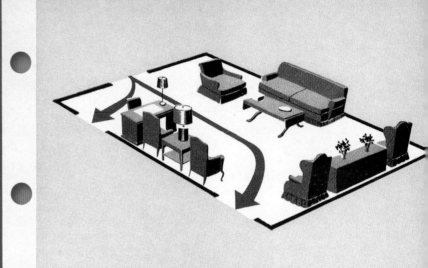

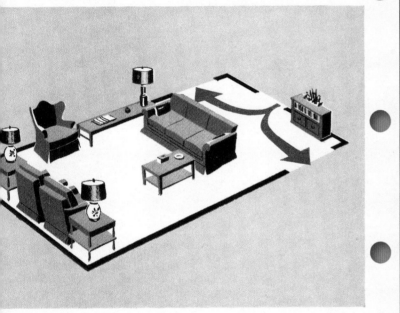

A massive focal point helps to alter the shape of a square room

A square room needs a heavy focal point to minimize its boxy look, to make the room appear longer. You can get a center of interest by pushing some long, low bookcases underneath a pair of well-dressed windows. Place a conversation grouping on either side of the window arrangement. If there are no windows on the opposite wall, balance the focal point with a large picture or a mirror. Then you can use the other wall areas for a writing desk or another major grouping of chairs

Make a long, narrow room seem wider with a compact arrangement

To make your long, narrow rooms seem wider, let the bulkiest furniture jut into the room at right angles to the longest walls. This seems to create the feeling of another wall there. If the sofa stands with its back to the traffic lane, the length of the room will be cut even more. Create your point of decorating emphasis on the end wall opposite the sofa. Here, pairs of chairs and end tables catch the eye. Complement this group with a series of pictures, or a dramatic sweep of draperies

The Focal Point

Whether life was simpler 50 years ago can be debated, but the first edition had a marvelously direct, simple approach to defining the focal point: *"The center of interest is that part of your room which you wish to play up—make dramatic—make the focal point of your decorating. It can be an architecturally natural spot, such as a fireplace, or a picture window with a view. Or it can be an arranged spot, such as a wall of built-ins with your sofa nestled in the center. It can be a magnificent picture on a long wall, which catches the eye as soon as someone walks into the room, and draws them to it."*

The editors encouraged readers to emphasize a spot in the room that played to personal taste. Strip away 50 years of muddied discussion of focal points, and return to this straight-to-the-point definition.

Fireplaces are natural focal points. They so dominate a room that you really must give them their due.

If other areas of the room also require focus, a couple of comfy chairs flanking the hearth are a sufficient nod.

Seasonal Shift

Add a little variety to a room by changing the setting with the season and with it a room's focal point. For most of the year, the seating pieces in this room gather around the fireplace for warmth and coziness. Come spring and summer, the pieces are turned around and the room focuses on the great outdoors. The conversation group now faces a large window that brings in the light and beauty of the season. As an added bonus, the wear on the carpet is distributed more evenly—and everyone gains a whole new perspective!

Plan for People

People require space, too

Odd how decorating books and magazines show all these fabulous rooms with exquisite furnishings and posh furniture—and rarely a human being in sight. The occasional family pet strays into the pristine space to get 15 minutes of photo-flash fame.

Rooms are for people to live in. Yes, it's easier to show how room arrangements work and how lovely the furnishings are without people wandering through or sitting down and messing up a shawl perfectly draped over the chair. So even when viewing unpopulated pictures, think about allowing adequate space for people passages and creating conditions for interpersonal interactions. The solution is a matter of a few measurements. Use these numbers from the original book as a starting point for your new room settings.

Conversation groups

Sitting down for a nice chat is so much more fun if you don't have to shout across the wide, open spaces. For easy sociability —and normal hearing—there should be a maximum of eight feet between conversation groups. Any more than that, and you'll have to strain your voice to be heard and sit forward in your chair to catch the conversation

Getting up from the table

Give the man a chance to be gallant. Getting up from the table uses up 3 inches. And the gentleman needs room to walk behind your chair, too. In all, that requires a minimum of 5 inches from the wall. Give yourself room to serve and clear the table. Children will need even more space

Pulling out a drawer

You'll need 36 inches to stand in front of even a partly opened drawer. This is the minimum and you'll probably want enough room to open the drawer completely. You'll avoid frustrating moments if you keep this in mind when arranging furniture with drawers that pull out.

Passing between furniture

For one normal-size adult, you'll need to leave a 30-inch traffic lane. That's what comfortable passing between two pieces of furniture requires. Of course, if it's the traffic lane from the kitchen, you'll need enough extra space to accommodate trays and plates and elbows, too. When planning traffic lanes around doorways, be sure to allow space for several people to pass at once.

Sitting at a coffee table

If your family is of usual size, be sure to allow 15 inches between chair or sofa and your coffee table. Otherwise, watch out for barked shins. Remember . . . the first rule of furniture arrangement is ''comfort.'' And that means comfort for people to sit and enjoy themselves.

Let's Talk About It

The furniture grouping where people gather to talk should facilitate chitchat not impede it. The "conversation group" is decorating lingo for chairs, sofas, and/or love seats in an area no more than eight feet apart, all facing each other so no one is out of view or earshot and everyone has room to lounge comfortably.

Big rooms can have more than one conversation area. For example, pair a main grouping of sofa and chairs with a smaller tête-à-tête space using just two chairs and a table snugged into a corner for more intimate exchanges.

Whatever the size of the conversation group, direct the traffic flow around the space, not through it.

Coming to Terms with the TV

The 1956 technology dates the images, but the editors' advice for accommodating a TV is practically hip! Who knew?

". . . your family gathers together for its entertainment, cozy against the outside world. To make the most of this pleasure, be sure everyone is comfortable."

The original editors clearly understood that the TV set was destined to become an important fixture in American homes, and the smart money was on encouraging readers to create attractive, comfortable settings for TV viewing.

What they didn't consider (and couldn't possibly foresee) is the challenge of decorating around behemoth screens and the wide array of electronic entertainment machinery that have found their way into today's homes.

One solution is, ironically, the revival of an idea first popular in television's early days: the TV room. Of course, now it's called the media room, but the concept is the same. Since big TVs with surround sound and all the accompanying stuff dominate a room (when they're on, no one can do anything else in that room), why not dedicate a space to electronic entertainment.

Another solution is a built-in cabinet with doors or shutters to hide (and protect) the TV when it's not in use. Built-ins and entertainment armoires provide shelving for the equipment and corral the snarl of cords modern systems require.

Your television set can become an integral part of your furniture arrangement. It can be featured as an element in your major decorative center. It can serve more than one room. It can stand free, or it can be built into a music or storage wall.

The first consideration, as in all furniture arrangement, is comfort. The set should be placed where the whole family can see it easily, and where there is no glare on the screen. There should be enough seating units for everyone in the family, and they should be the soft, lounging kind.

Plan for placement

If your room is L-shaped, and you would like to watch television from both sections of the room, try placing the set at the corner of the "L." A swivel base, or a table with wheels, will let you turn the set toward either one of the living areas for viewing.

You can use your television set as a divider in a long, narrow room. Place it facing in toward the major living area. A divider solution might be to put a big picture or decorative panel on the back of the set. But if you do, be sure that the panel or picture is installed on extension brackets, so that there is plenty of ventilating space behind the television set.

A television set is most oft placed against a wall, facing major furniture grouping. If t set is freestanding, rather th built into a storage unit, treat as you would any other cabinet chest.

Unplanned Obsolescence

Here are a couple of points from the 1956 edition that you no longer need to consider when placing a TV in a room today:

- *Have a comfortable chair near the set so that one viewer can work the controls without getting up.*

- *Allow extra ventilation around the set in case you'll soon be replacing a black-and-white TV with color.*

- *Permit easy access to the back panel for replacing blown TV tubes.*

Team up your centers of interest by an arrangement that focuses attention on both fireplace and television

In a small room, there isn't room for more than one spot of decorating emphasis. Your furniture arrangement naturally turns toward this focal point, at-
tracting attention to it. However, you'll want the seating group to face toward
the television set, for comfortable viewing. So team them up and give the
room a unified, spacious look. This will mean more convenience for conversation

Scale lamps to tables

Tables should be selected to ensure comfort. An easy chair needs a table for there are always books, magazines, and ashtrays to cope with.

For convenience a table should be approximately the height of the arm of the chair by which it is used. When seated it is uncomfortable to have to reach up or down when you want an object on the table.

Consider the function of the table before deciding how large a top surface it should have. The decorative aspects of a table are important but keep in mind where and how you wish to use it, choosing accordingly.

The same requirements for comfort guide you in the selection of lamps for your rooms. The choices of color and style are personal ones. But apply the same yardsticks of placement and size that you did in selecting your tables.

Most seating arrangements need adequate illumination. The lamp you select should be of sufficient size and height to cast enough light on the reading and working areas.

Balance and scale are important when combining lamps and tables.

A table can serve more than one chair

Twin chairs and a long, low coffee table make an attractive grouping for conversation or reading. A large box base added to the lamp raises it to more correct height. This arrangement could also serve as a room divider

This table is too low and too small for comfortable use

Every chair deserves the *right* size table. This one is too low. Lamps and ashtrays are likely to be pushed off. The table is also too delicate in scale for such a massive chair. The top surface is too small to hold all of the items usually needed next to a lounge chair—lamp, ashtrays, books

This table is just the right size and height for its chair

The table that you select for any chair should be of the right scale and proportion to the size of the chair itself. It should be approximately the same height as the arm of the chair. And its surface should be large enough to hold all necessary items. For a reading chair, a table with a shelf for books is a particularly good choice.

This lamp is too low to throw enough light for reading

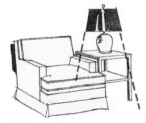

Every table deserves the *right* size lamp. Now we have a table that is exactly suitable for this chair. But this lamp, while handsome in design, is not a good choice here. Notice how the light falls only over the arm of the chair. A lamp should be tall enough, and the shade big enough to throw plenty of light on handwork, reading material, surrounding area

This lamp will send a wide gleam of light over work or reading

When you go shopping for new tables and lamps, take your chair measurements with you. First select the table, then the lamp. Every table should have a lamp that is good for reading, one that lights up the whole chair area. Now we have the right chair, the right table, and the right lamp, all together in one place. The result, years of comfortable service

A perfectly proportioned room with neatly arranged accessories can still be a complete decorating disaster if you're not comfortable in it. Sit on the sofa before you buy it. Have other family members give it a test-sit, too, before you buy.

efinitions sometimes fall short of facilitating understanding, especially regarding concepts. In decorating, balance and scale are two such concepts. Illustrations of poor choices along with good help convey these ideas better than mere words.

Evaluate scale and balance in a room beginning with the largest piece. In a living room, for example, where is the sofa placed and how do pieces group around it (balance)? And do those pieces fit the size of the sofa and the other pieces (scale)? Run that exercise through your mind as you choose new items for your rooms.

These two-tone sketches, unfortunately, remove one other key factor in scale and balance: color. Dark colors add weight to a room; pale colors and neutrals can lighten even large pieces. Getting comfortable with these elements of decorating is accomplished over time with practice, practice, practice. Keep these concepts in mind as you look at images in magazines and books. Soon your eye will be able to assess scale and balance in the images.

Formal balance—everything in pairs

Every item in this room is in perfect formal balance. The sofa and the tall picture above it serve as the fulcrum. On either side, matching end tables hold matching lamps. Lounge chairs, exactly alike, face each other across the coffee table. Pictures, framed alike, line up on either side of the center, forming a solid oblong that balances the sofa

Informal balance within a formal frame

At first glance, this room also is in perfect formal balance. Again, pairs of end tables, lamps, and chairs appear. The picture grouping over the sofa is, in its entirety, balanced formally to the sofa. But variety is gained, and informal balance introduced, by the pictures. The biggest frame is in the upper corner, with smaller ones grouped around it

Here is informal balance in furnishings

This is a good example of informal balance, and the variety it can give a room. The sofa is still the fulcrum of this group. On one side is an end table, with a lamp. On the other is a floor lamp, tall enough and massive enough to balance the end table. One chair has square arms and is covered in a plaid. The other is covered in a plain textured fabric

Divide and Define

A room that multitasks is not a new concept; it was referred to as "multiuse" in the past. In 1956, the new thing in home design was contemporary architecture that embraced fewer, larger rooms intended to accommodate lots of family functions—children at play, the family enjoying time together, and quieter activities such as homework and reading—all taking place in the same room, perhaps at different times. Newer homes often take open design a step further: Even the kitchen is exposed to public view. And that multipurpose room is now called the great room.

Carving out spaces for separate activities makes big rooms feel friendlier, small rooms seem larger. Each space should be defined as well as connected to the other spaces. To keep the solution simple, two options are as good now as they were 50 years ago. A row of bookcases strongly defines the divide between spaces; using a piece of furniture, such as a sofa or a console table, makes a softer defining line. This option maintains the visual contact between spaces while still keeping the areas separate.

For activities that need small spaces, use a room's natural balance to determine divisions. An out-of-the-way corner is the perfect place to tuck in a reading nook or desk; a folding screen can block out the rest of the room if desired.

Dividing a long narrow room takes away that "tunnel" look and maximizes usability. Freestanding bookshelves like these help shape the space. Make sure to choose enough items that face both directions.

Use dividers
to define living areas

Almost any room can serve more than one purpose. The open planning of contemporary architecture, with fewer but larger rooms, is emphasizing this multiuse. And the more "living" a room does, the more need for definition of these living areas. Suzy does her homework at the dining table—in the living room. Junior and his crowd listen to bop on the hi-fi—in the living room. Mother entertains at cards—in the living room. Father goes over the household accounts—in the living room. And, often, mealtime comes in the living room. Study, entertainment, conversation, homework, dining—all these can, and sometimes do, go on at once.

You can gain privacy

"Divider" is a term used for anything that "divides" these areas from one another, giving at least the illusion of some privacy. The divider can be a series of shelves, or a bookcase, a piano, or a built-in. Today's built-in divider is often a freestanding storage wall, with turnabout television and covered cabinet.

← *Shelves and sofa both serve as dividers here*

This big around-the-corner sofa divides the conversation area from the traffic passageway. High, open shelves separate a teen-age area from the family living room. Although high and massive, shelves keep contemporary spacious look

A piano doubles as a partial room divider, leaving valuable wall space free. This arrangement also lets the performer share in fun, instead of staring into a blank wall. Cords of lamps meet behind music rack →

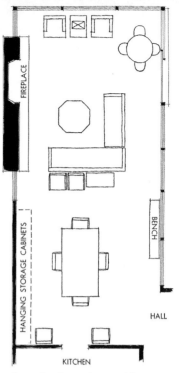

Open planning makes careful attention to traffic lanes important. This arrangement lets all traffic flow freely

Floor Plans

It is logical and obvious to place the dining end of this room next to the kitchen. There are four people in this family, and they entertain often, so a good-size dining table was indicated. Because the table was fairly large, space was saved by using hanging storage cabinets, instead of a buffet.

Living area serves three uses

The living area of this room serves as family room, as a place for televi-sion viewing, and for card playin The major conversational groupir of two sectionals forms a divider b tween this area and dining roor Fireplace is center of interest.

Television is installed on the wa to the left of the fireplace, providir an excellent view for everyone. Th permanent game table goes whe light is best, and also has its ow ceiling spotlight.

The passageway along the windo wall looking onto the terrace is le clear for traffic.

Turning room-arranging concepts into reality starts with creating a floor plan. There are computer programs galore in addition to the tried-and-true paper-and-pencil models. Really, truly, this is the best way to understand how furniture will fit in a room—aside from buying it and trying it in the room when it's delivered. In the exercise of virtual reality, measuring compensates for imagination and visualization: If it doesn't fit on paper, it won't fit in the room; and you can see the relationships between pieces of furniture.

Tri-Perfecta

Getting the relationship between pieces and spaces can be tricky. These three tips go a long way toward increasing understanding of how furniture works in a room.

Fit furniture to space

Just as important as the dimensions of the individual pieces you buy are the dimensions of the space where they are to go. These space measurements are not flexible, as are those of the individual pieces.

Use a yardstick

Get out a yardstick and measure the outside limits of your conversational group. Then fill in with the dimensions of the pieces of furniture you are going to buy.

Be sure to leave traffic lanes, and give enough space for people to sit without bumping their knees on low coffee tables.

We show you here three ways of arranging sofas in conversational groupings. Check the measurements of your room against ours, and you'll find the selection of an arrangement and the placing of furniture easier.

In a corner, fill the gap between sofa and chair with a table at least 30-inches across — anything smaller will leave an awkward hole. Place on it a lamp large enough to give good reading light for at least two people. Placing the coffee table off-center balances the group and is convenient for the person at the far end of the sofa. Center the picture grouping over sofa, even though this may not be center of total wall

Against a long wall or group of windows, your sofa can be flanked by tables and chairs. It's the ideal setting for conversation, but it does take space — and don't try to squeeze it too close to a doorway. Be sure the grouping has an area of at least 6½x14 feet, clear of traffic lanes

When sofa projects use tables in back

When the sofa projects into a room, save space by placing the tables at the back of the sofa instead of at the ends. Actually, these are the same tables and the same 80-inch sofa pictured on the opposite page. Placing sofa at right angles to fireplace requires a room at least 14 feet wide. Keep the lamp related in height

Furniture Placements Plans

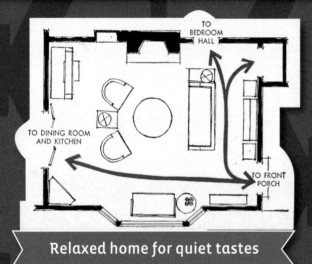

Relaxed home for quiet tastes

I n the unfailingly wise words of the original editors, *"Every home should be furnished to suit the taste and way of life of the people who live in it."* And the following examples show how two families might create living spaces following the fundamentals of furniture placement.

This example is for a fictitious family of three in a Colonial house. They're a quiet family looking to spend time home together or with a few close friends. Although the living room is of good size, the placement of the doors creates long traffic patterns along two sides. Here is how a real family with a similar situation might accommodate its needs and create a comfortable living room.

1

As an empty room, you can see how the bright room-size rug sets the color theme, defines the living area, and directs foot traffic around the center space. The wallpaper picks up on the lively pink in the rug, adding to the cheerful feeling.

2

Because of space limitations, the conversation group is anchored by a love seat. And the grouping is centered in front of the fireplace to emphasize the hearth wall. The setting is cozy with plenty of room to easily move around the furniture without disturbing the conversation.

With accents and accessories in place, the room comes to life. The china hutch is full of favorite antique pieces, and is flanked by antique black side chairs. Blue lamps and accessories pick up the blue in the fireplace surround. And the round coffee table makes it easy to move around the space without clipping a shin.

3

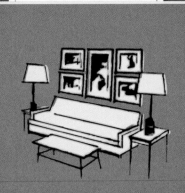

My, How Times Have Changed

The rule was that big rooms needed big furniture and small rooms should have only small furniture. New thinking makes way for a larger piece in a small room. With a large piece in a small room, don't upsize everything else or you'll never be able to move around.

Avoid making a large item look like Gulliver in Lilliput: Don't surround it with tiny furniture and small accessories. Better to have a few mid-size furniture items for balance. Choose lamps and accessories to fit proportionately.

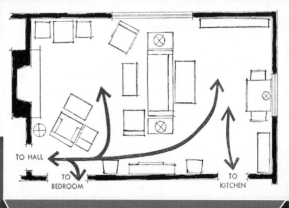

Comfort and informal living

The tastes of the second fictitious family run more to modern, and their lifestyle is more outgoing. This family entertains a great deal so they need plenty of seating and maximum open floor space for guests to mingle. Their ranch-style home is conducive to those needs. The large living area has an open floor plan and one main traffic path, so only one side of the room needs to accommodate people passing through.

1

Warm gold carpet visually expands the room to its maximum size. The color is close to the stone on the fireplace wall, maximizing the visual length of the room as well. The cool blue on the outer wall is a subtle shade that contrasts without advancing.

2

A large sofa anchors the seating area; it's a sleep-sofa to accommodate overnight guests. Lightweight side chairs can easily be moved around as conversation groups develop and disperse over the course of an evening's party. The console behind the sofa can be used as a buffet.

The final touches are bittersweet—the color bittersweet, that is. The dramatic orange-red is opposite the blue-green on the color wheel and relates well to the warm gold in the room. Black accents (lamp bases, TV, fireplace accessories, and side chair) bring out the vibrancy of the color scheme.

3

With plush carpet underfoot and warm wood tones on the walls and ceiling, this family room shows just how inviting smart background choices can be.

The Background
Walls, Floors, & Ceilings

A room is, essentially, a cube that you decorate on the inside: six sides to cover. Obviously, the top and bottom of the cube—the ceiling and floor—have different requirements from the walls and from each other. But all these surfaces play an important part in creating the overall look of your room; they're the backdrop that can pull everything together and define areas within a room and its adjoining spaces.

Today's surfacing materials—from carpet to paint to ceiling tiles—have improved durability and are available in a wider selection of colors and styles. But many of the considerations for choosing are the same today as they were in 1956. The advice and ideas offered by the original editors remains fresh.

Walls
Four Ways to Cover

Every wallcovering, no matter how grand or humble, should enhance a room's decor, usually without dominating the space. Good choices highlight the assets of a room, bring out the color in fabrics, and suit the style of the space. The four basic types of wallcovering defined in the 1956 edition still pretty much cover the territory:

1. Dado, or wainscot, splits the wall with a decorative treatment on at least the bottom portion. This treatment is popular in rooms where the walls might otherwise be bare. For example, in a dining room the chairs are tucked under the table, and walls are fully exposed.

Borders, wallpaper or stencil strips usually placed at the top of the walls, similarly wrap a room in color and pattern.

2. Contrasting trim and built-ins make architectural elements the emphasis. Interesting or elaborate trim can be used around the ceiling, windows, and doors to define those areas. Built-in bookcases and fireplace trim draw attention to a particular area within a room.

3. Solid color, often paint, lets other items in the room show off. There's no shame in plain, just don't slide into boring! Have fun with this no-nonsense option: Select a color that's interesting, paint one wall a more vibrant color, or try a textured treatment. Paint is the most popular wallcovering because it is so versatile (see page 87).

4. Companion patterns as used in 1956 were pretty staid: a fabric that matched wallpaper, with perhaps a slight change in scale or background color. Options have increased substantially: You can find groupings of complementary patterns, all color coordinated. Mix geometrics with prints for a unique blend.

Grass cloth blends in a transitional room

A combination of traditional background of beamed ceiling and fine wood paneling and furnishings of contemporary design give this room the feeling called transitional. Grass-cloth on the walls gives texture without too much pattern, blends warmth of color with the modern woven window shade

2

Oddball Walls

Small walls, such as this one by an entryway, are a place to boldly go where your creative heart leads you. Strong colors, vibrant patterns—all the elements that would overwhelm a room if used on all four walls—add fun and interest in a set-piece space. If you're wondering where these places are in your house, think of the ones that often get overlooked in decorating: entryways, hallways, stairways, and landings.

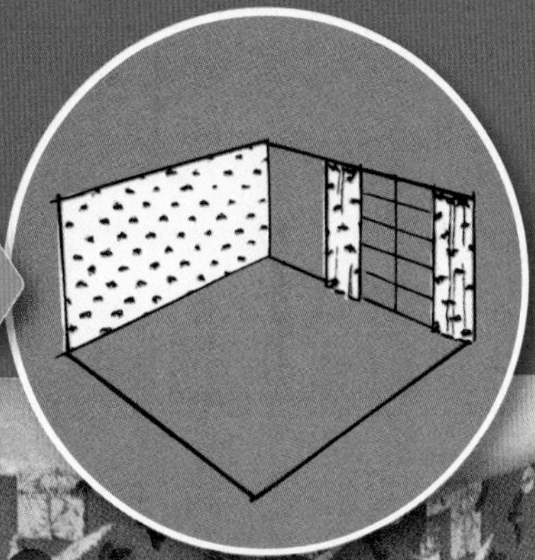

3

4

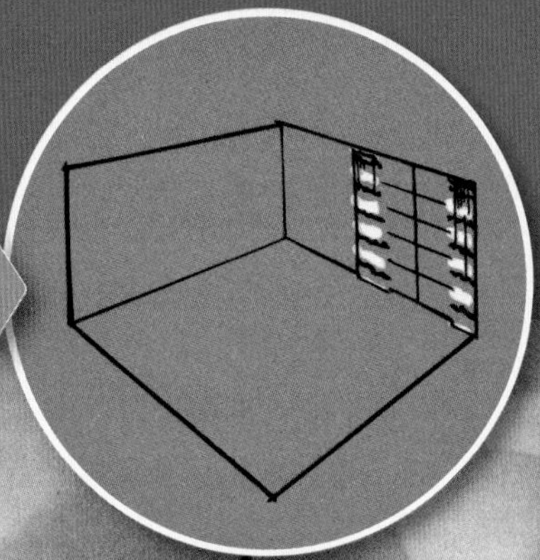

Walls
Creating Complementary Backgrounds

Put your wall treatments to work. Have them carry the tone and define the spaces they're in. As the original editors noted, wallcoverings can do one of four things: define, accent, blend, or connect.

Define

Subdivide a larger room into separate functional areas using wall treatments. Painting the dining area of this open living/dining room, *below,* a different color emphasizes the division of duties. Snippets and subsets of a room such as dormers and alcoves get a nice emphasis from this treatment too. Look for a natural break—doors or windows—to use as the dividing line. Without such breaks, the switch can seem forced. In those cases, use a change in wall material—switch from paint to wallpaper, for example—for a smooth transition.

Define

Accent

Accent

The wide-open space of a wall uninterrupted by window or door absolutely begs the use of a dramatic covering. Add spark with an outspoken wallpaper. This is also a great way to create style on a small budget.

   Big, bold patterns or particularly busy patterns generally do best with solid colors for the rest of the room—the furniture, other wallcoverings, and flooring. As in this vintage example, *above,*

Paint,
The Universal
Decorating
Solution

Essentially color in a can, paint is the quickest, cheapest way to change the look of a room. If you want a change but don't feel strongly about redecorating, choose a new color; you'll see the space in a whole new light. This room in deep green has a very traditional feel. That feeling lingers in the warm cocoa mid-range color, but it moves the look forward. With ivory-color walls, the room has a cooler, modern feel.

choosing a deeper tone of the main color from the wallpaper for the major upholstered pieces anchors the room; using a pale shade from the wallpaper and subtle tones on floor and window coverings cedes attention to the dominant wallcovering.

If you've used a daring, vibrant wallpaper, amp up the color choices on the other elements to keep the room's vibe on high.

Blend

Staining the wood a light blue blends the wall over the fireplace with the adjacent window treatments. A soft color switch like this creates a sophisticated look and emphasizes the elegant lines of the furnishings and grand height of the room.

Blend

When wall surface materials change but the goal is to keep the flow, use subtle variations of color to minimize the change. A shade of the room's dominant color makes for the most subtle switch. To both blend and define—if you want to define one area within a room, for example, but there's no clear break—use paint for one area and a subtly textured wallpaper, such as grass cloth, in the same color for a smooth transition.

Connect: Room to Room

Consider adjacent rooms and spaces, especially when choosing wall colors and treatments. To understand the effect find a pivotal point similar to the entryway in the image *opposite above*, a place where you can see directly into two rooms. When the wall treatments relate well to each other, the effect is cohesive, and people are naturally drawn into those adjacent rooms.

Modern architecture empha

BRICK GIVES FOCAL POINT TO LIVING AREA, BLENDS WITH WOO

There's a trend in architecture —toward bringing the outdoors inside as part of your decorating, and letting the natural beauty of trees and grass and sky frame your way of living. And the indoors, in its turn, serves as a frame, too— for the lovely view you planned when building.

As a result, the unadorned natural materials used in building are often used in interior decorating, as well as for the exterior of the home. In addition to being handsome, such materials as brick and stone, siding and paneling have the great advantage of being easy to care for.

Copy natural materials

For those of us who live in older homes, but are remodeling and rejuvenating our rooms, there are many copies of these natural materials that will give us the effects we want. Effects that will add new life to interiors.

Papers copy marbles, in many colors and patterns. You can find papers that resemble silver-gray weathered boards or highly polished knotty-pine paneling. Some papers even have three dimensions —with the individual bricks or pieces of stone jutting out into the room.

Real woods that have been shaved in thin sheets and mounted on a paper or canvas back, can be put on the walls as easily as paper.

USE EARTH TONES FOR WARMTH

Connect: Indoors to Outdoors

One decorating/design trend that changes but never disappears is the indoor-outdoor connection. In 1956 there was an emphasis on modern architecture using natural or natural-looking materials. Some ideas were perhaps better than others. (At least those less-than-perfect knotty-pine boards found good homes in rec rooms across America.)

Enhance the connection using colors and materials similar to the tones and textures of the great outdoors. New technologies make it easier: Composite "stone" is a lightweight alternative for use around fireplaces, decorative painting techniques give walls earthy textures, and wood paneling choices are truer to nature.

If the indoor-outdoor connection is more dream than reality—a basement rec room or child's bedroom, for example—have some fun. Wallpaper with the look of waving grass, and stencils of flora and fauna are fun choices to bring nature's appeal indoors.

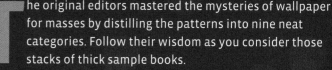

Wallpaper
Study to Simplify

The original editors mastered the mysteries of wallpaper for masses by distilling the patterns into nine neat categories. Follow their wisdom as you consider those stacks of thick sample books.

Pattern and color combined can do many things—camouflage architectural mistakes, cover up protruding beams and jags in walls, make a room seem higher, or push out the walls to give more apparent space. There are big patterns and little ones, bright colors and subtle tones. Each has its place in a decorating scheme. Take a good, close look; find your decorating problem. Is the room too small, too low—too long, or too wide? Pattern and color will help solve it.

1. "Fool-the-eye" adds space: If you like the feeling of space but your rooms are small, try a trompe l'oeil wallpaper. These papers give the illusion of another place beyond your wall and are designed to carry the eye out beyond the enclosing walls.

2. Allover patterns unify a room: Use these patterns to camouflage the sloping line of ceiling or make a jog in the wall look straight. Choose a nondirectional pattern—one that looks the same from any angle or any view. And these busy patterns should be the dominant pattern in a room, accented with solid colors.

3. Small patterns add interest: A small pattern, unlike an allover pattern, has a definite up-and-down and/or side-to-side direction. Small-pattern wallpaper is a good choice for subtly introducing color and symmetry in a room, such as a bedroom or office.

4. Textured patterns give variety: The three-dimensional look of textured patterns typically give the appearance of fibers or woven fabric. They add depth and interest even without much color; you'll often find them in neutral tones.

5. Some copy natural materials: Re-creating the look of natural stone or fine wood paneling can be easily accomplished with a few rolls of wallpaper. Not only is the wallpaper variety of "natural" style less expensive, hanging pictures or changing the wallcovering can be done with ease.

6. Definite patterns set the theme: When each design is a separate and distinct motif, it is called "definite." This kind of pattern is almost always used as the basis for a color scheme, and as the dominant feature in a room. Flowers, abstracts, and stripes are definite patterns.

7. Patterns serve as backgrounds: If you enjoy pictures and accessories on your walls as well as color and pattern, choose a background wallpaper. These patterns feature small motifs spaced far enough apart to not draw a lot of attention.

8. Border, dadoes act as accents: For a touch of vivid color and pattern, use a border. These are useful in rooms where the walls are mostly paint for maintenance reasons, such as a baby's room. Another choice is to use architectural dadoes to add an accent to a plain room, perhaps an otherwise unadorned dining room.

9. Large patterns give character: Create a decorative center of interest with a large-pattern wallpaper on one wall. These outspoken patterns tend to dominate a room, so choose a style that fits with the style of your furnishings.

Mural, Mural On the Wall

This fair wallcovering has come a long way with new technologies. Higher-quality reproductions and easy-to-apply sections in multiple sizes make this a fun choice to use in kids' rooms, basements, or hallways.

Use furnishings and accents in keeping with the mural to create a sense of place.

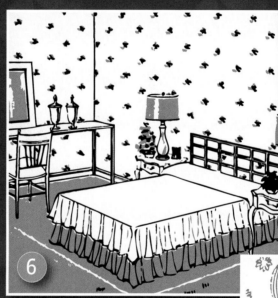

Ceilings
Look Up and Look Sharp

f there were ever a Rodney Dangerfield in decorating, the ceiling is it. Not only does it get no respect, popular choices focus on either making it disappear or, seemingly, making it look ugly. Ugly? Two words explain the point: "popcorn" ceiling.

Design aficionados may be the only ones to get worked up about such things: Unless you're in the Sistine Chapel, no one is going to strain a neck muscle looking at the ceiling. But put a little thought into choosing a ceiling treatment. As the original editors noted, fully one-sixth of the background area in any room is the ceiling—and that space is exposed, uncovered by furniture and accessories.

A formal pattern sets off a traditional room
Warm wood paneling provides the background for this traditional room, but needs large areas of color and pattern to set it off. A formal wallpaper pattern in red gives character, sets the decorating theme. Red and white are picked from the paper for the upholstery fabrics and for the cafe curtains

Six Ceiling Options

Ceilings are, with obvious reason, hard to work on. Choose wisely: With a smart ceiling finish, you won't be working overhead again for years. Also carefully consider how the material attaches to the surface. You don't want anything falling on someone's head or sagging over time.

PAINT is the most popular choice. Rather than using default flat white, choose a muted color from the room's palette. The daring among you may even wrap the whole room in a bold color. Paint techniques or stenciling can creep up the wall or slide from ceiling to wall for added interest.

WALLPAPER is a tricky-but-fun option. Tricky not just for the difficulty in hanging it on a ceiling but also for choosing the correct pattern. Ceilings with angled walls draw the wallpaper into a room, making it look like the inside of a well-decorated box top. Wide borders following the edge of the ceiling create the look of architectural details.

TEXTURED CEILINGS, such as the stamped tin associated with Victorian-style homes, add interest. Today you'll find metal ceiling tiles that replicate the look. Another option: Textured wallpaper designed to be painted; it comes in a wide variety of styles with as much or as little detailing as suits your room.

MOLDING AND PANELING, at the simplest level, add style to the seam between ceiling and wall with delicately curved cove molding. Or emphasize this transitional line using a grand assembly of molding pieces that carry a foot or more into the ceiling space. With either choice, fill the field with beaded board or planks to complete the look.

FABRIC OR ACOUSTIC MATERIAL reduces sound in open spaces. Thank goodness you won't have to settle for old-fashioned acoustic panels; manufacturers have created more attractive sound-baffling materials, so your ceiling won't look like the one in the copy room at work.

BEAMS, perhaps having been overly and unwisely used in the past, have fallen out of favor. Properly done, however, beams add a lot of visual interest overhead. Add grandeur to high ceilings with a crisscross of shaped beams and paneling to create a coffered ceiling. New wood-like materials make this choice a less back-breaking installation and bring the price closer to Earth.

Floors
Six Material Selections

Since 1956 the world has witnessed the creation of space-age polymers, the achievement of moon landings, and the appearance of nanotechnology and string theory. But there still are basically only six types of materials in two categories to cover floors. Yes, the fibers and materials have improved in 50 years, but sometimes it's good to know you can rely on some things to essentially never change.

1. **Area rugs,** the smaller soft floor coverings, define a space within a room. These rugs sit on top of a hard-surface flooring. The key advancement in area rugs is actually on the underside. Rug grippers and improved backings help these rugs stay put.

2. **Room-size rugs** serve the same purpose as wall-to-wall carpet without the permanence.

3. **Wall-to-wall carpet** has certainly become the most ubiquitous flooring. It's guaranteed to cover a multitude of things better left unseen while exuding warmth and comfort. Color and pattern advancements make carpet more appealing than ever, but what really improves its appeal are the advances in stain and wear resistance.

4. **Wood,** one of the most luxurious and lusted-after hard-surface floorings, has advanced in every respect: wear-and-tear protection, ease of installation, and variety of offerings.

5. **Tile** is made pretty much the same way as it has always been, but the number of shape and color options has grown exponentially; new adhesive and grout choices make it easier to install.

6. **Yard goods** as used in the 1956 edition refers to durable flooring such as linoleum, vinyl, rubber, asphalt, and cork that can be rolled out to cover high-traffic, hard-wear rooms, including kitchens and baths.

Using Soft Surface Flooring

Wall-to-wall carpet is a plush option that creates an uninterrupted flow of color. Choose a bold color in a deep pile for luxury underfoot. Or use a neutral color in a tougher texture to create a casual feel and maximize durability in high-activity spaces.

Room-size rugs can make a very large room look just a bit smaller. They also can add needed color and texture while still being easy enough to remove if needed, a good option for basements and rental homes.

The original editors also suggested that the room-size rug on the opposite page could be rolled to one end of the floor for teenage dancing. It's a nice idea, but considering the amount of furniture here and the average teenager's typical lack of finesse, one wonders if they had ever met a teenager before suggesting such a thing!

Area rugs define a space within a room, and part of their appeal is in their unique shapes and patterns. Area rugs, and their junior partner scatter (or accent) rugs, can allow for cost-wise lively and creative expression in flooring much as throw pillows do for upholstered pieces. At the other end of the economic scale are intricately woven rugs, such as Oriental rugs, used to set the tone for the room.

Area rugs also can effectively anchor a conversation area, directing foot traffic around the edges. Scatter rugs are designed to take the wear, often used at key standing places such as the kitchen and by doorways, where excessive wear is likely to damage an area of the flooring beneath.

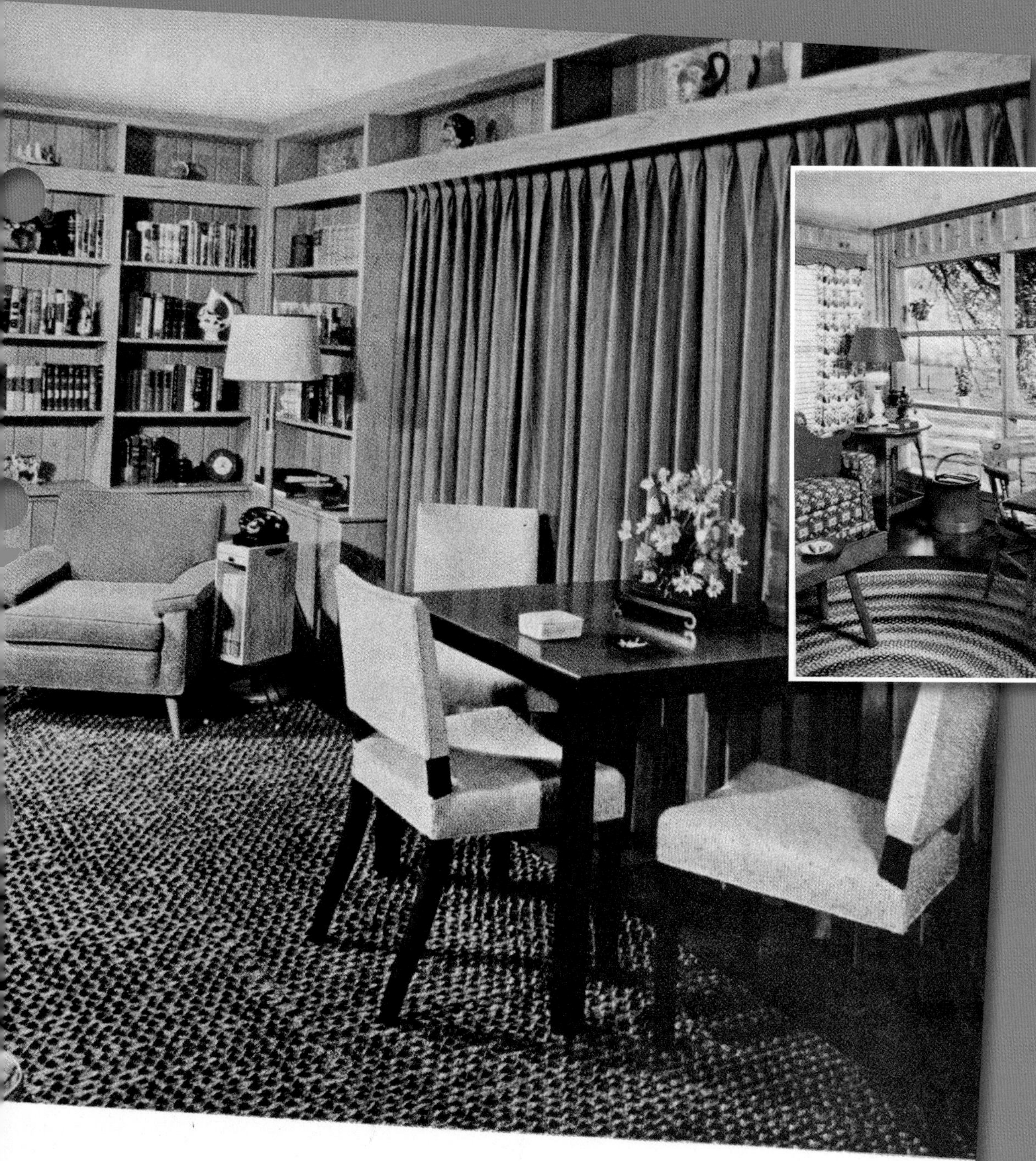

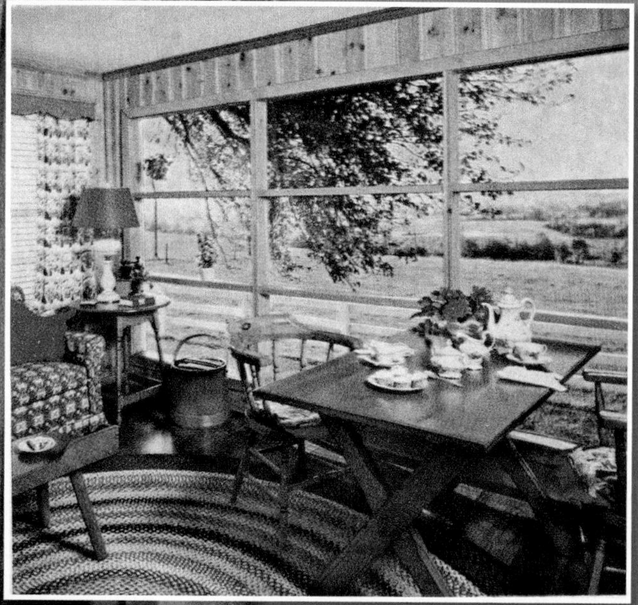

What's your choice—wall-to-wall carpeting, or snugly fit room-size rugs? Both have their advantages.

As a decorative element, carpeting gives a sweep of unbroken color from wall to wall, without the intrusion of another line or tone. And, no matter what the shape or size of your room may be, it *fits*, around all corners or curves or bays or jogs.

Rugs come in standard widths and lengths—6x9, 9x12, 12x15, and so on. And they can be custom-made from the standard carpeting widths of six, nine, twelve, and fifteen feet, and custom-ordered to any length desired. If you choose rugs, try to have not more than six inches of floor show at the edges. If there must be more, place heavy furniture to cover.

Natural Vs. Synthetic

Natural fibers for soft flooring include wool, cotton, and sisal.

Synthetics include nylon, polyester, and acrylic.

The naturals are not, generally speaking, as dirt-resistant as the synthetics. And improved fiber technology means many synthetics have the look and feel of much-desired wool at a fraction of the cost.

Using Hard-Surface Flooring

Durable, easy care, and apparently not a favorite of the editors in 1956 (they practically snubbed it with just a couple of images and a handful of copy), hard-surface is the underfoot choice for rooms destined to get dirty regularly—kitchens and kids' play areas, for example. Practically left out of the hard-surface flooring discussion was wood, an option perhaps almost too common then but now much desired in the 21st century.

Tile and vinyl are perennially good choices for work spaces and kids' rooms. Linoleum has a positive eco-factor (linseed oil is a major component) that has brought a resurgence in popularity. Cork, too, is making a comeback after some bad style days in the 1970s.

All hard-surface flooring (except for tile and concrete which require unbending support) shares an unseen improvement— better underlayment materials that allow enough give to make it comfortable to stand on for long periods of time.

Sometimes an idea just has to wait for its time. In 1956 new leather tiles, *above*, for floor and walls were touted as easy care and indestructible. The warmth and appeal are evident, but not much was seen of it again until fairly recently when some über-upscale designers have added it to the line of options—which gives you an idea of its price. Consider leather tile for an accent area or small den to create a feeling of richness and warmth.

Concrete Floors—Not Just for the Basement Anymore

Cool colors, interesting surface textures, and lighter-weight mixes have made concrete a presentable option for floors throughout the house, not just a default for work areas and basements.

Even unexposed, the new concrete mixes are popular. Often the underlayment of choice for radiant heating, concrete under carpet, wood, and tile, conducts heat evenly, keeping rooms toasty in cold weather.

Area rugs that are a smidge smaller than the full size of a room are good for keeping the emphasis on the center of the space. Oriental rugs, such as the one *above*, are eye-catching marvels that demand attention. Simpler, solid-color rugs, as at *right*, can subtly direct traffic in open spaces.

Mixing Flooring Types

For the convenience and comfort of wall-to-wall carpet but with sections requiring the dirt-repellent qualities of hard-surface flooring, install the carpet in a shape that accommodates both needs. For example, hard surfaces make sense inside exterior doorways, under dining room tables, and where plants are placed. What's particularly attractive about the vintage example *opposite below* is the lovely curve employed to accent the spaces and create visual interest rather than simply squaring off the line of separation.

If you're covering a portion of a hard-surface floor with a rug, keeping it in place can be a problem. Larger rugs held in place by furniture won't pose as much of a problem as small, thinner rugs that have edges exposed to traffic; use rug-gripping pads to hold rugs in place. If the corners are kept out of the traffic flow, the edges of a rug are less likely to curl up and become a tripping hazard. Curvy, fun free-form rugs, as shown *below*, don't have hard corners to worry about so are less likely to cause problems.

Bamboo: The New Wood

One reason the original editors may have snubbed wood flooring is that it was so commonplace. Around for centuries and abundant, wood was typically used for flooring in American homes. But wood needs care; it got dinged and dented from furniture and use. As wood supplies began to dwindle, however, real wood flooring became expensive and sought after.

Bamboo is a popular alternative. Actually a fast growing grass, timber bamboo flooring has a warm look similar to wood, and it is darn sturdy stuff. Its grain lines are more subtle than many types of wood, making it a complementary choice for use with stylish rugs.

This curvy rug clearly defines the conversation grouping and accents the room's modern look. It's easy to see how a well-chosen area rug can rev up a room's fun factor.

This striking space requires dramatic lighting. Overhead, a space-age built-in fixture splashes light throughout the room, and a string of fixtures under the sleek hearth highlight the floating feel.

CHAPTER 6 → Lighting

Knowing how critical good lighting is to successful decorating, the original editors made short work of their advice, then backed it up with lots of specifics to show how to create a good lighting scheme in any room.

Their wise words directed home decorators to create a lighting plan that achieved two key goals: Maximize visibility for tasks and make the most of your room's decor.

The basic hierarchy of lighting to reach those goals remains unchanged. *Ambient* is the overall lighting for a room. *Task* is lighting directed to a specific activity area. *Accent* draws attention to items or areas with focused lighting.

The list of things to consider along with recommended placement for lighting from the 1956 edition still provides a good starting point for your 21st-century lighting plan.

Light to Emphasize Decorating

1

Good lighting makes a room look well dressed: All the best features are highlighted and the lesser areas minimized. And the end result should look as though it fell into place effortlessly.

1. Round-the-Clock Lighting: You've spent hours matching colors, so give those colors enough light to enjoy them any time of the day. To re-create a sense of daylight at night, let some of the main lighting come from the areas near the windows.

Having a light source overhead also helps to replicate daylight. Recessed ceiling lights with low-wattage bulbs cast a gentle light all around the room.

2. Light Rooms Evenly: Contrast and glare in lighting are tough on the eyes. An evenly lit room reduces eyestrain and makes it easier to function. The approach is called layering light: top-down lighting to cover the room, and lamps to light the middle area at seated level.

2

③

To ensure you'll be able to place fixtures and lamps where light is needed, consider lighting needs as you create a decorating plan. Then you can have outlets and built-in fixtures in place to enjoy your new room from the beginning.

3. **Adjust Light Brilliance to Color:** Shiny and light surfaces reflect light and carry it throughout the room. Dark surfaces soak up light and seem to stop it near its source; plan for extra lighting to keep the room bright at night.

Light-color ceilings help reflect the light, hence the preponderance of bright white ceilings. Other ideas for spreading light around a room: include mirrors near lamps, translucent lampshades, and a set of spotlights on a stick—those floorlamps that are, basically, poles with three or more adjustable lights like the one in the vintage illustration *above*.

4. **Spotlight for Drama:** Dramatize your decorating with bright accents of light. Ceiling fixtures like this draw attention to a room's focal point.

Location and Light

Color is affected by light. That is probably one of the top 10 greatest understatements of all time. The perfect blue in the store is a hazy gray in your living room. The yellow that is an exact match for the background color in the fabric during the day looks completely different at night. Each light source affects color differently. Look at your samples in all kinds of lighting, paying special attention to daylight and the major type of lighting in the room.

With a dimmer, the spotlights' dominance can be reduced, allowing the light to simply supplement the ambient lighting and redirect the room's focus for an event. Dining rooms in particular benefit from this flexibility.

④

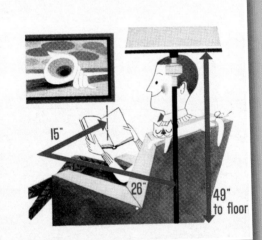

In the wise words of the original editors:
"As with furniture arrangement, the 'rule' for placing lamps is comfort. The effort of figuring out a few simple measurements before you buy lamps or place them will pay off in years of relaxation.

"Good looks go along with comfort. Place your lamps where they will be the most serviceable, and you will find the decorating effect quite pleasing."

Use the numbers they provided as a starting point. The goal is comfort and ease on the eyes for each task; adjust lamps and fixtures to your needs.

Lights by Seating Pieces

The distance from lamp to reader depends on the source, as noted here. Floor and wall lamps bring in light from above. Table lamps cast light from the side directly onto reading material; to avoid glare, the bottom of the shade should be roughly shoulder height. Adjustable-height lamps allow flexibility if people of different heights share a desk or reading chair.

My, How Times Have Changed

One thing the original editors would never have needed to consider was adequate lighting for a desktop computer. Computer screens are similar to television screens for lighting needs: Have soft lighting at the sides to minimize eyestrain. And for computers be sure the keyboard and nearby reference materials have adequate lighting.

Perhaps hand sewing has fallen out of favor, but someone doing handwork of any kind needs to be able to bring the light source close to the work. Swing lamps, as shown, are a good choice.

Lights for Working Spaces

Desk lighting needs to cast sufficient wattage over the entire work space. If you're the type to spread out over a larger surface, consider having more than one lamp or at least a lamp with a long, extendable arm.

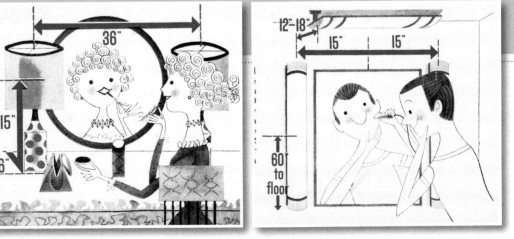

Must Beauty Lighting Be Brutal?

When it comes to light for applying makeup, the original editors felt honesty is the best policy:

"To avoid distortion of color when you are putting your make-up on, use a white light or white shades on lamps. This is one place where flattering light is not the answer. This will prevent the theatrical look of too-heavy cosmetics."

Fortunately, new lighting technologies provide clear and complimentary lighting. Look for coated or colored bulbs that cast a warm tone—and any bulb you choose should be frosted to avoid glare. Include fixtures at the sides of the mirror to cast a consistent light and reduce shadows. General bathroom mirror lighting benefits from the same overall approach.

Decorate with Balanced Light

A good lighting scheme works best when it isn't noticed. The lamps may be exquisite or the sconces may be the most expensive items in the room, but the real measure of success is even, clear lighting that draws people into the room and focused lighting that draws attention to the proper places.

The myriad of lamps, fixtures, and bulb options available now make it easier to create both gentle and bold lighting. Understanding the effect of lighting choices in a room, however, is still the hard part.

Evaluate the light in a room as you're decorating. If you've lived in the home for a while, you know where the "black holes" are that need brightening or the "hot spots" that need taming. Then experiment with lighting ideas before you buy lamps. Inexpensive clamp lights can be set up to get an idea of what accent lights will do; move existing lamps around or stack books underneath them to see whether some height will help.

Develop a list of lighting needs to use with your decorating plan so you can choose fixtures and lamps wisely.

Some New Things Under the Sun: Bulbs

In 1956, bulb options for lighting rooms were pretty much long tube fluorescent and round incandescent bulbs. Changes to those basic bulbs, plus the addition of halogen and other light sources, provide you with hundreds of options for creating a lighting scheme.

Here are five current popular lighting types. Each one comes in many shapes: halogen bulbs come in everything from tiny "peanuts" for puck lights to lamp size.

 **Incandescent** The classic choice for warm, soft light anywhere. Incandescent is, however, one of the least energy-efficient bulbs.

 **Compact Fluorescent** This subset of fluorescents comes in sizes to fit any fixture and offers pleasing light, little heat output, and energy efficiency.

 **Fluorescent** Standard tubes like this provide cool lighting—both to the touch and in color. Use this economical choice in utility areas.

 **Halogen** Clear white light and energy efficiency make halogen popular. But the bulbs get hot; allow for ventilation and protection.

Wake up your home with light

← after

Light-colored, semitransparent shades release light all over the room. New lamps are taller, because height was needed to shed enough light along the long sofa. Valance matches picture mats, conceals a glowing fluorescent light tube

before

The lighting here isn't doing justice to the room's lovely color harmony. Colors darken and look muddy — little areas of glare compete with vast spaces of dullness. The too-small lamps mean eyestrain when the family reads or works

Xenon A small amount of xenon gas enclosed in an incandescent bulb makes the light brighter and the bulb last longer, but energy efficiency is still low.

To find out more about the dozens of bulbs available for home lighting, visit the American Lighting Association's website: www.americanlightingassoc.com.

"ISLANDS" OF LIGHT

DRAPERIES LOSE DAYTIME GLAMOR

PICTURES IN DARKNESS

USELESS WALL BRACKET

LIGHT-STEALING SHADES BASES TOO LOW

TOO-SMALL DESK LAMP

COLORS LOST IN SHADOW

READING CHAIR WITHOUT LIGHT

Choose window treatments that complement their surroundings. Here, light-color draperies capped with a short, puckery valance neatly frame this picture window and nicely contrast with the wood paneling.

Window Treatments

Windows, the original editors noted, are designed to serve three practical functions: ventilation, lighting, and view. While the windows regulate airflow, window treatments let sunshine in—or moderate it when desired—and control the view to the inside to address privacy concerns.

Beyond the pragmatic, however, we also demand that window treatments be pretty. And those wise editors called beauty a function: Consider the role of windows from the inside and you can understand their smart thinking: Windows draw a lot of attention, so curtains, blinds, or draperies are highly visible as well. You can use window treatments to emphasize a room's decor or frame the view, disguise an architectural oddity or celebrate a great window shape.

The 1956 edition included a basic primer of ideas for window coverings with advice for what to consider when making choices; that's a good place to start. As with almost all aspects of decorating, you'll find so many more options today to address both the practical and aesthetic concerns.

Dealing with Window Styles and Shapes

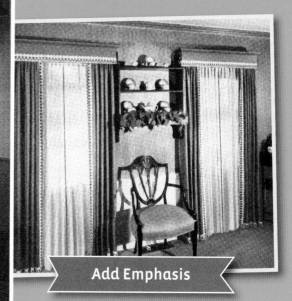

These two small sash windows, *above,* become dramatic decorative elements with layers of window treatments. The cornice adds height and formality; the fringe that skirts the lower edge makes each window look wider. Sheers and elegant draperies cover the windows and extend to the floor, continuing the illusion of height. The whole package of treatments also extends beyond the width of each window, adding an illusion of width.

Treat a door flanked by windows, *above left,* as a single unit for a cohesive look. This valance tops the full unit, and two layers of cafe curtains create privacy while allowing in sunlight and fresh air.

Function first: Start your treatment selection process by noting the style of your windows. Style is really a practical term here; it refers to how a window opens. Sash windows slide up and down, casement and awning windows swing out, and fixed windows do not open. Windows that open require treatments that allow ready access to the opening mechanism. An example of a less-than-perfect window treatment choice is a window shade set within the frame of a casement window; the crank for operating the window will always be catching the shade whenever it's down.

Then consider the shape and placement of the windows. While windows don't change shape or move, window treatments can create some incredible illusions: One window can look like two, two windows can look like one. Short windows can look tall, narrow windows can appear wide. With all these choices, simply covering a window at its actual size seems rather boring!

In some rooms, the windows aren't the center of attention. Here simple treatments matching the color of the surrounding walls will filter the sunlight or provide privacy. Reaching to the floor, these draperies keep the look formal even though they're made from cotton.

Combine Into One

Sometimes a room seems to have too many windows. In a simply decorated room such as the dining room *opposite below,* combining two windows with a clever treatment creates a cohesive look. While upholstered cornices aren't very popular and the curtain choice is rather stiff, you can see how a unifying top treatment (perhaps a plain valance), bookend treatments at each side, and an uninterrupted field of curtains create the illusion.

The lively pattern on this cornice, *left,* combined with sheers attached at top and bottom, helps these casement windows play up the geometry of a wall of built-in bookcases. This combination makes operating the windows easy and adds visual height to the room.

Soft Stuff: Curtains and Draperies

Curtains

W hile the terms curtains and draperies are used almost interchangeably, there is a difference. Curtains are lightweight fabrics, usually unlined, operable, and hung in a simple fashion. When the fabrics are heavier, lined, and hang to the floor, call them draperies. Take advantage of curtains' lightweight fabric and shorter length to cover windows high on the wall or where an open wall is needed beneath. Furniture can go right up against the wall, clearing more of the floor. And heating vents or radiators are safely cleared with curtains.

From a decorative standpoint, curtains have an airier look than draperies although the windows are often completely covered with either treatment.

Draperies often are dramatic and are an effective way to cover large spans of glass, often along with adjacent wall space, to effectively control ventilation, light, and view. Having more than one set of draw cords is the key to making these large swaths of fabric function well. In a bay window, *above left,* one opening at the center might be enough; draw the draperies open from a smidge to all the way, depending on how much light or breeze is desired. Another option is to have separate cords for the side windows to allow a cross breeze with a bit more privacy.

In modern homes with very large windows, like the one *above,* opening only the top tier of draperies allows light in while maintaining privacy during mealtimes. Close the top tier to moderate the light and open the bottom to enjoy the view during the day.

Cafe Society

Clearly a favorite of the original editors, these timeless tiers are a good choice for many rooms.

Place the lowest tier so it reaches from at least the bottom of the window (or all the way to floor) to viewing height. This gives anyone in the room a clear view to the outside while restricting the view into the room by passersby. Two or three layers complete the look.

Install cafe curtains using rings that slide on metal curtain rods so they can be easily drawn back for more light.

115

Flat Finishes:
Shades, Shutters, and Blinds

Shades, shutters, and blinds used to be pretty straightforward affairs: matchstick blinds that filtered light, opaque roller shades that blocked light, or venetian blinds with the mechanics to regulate light and ventilation. None was really designed to be used alone: These were utilitarian choices that looked best with proper draperies or curtains.

As window treatments lightened up, the options in this area have expanded more than in any other window treatment category. You can now find, or have custom made, Roman, London, and balloon shades in fabrics that accent your decor. Shade materials that insulate as well as control light come in a rainbow of colors and patterns, making practical pretty. And thin, lightweight slats make blinds an easy choice for many windows. Some types of "blinds" practically defy the definition of the term: They operate like venetian blinds but their flexible opaque fabric slats are held in place with transparent material, and they roll up as do shades.

The sun pouring through the big windows in this tiny room would be blinding. The white matchstick shades tame the sunshine while still allowing the view to peek through.

Outside The Box

Shades and blinds used to be confined to the exact size of the window, most often tucked inside the frame. New-style soft-fabric shades, such as Roman and London shades, can be hung outside the frame and drawn up and down without causing damage to the frame.

Shades can be chic. At night, these cool gray shades are pulled down, and the wall becomes a dramatic backdrop for the jewel-tone furniture and crisp white draperies.

The classic, formal arrangement a window is a layer of solid color sheers topped with a valance and full draperies in a patterned fabric. For maximum drama, cover the wall completely, top to bottom, side to side. The look is always lush.

Layer On the Look

Window treatments are a sociable sort. Where you find one, you're likely to find at least one more. A valance with swags over draperies *and* a shade tucked behind is not considered a rare decorating choice. In the 1956 edition, rarely more than two layers were featured on a window. Perhaps it was the fashion of the times; perhaps the choices were more limited—but layering always makes a window look more joyful.

Ruffly sheers are a pretty choice but offer little privacy. A simple roll-up shade tucked behind discreetly adds privacy.

One designer item that is surprisingly easy to get and within the means of many is custom window treatments. Rather than rummaging through a stack of packaged curtains or draperies in a department store, you can sit in your own home and choose custom-made window treatments in a wide variety of fabrics or wood tones.

To finish the look, add the rods and finials, rings and other hardware that you want. In as little as a week, all this will show up at your door.

Measuring carefully is more than critical; sometimes custom items are not returnable, so mistakes can be downright expensive.

Behind this flock of shutters and tiers of cafe curtains is a series of sash windows installed at a low height. This elaborate treatment gives the impression of one large window.

A well-accessorized room has the right balance of items to enhance the decor and express the homeowners' personalities.

CHAPTER 8

Accessories

As you decorate, you may worry about where the sofa should go, or fret about the window treatments. But true decorating anxiety really bubbles over when you start selecting and placing accessories.

To make accessories really shine in a room, consider them from the very beginning of your decorating plan. Sometimes an accessory or a collection even directs the decor. Conversely, if you've collected a few too many items, you may need to get rid of or store some. Decorating writers call this "editing." Decorating is the opportunity to evaluate these items and keep only those that still hold meaning for you and that will look good in a room.

The original editors had a three-pronged approach for choosing and displaying accessories based on location, location, location: deciding what goes on the walls, on tables, and on the mantel. That, of course, succinctly covers the territory.

Accessories for Walls

Another Obvious Advice Alert! The most frequently used wall decoration is framed pictures. That, however, is no constraint to your choices. The images, how they're grouped and framed, and the wallcoverings behind them all have an impact in a room. Create balance in your wall displays. Find the centerline of your display (over the mantel or the center of the sofa, for example); if the placement of images on one side of that center line mirrors the placement of items on the other, the arrangement is *symmetrical*. If there are more images on one side, or they're at varying heights, the arrangement is *asymmetrical*. Either way, the visual "weight" of the grouping should be equal.

Using a single large image, such as the one at *right,* dominates a wall and simplifies the look. It was chosen because it played up the room's color scheme and added to the desired sense of calm in this room with subtle tones.

Of course, not all wall decor is initially chosen with room decor in mind. A collection requires the right place for display. Designate an area large enough to show your collection; if you're still collecting, think of other places for display or plan for flexibility to rotate items.

Compare the two images *above*; the effect of wall hangings on the feel of a room is obvious. Neither is "better"; rather, each expresses the choices of two very different people.

Note how this art collector lined up images at eye level down a long wall; most of the tops and bottoms of the frames are at different heights so if a picture is changed, there's no worry about lining up the frame with the others. Also the subject matter and colors in the images are diverse, eliminating the expectation of similarity.

Perfect Placement

Smaller pictures can get lost on the wide open range of a wall; creating an arrangement that makes them all part of a whole gives them visual importance as well. Achieving good balance using large and small images can be difficult to visualize; that's where good grouping comes into play—and where the original editors shared the technique that has been passed down almost unchanged from the first edition.

Cut pieces of paper to match the sizes of the pictures. Label each one. Lightly tape the paper on the wall, and move the pieces around until you achieve the desired result. With a pencil, lightly mark the corner placement for each picture so you can place the real pictures precisely once you've removed the paper.

Color and spacing show off each
piece of this striking collection.

For an array of small items, collect them in a unifying
element, such as these seashells on a pretty glass plate.

This shelf unit arrangement, *below,* shows the pleasing
effect of placing accessories in the right space.

Accessories for Tables

In the words of the original editors:
    *"There are two kinds of accessories ... those that are purely
decorative and hold their usefulness in the satisfaction
beauty always gives, in the necessity of mankind for more
than pure function. Then there are the accessories that perform
a direct service for you, but contain and reflect beauty as well."*
    For both kinds of accessories, proportion and function are key.
An abundance of small items will crowd a tabletop and look
messy. Big items leave no room for anything else. If someone
will regularly be setting items on the table (papers, a remote
or two, glasses), leave room for these items so no one needs
to push things around to make room or to find things. The
tabletop is one area where less is almost always more.

adding accessories

r convenience and looks

personality with its own useful accessories

wrong

Avoid decorating with objects that are too small and pieces that are too ornate, or poorly proportioned. Functional objects can be pretty as well as practical

right

Put pieces from your hobby collection to work. Here an Early American bread trough holds potted plants, copper warmers brace books

Keep whatnots off your table, and house plants low

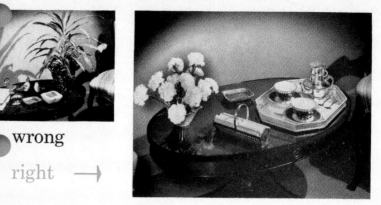

wrong

right →

Keep your table accessories selective; place them so you can easily find room to set needed things. On this small table, the removal of a magazine or book makes room for a coffee tray. The flower arrangement is in scale with the small table, low enough to see over

A large table calls for a few but important objects

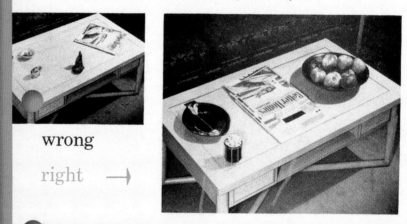

wrong

right →

Little ashtrays and figures appear lost on this big table. A few good-size objects, in different shapes and sizes, are a better choice. Here a black porcelain ashtray, a pottery cigarette cup, and a painted wooden fruit bowl help to carry out the casual contemporary theme

Pillow Talk

There's just something about pillows. Any chair or sofa seems bare without at least one. Use pillows to accent your decor and add flair. Be sure your pillows have a comfy, squishy feel so you can use them for lounging and leaning, not just for looking at. Use different sizes and shapes and a variety of colors to make pillows a vibrant part of your decor.

Accessories For the Mantel

The original editors recognized that people might look askance at the idea of books as decor. So they were quick to point out that a full bookshelf's visual appeal is an additional pleasure to what's inside the books.

Decorating the mantel involves decorating the whole fireplace wall. In many instances, the fireplace is the dominant point in the room, so what's on the mantel (or above it) is prominent in the room. Choose accessories for the mantel that relate particularly well to the space and put extra thought into the size. Items need to be substantial enough for this spot, but shouldn't overpower the room. For example, a large, very active picture that covered the entire wall above the fireplace could look as though it would topple over, but a grouping of images such as on page 122 covers the same amount of space and is visually pleasing.

At the other extreme, avoid items that are too small. Even if you keep things simple, such as the three pieces of pewter on the mantel in the Colonial-style room, *opposite top,* the items should contrast with the background and keep the mantel from looking empty. Note that although these pieces aren't large, they are substantial enough, so the space doesn't feel bare.

Bookshelves over or next to the fireplace are another pleasing option. This option puts the books you'll be reading in a place you'd like to read them—next to the fireplace—and gives you lots of decorating options. Break up the march of books stacked on the shelves library style with decorative items, plants, and books stacked on their sides.

A simple mantel arrangement is in keeping with the room's Colonial decor. That simplicity nicely contrasts with the busy patterns in the rug and fabric.

Modern mantel-less fireplaces still require interesting accessories. This school of fish swims horizontally across the vertical lines of the paneling to break up the space. The effect is of a floating mantel.

The mix of old and new, the bright inviting colors, and the smart room arrangement make this room a perfect choice for 1956 and today.

CHAPTER 9

Reality Check

In the last chapters of the first edition of the *Better Homes and Gardens Decorating Book*, the editors displayed a sure-footedness in the practical matters of decorating a home. The chapters titled *Space Makers, Dollar Savers,* and *Redecorating,* thoughtfully presented real rooms as attractive as those in any designer showhouse. They didn't skimp or breeze over everyday decorating concerns: With the same unfettered enthusiasm, they presented advice on repurposing furniture, squeezing out more space, and giving a plain room a major pick-me-up for pennies. Perhaps they liked nothing better than a good challenge!

The lesson: While there's nothing wrong with over-the-top design intentions, don't give up on your decorating dreams because you can't have everything. A little reality check and some clever thinking will curb any irrational decorating exuberance and lead the way to achievable style.

Space Makers
Creating Rooms that Multitask

To make small work of this topic, the editors photographed the same room from no less than six viewpoints. (Four are shown here.)

This was not just a savvy budget decision for creating images for the book; the variety of viewpoints made it easy for readers to see how several design and decorating lessons can be applied in a single room to make spaces seem larger and work better.

The overall shot at *right* shows how to make a small room with an L design look like one large space and function as several separate rooms.

Starting at the back, the dining table is informal and made of durable materials so it can be used for other activities such as game-playing (looks like they're engrossed in a game of Scrabble®!), or crafts. In the middle, storage pieces and a bookshelf along the wall lead into the desk right where the room turns, an area that was "dead" space before.

In the living room area, the sofa is a sleeper to accommodate overnight guests. Every square foot is used, but the feel is open and spacious.

Before

After

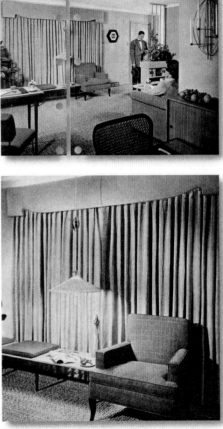

A few bright elements pop in this L-shape room, but the reason everything holds together is the flow of color on walls and furnishings from one end to the other. Flooring is important too: Notice how the two matching room-size rugs meet to keep the flow uninterrupted and make the rooms feel larger.

Perhaps this monochromatic choice is a bit extreme. Still it drives home the point: Keep your color scheme uncomplicated to maintain the connection between spaces and elements.

Good lighting is another way to maximize the spaciousness and usefulness of a room. Two good-size ceiling fixtures that can be raised or lowered provide most of the lighting for these rooms. In the lower positions these fixtures serve as task lighting; when raised they cast light throughout the rooms. Table lamps by task areas provide focused lighting and minimize dark spots.

Space-Makers
Savvy Furniture Choices

Clearly guests have arrived for the holidays, but the rest of the year this small room is a study and TV room. Smart furniture choices and placement mean neither function is compromised.

Not every piece of furniture in a small room has to multitask, but every piece has to effectively serve a purpose. End tables need to be large enough to hold a lamp and miscellaneous items; coffee tables need to be either small enough to move out of the way or large enough to hold reading materials, remote controls, and anything else needed in the room. Mostly solid colors and simple lines help keep furniture visually underwhelming.

Built-ins like the bookcase in this study/TV room/guest room, *opposite*, are another popular choice for small rooms. They provide storage and display space without taking up floor space. The dramatic color scheme and use of patterned draperies show how a small room can be visually interesting.

The quintessential multipurpose piece of furniture is the sofa bed. If you're buying one for your guest room/whatever-else room, consider first the comfort of your guests. A cheap backbreaker could break your relationship.

The Magic Of Mirrors

Double the size of a room, multiply the light from lamps and windows, or bring a great outdoor view right into a room. These aren't decorating tricks, rather things you can do with well-placed mirrors. And that makes mirrors such an appealing choice for small rooms.

When deciding where to place a mirror, look across to see what will be reflected from several angles to avoid a dull view. Nothing is more boring than seeing a plain wall twice.

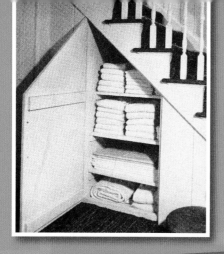

Space Makers
Storage Ideas

Nothing frees up floor space and opens up a room as the smart use of storage. There's at-hand storage for things you use frequently. Kitchen cabinets hold cooking utensils and dinnerware that's used every day, for example. Then there's storage for everything else—out-of-season clothing or linens, special occasion dinnerware, and so on. Incorporating good storage of both types will make your home function well. Comfort and convenience, the bywords of the original editors, are maximized with good storage.

In the 1956 edition, floor-to-ceiling, long wall storage was offered as the option of choice for long-term storage, and with good reason: *Everything* could be stored there. By creating a centralized storage area, you'll be less likely to be scrounging around closets to find things. Building a corridor of closets also allows for a quiet style choice; painted panels or lush wood tones add to the serene sense of organization behind those doors.

Storage should come in various sizes: big spaces for coats, little spaces for a stash of Christmas cookie cutters, and everything in between.

Short-Wall Storage

Even if you don't have a long hallway wide enough for a closet, you usually can find a small area to squeeze in a sliver of storage. The proverbial favorite is under the stairs. Older homes often have sloped walls or under-eaves spaces.

Use these areas to extend the storage for that room; that way you'll remember what's being stored behind the door.

Dollar Savers
Rev Up Rejects

Paint and fabric can turn less-than-fresh furnishings into perfectly new-looking items for your home. If you fill a room with these revived pieces and cover the walls with fresh paint, drab spaces look new and inviting.

If your decorating project begins with an entire room filled with an odd-lot collection of furniture, start at the same place you would if you were buying new furniture: color. Establish a color scheme for selecting fabrics to recover or slipcover the upholstered pieces, as shown in this vintage example *opposite*. For pieces with exposed hard surfaces (wood, metal, plastic) in a variety of colors or for furniture in several styles, consider painting them all to create a more cohesive look. (Many wood pieces can be stripped and stained to maintain the appearance of the grain.) Think of a half dozen dining room chairs, each a different style, all painted the same color—suddenly, you have a dining set!

The only caveat to resurfacing every piece in a room is this: Be sure you're not stripping away the value of a precious piece. Even some of the tables and chairs featured in the 1956 edition are now valuable pieces. If you think you have something of value, have it appraised.

Secondhand Savvy

Back in the day, used furniture often was called castoffs or hand-me-downs, and people came by them from friends and family. Rare was the person who spent Saturdays hunting down decrepit dressers or dilapidated light fixtures with plans to revive or repurpose them, much less think about bragging rights for the day's finds.

Today, haunting flea markets, tag sales, and secondhand stores is a popular way to find home decor. Low cost, the wide variety of unique options, the thrill of the hunt—it's easy to see the reason behind the popularity of secondhand shopping.

When you head out on a tag-sale expedition, have an idea of what you'd like to buy and know the size of your rooms. Have a tape measure in hand to ensure things will fit. Make sure drawers open and that you can sit on chairs or sofas without causing a collapse.

Perhaps most importantly, try not to get swept up in the moment and buy too many things that you'll never have time to fix up and enjoy.

Dollar-Savers
Ideas for Inexpensive Accessories

What really makes any room unique is the accessories. These miscellaneous items speak to what you and your family members find important, inviting, and expressive. To keep the budget in check, look for clever ways to use things you already have or to repurpose inexpensive items you find.

Displaying collectibles such as arrowheads, foreign currency, and antique maps is a good way to enjoy what you've gathered rather than keeping them in drawers and looking at them only occasionally. Grouping collections adds emphasis without expense.

For wall decor, look for interesting items at flea markets. Old prints of plants or animals from books, and decorative tiles are a few ideas for unusual artwork. Elaborate picture frames, pieces of decorative metalwork, and molds are more sculptural options.

China: The Reliable Standby

Beautiful china often spends much time behind cabinet doors, only seeing the light of day on special occasions. Dollar-savvy decorators have been putting it to decorative use for years. If you have an unused treasure trove of china, display it in a cabinet or on a rack if you want to be able to use pieces for special dinners or hang a few pieces on the wall if your service is no longer in service.

If your china cupboard is bare, tag sales and flea markets are full of incomplete sets of these graceful items often at very reasonable prices. Soup tureens make great planters, pitchers are perfect vases, and serving trays and bowls are colorful catchalls for hall tables.

Simple accessories become dramatic focal points when they are grouped in a visually interesting way.

Do You See What I See?

Some pieces can be repurposed and the style changed completely with just paint and hardware. In this example, the legs were cut down, and the piece gained an Asian flair with black paint accented with gold trim. If you came across such a piece at a garage sale, you might have to consider it carefully to see the options.

To make sure you don't overlook a decorating opportunity, keep a list of items you want to add or replace in your home. When you're checking out a flea market and something catches your eye, think about how it could serve a needed purpose, and inspiration may strike.

Dollar Savers
Some Assembly Required

The tradition of do-it-yourself is tried and true even for decor: Every dollar goes further when you can do some of the labor yourself. With a little practice, for example, you can paint a room for only the cost of materials. With a little more practice, you can paint furniture. The options shown in 1956 may pale in comparison to what you'll find today but the promise of a fresh piece is constant.

Beyond the revamping of pieces is the imaginative combining of elements. Call it *MacGyver Decor*: creating marvelous pieces out of simple, nondescript items. These examples from the first *Better Homes and Gardens Decorating Book* show how the concept of do-it-yourself decor works.

1. You'll need a little painting and papering finesse to create a similar wastepaper basket, but the only materials you need are a length of heating duct that's been capped on the bottom, two cans of glossy paint in contrasting colors, and a decorative print.

2. An unadorned dresser becomes entryway-worthy with a coat of glossy paint, shiny brass knobs, and a faux marble top. In 1956, the look was achieved by varnishing a sheet of plastic veneer to the top. Today, a faux painting kit will do the job.

3. Simply painting a square of pegboard in a contrasting color gives the antique car enthusiast a place to display select pieces and flexibility to rearrange the collection.

4. Ingenuity and imagination really come into play for combining materials to create this hanging shelf. It's a wire-mesh frame for drying clothes (an item probably not as readily available these days) that's been painted with black lacquer for a shiny finish and topped with a piece of cut-to-size plastic. The look is elegant and sleek, although the materials are plain.

When you find (or already have) a good item that needs some dressing up, consider where you're going to use it. Painted a bright color, this dresser would work just as well in a child's room.

④

Where Do You Shop?

The editor for this chapter of the 1956 edition seems to have had a scientific leaning: Several of the items are from a chemist or druggist supply. The mortar and pestle, the chemicals flask, and the tall powder jar shown here are inexpensive and elegant.

If you're looking for interesting, inexpensive accessories, shop at interesting, inexpensive places. Home centers have become popular decorating hot spots, as have office supply stores, restaurant supply houses, and gardening supply shops. Snoop around these stores to spur your imagination.

Another option is auctions for commercial as well as residential items. You'll find plenty of money-saving ideas even if you don't buy.

③

It's all in the display. The central point of this grouping is a piece of pegboard. The smooth white surface pops out against the bright red wall. Black frames on the prints and the straightforward display carry the formality.

141

Redecorating
Change the Background

Before

After

Most decorating is redecorating: Once you've acquired furniture and decorated a living room, for instance, chances are you'll be adding or deleting items from then on. When you move, much of your furniture moves with you. To use some of those items in new rooms or to refresh existing rooms, you'll need a decorating strategy. The original editors offered three basic approaches: change backgrounds, pep up with fabrics, and combine old and new. All are truly timeless, and many redecorating projects incorporate all three.

The first strategy, change backgrounds, includes changing window treatments as well as wallcoverings. If your furnishings are in good shape but you're moving to a new place, this is a money-savvy option. Paint and wallpaper readily bring the walls into your color scheme. Windows can be a little trickier. Chances are any existing window treatments won't fit the new windows, but save them anyway. Fabrics can be redone to make valances or swags to minimize your cost.

In this dining area, the new paint color accentuates a new two-layer window treatment that groups three sash windows into a single, lovely focal point. Covering the radiator also smooths the view of the room. The whole arrangement becomes cohesive and inviting with only a few small changes.

Changing backgrounds can be an especially effective technique for redecorating kitchens. With all those built-in cabinets and expensive appliances, kitchens tend to remain unchanged for long periods. Changing the paint or wallpaper and the window coverings, however, can revive the room. This lively lavender vintage image is a good example.

One-Bold-Move Decorating

There's drama in decorating and there's over-the-top, look-at-me! drama in decorating. Living with the former is easier, but the ideas in the latter can be so appealing. Fortunately, decorating isn't an all-or-nothing event. Choose the things you like and incorporate them at judicious levels. One key example is coloring one wall in a dramatic color. This amazingly red wall works because the ceiling was painted in a toned down but complementary pink. The gentle geometric pattern in black and white on the draperies softens the transition from red wall to white. The room has drama without being jarring or harsh.

The soft, flowing trees in these draperies established the color scheme for this room.

Redecorating
Pep Up with New Fabrics

Upholstery, pillows and cushions, and window treatments aren't just textiles that conform to the shapes they're used with. Fabric can be used to reshape furnishings. Even without reshaping, simply the change of color and pattern can give a piece of furniture an entirely different look.

A bunch of playful geometric pillows in bright jewel tones give this family room, *right*, a casual modern look. If the pillows were replaced with square back cushions in more subdued colors, the look would become more formal. And even though the benches are very modern, if pleated skirts that reached the floor were added, the look would be traditional.

Probably the most versatile use of textiles is window treatments. Rarely do decorating books and magazines recommend simply using curtains or draperies cut to the precise size of the window. Several small windows can be linked together to look like a single large window, short windows can appear to reach from floor to ceiling, narrow windows can look wider, and large walls of windows can be divided into manageable bits—all accomplished with fabric.

Slip into Something A Little More Comfortable

If your redecorating plans don't include replacing the upholstered pieces, check out the wide range of slipcovers on the market. Whether loosey-goosey, plop down comfortable canvas or snug-fitting prim-and-proper tweed is the look you're after, it's available. New fabric finishes also resist stains remarkably well.

Slipcovers are also an inexpensive way to try on a new look or to change the look of a room with the change of seasons.

Bedrooms can be readily redecorated with a change of background. The fresh white accents play up the new yellow walls and a hint of rose in the carpet. The color choice came from the fabric, copious amounts of which were used for window coverings. Keeping the bedspread simple and in style with the Colonial furnishings is a quiet counterbalance to the print.

Redecorating
Combine Old and New Styles

Something old, something new, they'll live in harmony, if they share scale and hue. In the first chapter, the concept of blending styles related to choosing a style. Here, the approach is from a practical angle: You have a few pieces of this style, and a few pieces of that.

Fortunately, the same strategy for success applies: Look for items with the same level of formality or informality, use color to tie the items together, and, generally speaking, choose items of the same scale.

Since these items are from various sources, remember that you're looking for jazz harmony, not barbershop quartet harmony. It's the unexpectedness of a traditional piece in a modern room that adds visual interest. Like an underlying theme, these rooms work best when one style is dominant. In the living room at *right*, just a few traditional family pieces fit in nicely with the mostly modern setting. Fabric is a great equalizer; recovering the traditional sofa in a modern color blends the piece neatly into the room.

Lampshades

New lampshades can go a long way toward changing the look of a room. After several years over a hot lightbulb, lampshades can yellow, dulling the light. If you don't find the right shade locally, look in decorating catalogs or on the Internet. You also can change the shape of shade for added interest. If you're not sure that a catalog lampshade will work, first measure to be sure it's about the same size as the current shade. Then look for similar shade-lamp combinations in photos.

Barrel Straight-sided barrel lampshades can add a modern look to a lamp. Wrap the shade in stripes to maximize the look.

Cone The soft slant of cone-shape shades is a gentle, classic choice. Pleated cloth softens the look even more.

Flared Jaunty curves and sharp corners make flared shades outspoken. Add interest to a plain lamp base with a flared shade embellished with ribbon.

If you need another piece of furniture in a room, look for something with clean, simple lines so it will accent the style of the other furniture.

Modern tables accent traditional

Against the sharp, clear background of primary red and white, an elegant traditional sofa lives well with sleek lines of tables in contemporary design

An informal setting combines old, new

A lady's desk in the Colonial tradition combines with a lightly scaled contemporary lounge chair in a setting which expresses the lively and all-embracing tastes of the homeowners. Accessories contrast, adding interest

Remodeling
The 800-Pound Redecorating Gorilla

Decorating, alas, cannot always resolve the problems in a room. Truth be told, some redecorating projects rightfully evolve into remodeling: Why make cosmetic changes to a room that doesn't function well anyway? The original editors recognized that a room's design flaws cannot be corrected with decor. As well, fine tuning just a portion of a room's design can greatly improve usability and appeal.

As you prepare to decorate, you may realize that a room's major feature is being completely overlooked, or perhaps there is no good way to make foot traffic move smoothly. Stop and consider whether what's really needed is remodeling: Don't ignore the proverbial 800-pound gorilla sitting in plain sight.

A fireplace wall redo and a living room remodeling project featured in the 1956 edition created new spaces that were comfortable and convenient—two things that repainting the walls or reupholstering the furniture could not accomplish.

Before

DINING
10 x 10

LIVING
20 x 21½

KIT
10 x 13½

UP

PORCH

PORCH

After

DINING
8½ x 13

LIVING
20 x 21½

KIT
10 x 15

UP

PORCH

PORCH

Adding windows and reconfiguring the entry hall maximized the view and improved traffic flow. In a home with these kinds of design problems, the homeowner was wise to invest in remodeling before redecorating.

The One-Wall Renovation

Because of their room-dominating nature, fireplaces are hard to hide—especially when the style doesn't fit with a new decorating scheme. Fortunately you can change the look without tearing out the working elements.

Even a surface redo like this, however, can add significantly to the cost of a redecorating project. Removing and replacing wallboard, and installing specialized materials, such as brick or stone, often requires skilled labor to get the right look. If any electrical work needs to be done (adding lights, for example, or moving outlets) you'll need a licensed electrician too.

CHAPTER 10

Everything In Between

1956

1962

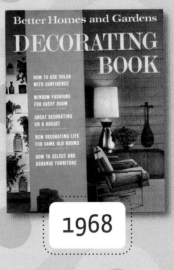

1968

1975

From a strong beginning in 1956, the *Better Homes and Gardens Decorating Book* became the standard-bearer of real-life decorating advice. As trends changed, the book kept pace with fresh editions, as this gallery of covers attests. Beyond styles, successive generations of editors incorporated advances in technology and changes in what homeowners required of their houses.

Each new edition showed the changes, and putting images from each book together gives one a sense of progression. And by looking at each edition individually, you can get a clear picture of what the style trends were at the time. Beyond the photos here, however, the advice for creating comfortable, convenient rooms—the motto of the original editors!—is pretty much unchanged. In every edition you'll find timeless design advice with timely decorating styles.

1981

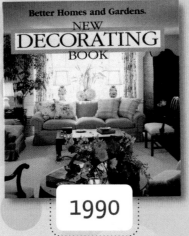

1990

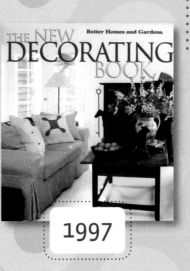

1997

2003

1962

Six years after the first edition was printed, it was already time to update the book. This edition included many of the illustrations from the first edition, but many photographs were new. Particularly, the miniature sets for furniture arrangements were replaced with full-size rooms. That helped the book become brighter and more inviting.

Whether it was for office work or homework, the home office gets major play in the 1962 edition with a wide variety of stylish options. Then as now, organization was the guiding force. In kids' spaces, it was hoped that access and fun colors made homework less dreaded.

The sleek lines clearly in evidence in the first edition get even sharper. The look is almost techno and the first signs of pop art show up.

153

Blurring the line between indoors and out, living spaces on patios resemble indoor living rooms.

Budget decorating adds the "save-on-item-A-to-splurge-on-item-B" twist. For example, this dollar-savvy bookcase allowed the homeowner to spend more money on furniture elsewhere in the house.

Plan a traveling decorating scheme

Even if your family is one of the many that must often uproot and move to a new town, it's possible to take your decorating scheme along.

A series of rugs in the same color, enough matching chests to be dramatic when grouped in a big room—separated for a small one, pair of loveseat-size sofas rather than one big one . . . all will allow a repeat of your decorating theme. Just add chosen color to the new walls.

The book took on a more personal touch as more people were featured living and interacting in the rooms.

Groups of storage pieces will fit in any home

Tall and important, the color-paneled wardrobes are designed for hall storage here, can double as extra closets or an entertainment wall in another home. They can also be used separately. Grass-square rug can be resewn to fit space requirements.

1968

While only another six years passed, the changes in styles and focus were significant. Not surprisingly, the third edition got a whole new look, and the chapters showed a change in emphasis: Furniture and furniture arranging each got a chapter; walls and floors received individualized attention as did apartments.

These illustrations for warm and cool colors attest to the strong influence of pop art in this edition.

To address not only small spaces, but also to show what furnishings alone can do, decorating apartments gets its own chapter.

Perhaps this should be called the 1968 Color Edition! The color schemes showed the drama of pushing extreme in boldness and contrast.

Where Are The People?

As quickly as they appeared in photos, they disappeared. People in images can interfere with readers seeing themselves in a space. Perhaps that's why most rooms again were photographed unoccupied.

Children's rooms get a section to address the needs and styles of the rooms of the youngest members of the household.

Personal space became more important in homes, and the 1968 edition reflected the change by introducing advice for decorating master suites.

158

What was then is new again! Decorative paint techniques appear in this edition.

342

SPECIAL EFFECTS

Marbleizing is easier to achieve than it looks. Start with flat black enamel as an undercoat. When dry, paint on white glazing liquid or flat white enamel thinned half and half with turpentine. Crumple a piece of plastic drip cloth, shake it out, and lay it on the glaze. Leave some wrinkles in the cloth. Pick cloth up carefully. Spray with clear finish when dry.

Crumble texture is made the way it sounds—by crumpling paper toweling, terry cloth, or tissue paper. Jab it straight down into the glaze in a random, overlapping pattern. By varying the material you use, the amount of glaze, and the pressure, you can make a wide variety of patterns. A light glaze coat and fine texture looks like old leather.

Splatter is put on over other patterns to add more interest and character. It's especially effective with simulated wood grains and over distressed natural wood. Use the splattern technique (page 343), but dip the brush into a glaze. The spray should be fine, but fairly dense. Concentrate along edges and into corners. Flip off excess glaze on newspaper each

343

Tortoiseshell pattern is striking used in small areas such as in door panels or on small drawer fronts, but would be too much for large areas. To make the pattern, put on a heavier than usual coat of glaze, then tap lightly all over the surface with the tips of your spread fingers. Change the angle of your hand on each tap to give a more random effect.

Splattern works only on a horizontal surface. Wipe glaze coat leaving a little more on than usual. Dip small stiff brush in plain mineral spirits. Shake the brush out, then strike with your thumb or a nail to spray the mineral spirits on the newly glazed surface. The undercoat will show through in irregular dots. Wait between sprays to get the effect.

Stippling with a short-bristled stiff paintbrush creates this effect. Buy a stencil brush or make your own by cutting off the bristles of a cheap paintbrush close to the metal ferrule. Jab the brush lightly straight down into the wet glaze, rotating it a little between strokes to make a random pattern. A very light pattern, with almost all glaze wiped off beforehand, looks like leather.

Distressed wood, even on pieces that already have a clear finish, can be done with nothing more than a tube of artist's raw umber oil color. Make random scratches with the point of a nail, dents with pieces of walnut shell or crushed rock pounded into the surface. Sand lightly, then rub raw umber into all dents and scratches. Rub off vigorously. Blend in streaks with turpentine.

A glossary of decorating lingo was included for the first time in this edition.

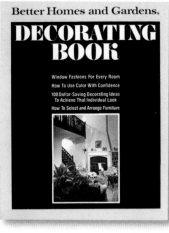

Better Homes and Gardens.

DECORATING BOOK

Window Fashions For Every Room
How To Use Color With Confidence
100 Dollar-Saving Decorating Ideas
To Achieve That Individual Look
How To Select and Arrange Furniture

1975

Seven years later, the fourth edition showed the impact of styles and colors at the extremes. It's the pinnacle of richness and boldness in every aspect of decor. The book took on an outspoken tone, too, encouraging readers to express personal styles with a call to action that had a very immediate tone.

Even the best home decorator might be able to do better with the help of a professional. Acknowledging this, the idea (along with advice) for working with an interior designer first appears in the 1975 edition.

As truly "far-out" decor became readily available, decorating with an exotic flair got attention.

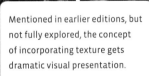

Mentioned in earlier editions, but not fully explored, the concept of incorporating texture gets dramatic visual presentation.

To draw attention to the decorative power of everything from molding to fireplaces, architectural details got their own chapter. In keeping with this edition's tone of extremes, this concept is expressed in terms of what can be highlighted and what can be hidden.

GUIDELINES FOR IDENTIFYING FURNITURE STYLES AND COORDINATING PERIOD ROOM SETTINGS

	Identifying characteristics	Woods	Colors	
V 74	Rococo movement brought small, dainty, ornate furniture with curved legs, marquetry, inlay, painted panels, gilded caning, and Chinese lacquer.	Satinwood, ebony, walnut, mahogany, and fruitwoods.	Grayed tones of blue, green, yellow, rose, and off-white.	◐
VI 33	Simple, rectangular forms decorated with Greek, Roman, and Egyptian motifs. Straight, tapered, and fluted legs. Black and gold lacquer decorations.	Mahogany, ebony, rosewood, tulipwood, and fruitwood.	Either muted or strong. White, gold, green, pink, blue, and crimson.	
Anne 14	Graceful, curved line. Legs—cabriole, ''S'' curve, and claw feet. Beauty of wood—carving, veneer. Very little ornamentation. Motif—scalloped shell.	Walnut, oak, pine, cherry, and mahogany.	Soft crimson, blue, green, and deep yellow.	◐
ndale 79	Solid, graceful forms. Chinese influence. Much carving, fretwork, and grooving in scrolls. Legs—Chinese or cabriole with claw and ball feet.	Mahogany; some Chinese lacquer and gilt pieces.	Rich, muted tones of red, green, turquoise, blue, and yellow.	
an 40	Designs of Sheraton, Chippendale, Hepplewhite, and brothers Adam. Graceful, dainty pieces with carving, inlay, and spade feet. Legs—straight, tapered, round, and fluted.	Mahogany, rosewood, satinwood, walnut, and exotic veneers.	Soft shades of blue, gray, yellow, green, and rose.	
an 00	Crude, unadorned adaptations of English styles—Jacobean, and William and Mary. Simple straight lines. Rush seats. Ladder and banister chair backs.	Pine, maple, cherry, and oak.	Warm shades of red, blue, green, yellow, and brown.	◐
an 31	Adaptations of Queen Anne, Georgian, and Chippendale styles. Spindle backed. Windsor chair, and rocking chair.	Mahogany, maple, walnut, and pine.	White, cream, mustard, red, blue gray, and green.	
y 5	Dominated by designs of Duncan Phyfe who was inspired by English and French Empire styles. Motifs—eagle, lyre, swag, star, and pineapple finial.	Mahogany, oak, ash, hickory, walnut, and fruitwood.	Soft to rich shades of red, blue, green, yellow, and brown.	
n 1	Overly ornate curves and ornamentation, heavy carving and turning, mother of pearl and brass inlay. Motifs—scrolls, flowers, leaves, and grapes.	Black walnut, rosewood, mahogany, and oak.	Somber shades—black, maroon, red, green, blue, and brown.	◐
al	Simplified versions of Louis XIII-XVI. Emphasized beauty of wood. Natural wax finish. Avoided gilt, paint, and marquetry. Ornamentation—simple carving. Legs—straight or cabriole.	Walnut, fruitwood, oak, pine, and chestnut.	Soft shades of dove gray, rose, silver, powder blue, and light green.	
ranean/	Large-scale pieces with Moorish influence. Lavish ornamentation, rectangular forms, and turned spindles. Hardware is heavy—brass or wrought iron.	Oak, pecan, chestnut, walnut, and red pine.	Rich red, gold, turquoise, emerald green, and black.	◐

80

NEW DECORATING BOOK

1981

Cool breezed in with the fifth edition. A larger page format and quieter tones gave the book a new relaxed, laid-back look. The mix of styles still prevailed. And the call to decorating action was backed up with how-to projects. With a nod to the increase of products for sale, the editors expanded their advice to cover more elements—everything from bleaching wood floors to buying

New, larger page format is introduced

Creating a room that has a certain personal feeling has long been a main goal of decorating. In this edition, the concept of decorating for ambience by style is described in detail.

TYPE
astic
rk Wo
ahogar
aple
l

TYPE
ater Ma
hite Ma
lk or A
garette
eat Ma
icking
ail Poli
aint Sp
andle V

FURNITURE FIRST AID

SH

PROCEDURE: SCRATCH REMOVAL

Regular applications of automobile wax fill in minor scratches.

Rub nutmeats (walnut, Brazil, or butternut) into scratch. Or touch up with furniture crayon, eyebrow pencil, or shoe polish in shade to match finish.

Apply aged or darkened iodine.

Apply aged or darkened iodine diluted 50 percent with denatured alcohol.

Using a fine steel-wool pad, rub lightweight mineral oil, boiled linseed oil, or paraffin oil into scratc[h]. Wipe dry.

N

PROCEDURE: STAIN REMOVAL

s

Place clean, thick blotter over stain and press dow[n] tion of cleaning polish or wax. Or apply camphora[ted] grain. Wipe dry. Repeat.

Rub with thin paste of wax and mineral spirits. Wher[e] rub with cigar or cigarette ashes, using cloth dipp[ed] lard, or salad oil. Wipe off immediately. Rewax.

Using fingers, rub liquid or paste wax into area. If rottenstone (available at most hardware stores). U[se] Polish. Or apply ammonia with damp cloth. Polish

Rub area with scratch-concealing polish. If that fail[s] burn is deep, area may have to be refinished.

Rub area gently with dry steel-wool soap pad a tiny that fails, rub with cloth dampened in camphorate[d] Repeat. Or rub gently with fine steel wool. Wipe of[f]

Saturate paper with lightweight oil. Wait. Rub area

Rub area gently with fine steel wool dipped in liqu[id]

If paint is wet, treat like nail polish stain. If dry, soak away paint with cloth dampened in linseed oil. If a[ny] and rottenstone.

Harden wax with ice cube, catching moisture as i[ce] remaining wax gently with old credit card. Rub w[ith] clean, thick blotter over stain and press down wi[th]

The buymanship and care information introduced in earlier editions became more detailed and comprehensive.

FINISHING TOUCHES
ACCESSORIES

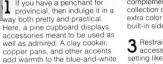

1 2
3

1 If you have a penchant for provincial, then indulge it in a way both pretty and practical. Here, a pine cupboard displays accessories meant to be used as well as admired. A clay cooker, copper pans, and other accents add warmth to the blue-and-white china and glassware.

2 With a little help from you, down-to-earth objects can make delightfully decorative accents. Here, a cluster of old daisy-filled milk bottles becomes a refreshing centerpiece. Much more at home than a contrived floral arrangement, the grouping complements the antique table. A collection of old Mason jars adds extra color and interest to the built-in sideboard.

3 Restraint is the key to accessorizing a contemporary setting like this one. The simplicity of the all-white scheme has been carefully punctuated with a few well-chosen items of interest—an elephant sculpture, a round glass bowl filled with irises, and a colorful quilt that is actually a mattress pad to which seaming and iron-on tape have been artfully applied. Stacked pillows provide extra seating.

Room tours introduced.

1 First, prepare the walls: Fill cracks, patch plaster, scrape and sand damaged areas, clean off dirt, and coat surfaces with the necessary primer. Then assemble your painting supplies. In addition to brushes, rollers, paint pads, and pan, invest in plastic drop cloths and an extra roller "sleeve" for each different color or type of paint you use.

2 Fill roller with paint by rolling it into the lower end of the tray, then smoothing the load on the slanted surface until paint is distributed evenly around roller. Fill roller with as much paint as it will take without dripping.

For the first time, illustrated do-it-yourself information is incorporated.

For the first time, creating style on home exteriors was addressed.

Detailed project information is included for several small projects.

LIGHTING/DO-IT-YOURSELF IDEAS

With a few basic tools and some do-it-yourself skills, you can create your own ingenious lighting. You can even build recessed and track lighting at a fraction of the cost of conventional models.

Put your imagination to work and scour your house for items to convert to lighting use. Visit your neighborhood hardware store, lumberyard, tile works, or business supply company. The number of items available for only a few dollars will surprise you.

Galvanized pails and stovepipe elbows, old rooftop ventilators, food graters, cans of all sizes, flowerpots and baskets are only a few of the things you can use as decorative lighting fixtures.

If the lights will be some distance from electrical outlets, buy long electrical cords. An extension cord may not be strong enough, especially if you attach the wire to the wall or ceiling or thread it through a hole in the wall.

Don't twist wires or pull them too tight. Fixtures should never hang from the electrical wiring, but from a chain or other support.

Always use low-wattage bulbs under do-it-yourself shades, unless you line the interiors with asbestos. And remember to paint interiors of pails, tiles, stovepipes and such items white, so they will reflect light efficiently. For ceiling fixtures, wiring will be less conspicuous if it is painted to match the walls, run from the fixture to the ceiling molding, and then down to the wall outlet.

1 Ready-made lighting fixtures may be beyond your budget, but with a little work and imagination, you can create clever lighting effects that cost very little.

This versatile accent light is simple and inexpensive to make. Buy a terra-cotta drainage tile from a building supply store. Then cut a plywood disc to fit inside the tile and nail the disc to a larger disc that will form the lamp's base. Route the wire through a hole in the base, attach a line switch and plug. Screw in a mini spot bulb, plug in the light and presto: You have an instant accent light.

You can use the same basic idea with clay half tiles and turn them into reflector lights for the yard. Simply bury the flared end in the ground, so the opening faces the area you want to light. Use outdoor stake-type fixtures and landscape around the tiles with pebbles.

244

167

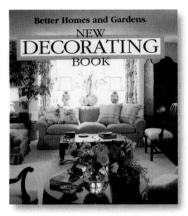

1990

The cool Zen morphed into a cozier look for the sixth edition. Warm wood tones, layers of textiles and collectibles gave a vintage look—with notably vibrant exceptions. A new section of whole-house tours showed the flow of style from room to room. The design principles were shown in photographs; illustrations were reserved for how-tos.

The cool colors continued, but wood tones and layers of fabric added warmth. The modern influences were tamed in many places to reflect the cottage influence.

Perhaps reflecting
improved photography
and printing processes,
the book starts with
several pages of larger
inspirational photos.

Many of the rooms possess
a softer, more romantic
mood. The look was busier;
patterned fabrics, and lots
of items on display.

Even the once exuberant Bohemian rooms that reflected international styles became more sophisticated and shown in subdued tones.

The room-by-room approach was supplemented with personal stories of whole-house decorating strategies.

As collecting fever gripped home decorators, this edition offered more advice on creating vignettes, displays of growing personal collections.

171

THE NEW
DECORATING
BOOK
Better Homes and Gardens.

1997

The seventh edition saw a little housekeeping. The new organization: Section 1—By room. Section 2: Design topics and reference materials. Now inspiration and hard-working instruction flowed throughout. The images reflected the cleaner, more straightforward approach. More streamlined, a room's beauty shone through and the clean design emphasized the

New —
Take the quiz! Learn your decorating attitude to help focus your decorating choices.

Where do you like to vacation? What's in your wardrobe? And what do these questions have to do with decorating? Learning about your inner design self may offer a guide to new decorating choices.

The decorating attitudes—eclectic, slick, formal, casual—aren't style specific. Since they speak more to lifestyle, you can build a personal style from your attitude. This edition featured examples for every room.

Since the style "rules" had long since relaxed, the rooms themselves seemed to kick back more, even the more formal-style rooms.

With stylish furniture available in a wide price range, it became easier to achieve a lush look even on a budget. And with the now long history of save-on-item-A-to-spend-on-item-B, and flea-market finds, home decorators could really amp up the style while squeezing the budget.

Room functions blurred as much as styles. As well, storage became a style statement in every room.

New technology in color scanning began the era of personalized paints.

Room
by Room

Fresh ideas for every space

Every room serves a purpose. Living and family rooms are for gathering. Bedrooms and baths are for quiet escape. The first step to successful decorating is accommodating those functional requirements. Next is adding personal style. Look at these examples for ideas to combine the practical with the beautiful in your home.

Living rooms

Your living room can be one of the most versatile rooms in your home. Whatever your style, the space can be as cozy for conversation, as gracious for entertaining, and as comfortable for relaxing as this New England-style classic. What else would you like it to be? Could you add a home office or library? Could it become a music room too? Whether your space is big or small, the right furnishings can help you put more life, style, and function into your living room.

Express Yourself

A well-designed living room lives and entertains the way you do. What's in the script for yours? Is it a guests-only space? Is it the family's everyday gathering spot? You'll put yourself and your guests at ease by tailoring furnishings to the way you use your living room. Analyze your space and decide if the furnishings and the arrangement work. If you're a put-your-feet-up, casual type, a room with white upholstery and no ottoman in sight may be a bit too formal for you. However, if your living room is more for entertaining than for watching television, the formality of classic furnishings and traditional arrangements could be the best choice.

ABOVE LEFT: Classic forms and details in the upholstery, window treatments, Louis XVI chairs and console, and the symmetrical arrangements exude formality in this room. **ABOVE RIGHT:** Neutral walls set a serene backdrop for a simple room where shapely, comfy seating is a priority. Accents are edited to a dramatic few.

ELEMENTS OF YOUR STYLE

Whether your design style is formal, casual, spare, or a funky mix, take a thoughtful look at the design elements and furniture arrangement in your living room. Is your room in sync with your style? If not, use these tips to do a little redecorating.

■ **USE FABRICS CREATIVELY.** Fabric weaves, finishes, and patterns express different degrees of formality. Linen, for example, is a good choice for an eclectic room that's sleek yet casual; use it in natural hues in understated window treatments. To express a casual attitude—whether your style is contemporary or country—dress sofas and chairs in the same textural denims, plaids, and cottons you wear on weekends. Mix patterns for eclectic and casual styles. Matched fabrics convey a formal look, as do elegant silk, damask, and glazed chintz. *(For more tips on choosing fabrics, turn to "Fabrics" on page 416.)*

■ **FRAME A NEW VIEW.** Window treatments play a major role in building your style. Loosely draped curtains express a casual, clean, or eclectic look. For a minimal look, stick to unadorned shades, blinds, or shutters. For a formal, traditional feel, consider traditional draperies with flowing floor-to-ceiling panels, valances, and elegant trims.

■ **LET FURNITURE TELL YOUR STORY.** Create a formal look with antiques and reproductions featuring classic details: camelbacks on sofas, cabriole legs, ball-and-claw feet, or shield- or lyre-shape chair backs. Make a formal yet modern statement with 20th-century classics such as Barcelona and Wassily chairs. Oversize roll-arm sofas with squashy cushions can set a casual mood.

■ **FACTOR IN TEXTURE.** Rough textures such as berber carpet, natural-fiber rugs, and twig furniture work in casual and eclectic rooms. Smooth textures—lacquer, glass, mirrors, and polished woods—can combine to convey a sleek yet formal attitude.

ABOVE LEFT: Classic, sink-in seating and a bright mix of colors and patterns give this room its outgoing look. The upbeat mood is enhanced by yellow paint on the end wall and on the back wall of the open shelves. **ABOVE RIGHT:** A Victorian sofa, a sleek ottoman, and graphic pillows add personality to a romantic room.

Formal or Casual?

To put your best "style foot" forward in your living room, would you wear a silk pump or a cross-trainer?

Most living rooms fall somewhere between formal and casual. Whatever their degree of formality, they all share a goal—gracious comfort and ease—but take different paths to get there. What's your lifestyle, and what are your entertaining needs?

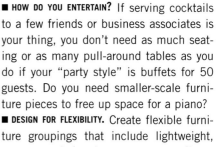

FORMAL FLAVOR

A living room used for formal entertaining demands a few special considerations.

■ **HOW DO YOU ENTERTAIN?** If serving cocktails to a few friends or business associates is your thing, you don't need as much seating or as many pull-around tables as you do if your "party style" is buffets for 50 guests. Do you need smaller-scale furniture pieces to free up space for a piano?

■ **DESIGN FOR FLEXIBILITY.** Create flexible furniture groupings that include lightweight, open-arm chairs that rearrange easily as guests gather during a party. Upholstered ottomans work as tables and extra seating.

■ **MAKE IT EASY FOR GUESTS.** Put tables within reach of sitting areas. A sofa table can be a mini oasis for plates and drinks.

CASUAL DAYS

Live and entertain casually? Remember that any style, including traditional, can be casual if you decorate with these ideas in mind.

■ **ARRANGE CASUALLY.** Instead of placing sofas in a formal face-off at the fireplace, let seating mill around informally. Add a sturdy ottoman or coffee table for a footrest. Arrange collections and art asymmetrically.

■ **MIX IT UP.** Toss a wicker chair, a wood rocker, even an unexpected log chair into an upholstered grouping to loosen things up. Mixing knotty woods and painted or distressed finishes relaxes the mood, as do gathered skirts on traditional sofas.

■ **ADD FAMILY ROOM TOUCHES.** Add a dining or game table to a corner of a traditional room. Pull a table up to a bookcase for a snug reading, homework, or dining spot.

ABOVE: Free-spirited color beckons from this easygoing room. A playful mix of fabrics on the slipcovered sofa and pillows contrasts with the textures of distressed wood and wicker. No window treatment is needed; a folding screen easily moves in front of the windows to add privacy or fend off harsh rays. **OPPOSITE:** Classic furnishings, antiques, and gilt-framed art give this room a formal air; seating reupholstered in highly textured chenille relaxes the mood. The modern cocktail table makes a delightful and unexpected contrast to the oversize French mirror behind the sofa.

Design for Flexibility
Pull together the versatile basics in furnishings and other design elements,

and your living room can sail gracefully from casual daytime living to dressier evening entertaining with only a subtle change of accessories. Whether your style leans toward traditional or modern, your living room can be inviting around the clock if you make comfort a priority and keep backdrops simple.

■ **GO LIGHT.** Neutral, or at least subtle, backdrops entertain well, day or night, making it easy to add more color and pattern in accessories. White walls, ceilings, mantels, and window treatments are crisp and appealing with any decorating style.

■ **STOW IN STYLE.** Storage ottomans and window seats, armoires, and bookcases with enclosed compartments hide daytime clutter when company arrives.

■ **PUT COMFORT FIRST.** Use overstuffed versions of traditional seating pieces, such as roll-arm sofas and club chairs. For long wear and beauty, make your biggest decorating investment the sofa and cover it in a durable fabric, such as tapestry or cotton.

■ **DRESS UP ACCESSORIES.** Substituting silk accent pillows for daytime cotton ones or arranging candles and collections on the coffee table sets a special-occasion mood. Build a fire or fill the fireplace with a cluster of candles.

■ **PLAN FOR LIGHT, DAY AND NIGHT.** Minimal window treatments, from classic swags and jabots to chic window-framing drapery panels, invite the most light by day, yet they still look dressy for parties. Turn on accent lights at night; a picture light over your favorite painting adds drama to a dark wall.

ABOVE: When the owners of this home chose the room's main focal point, the fireplace lost out to the view, but it's the center of attention in an alcove that includes a desk and striped seating. The fireplace wall glows in sun or candlelight thanks to pearly paint used in the cloud-effect finish. RIGHT: Striped, floral, and plaid fabrics make a friendly mix against the sail-white backdrop, wicker and wood tables, and yellow berber rug. An unexpected and witty touch, a frilly yellow lampshade tops a floor lamp. OPPOSITE: Golden sunshine and ocean blue inspired the palette and breezy attitude of this living room. The slipcovered sofas are angled to focus on the spectacular Pacific view. The arrangement also keeps this main conversation area open to the action at the other end of the long space.

Choose Your Focus

Every sitting spot needs a focal point. Think of it as the sun in your furnishings universe—an anchor around which all your furnishings revolve. If your living room has a natural architectural focus, such as a rustic fireplace, built-ins, or a great view, group seating around it. If not, accept the challenge and create your own focal point. Arrange seating to focus on a bold painting, a grouping of colorful prints, a large decorative mirror hung above a console table, a bookcase, or an armoire. A focal point gives the eye a starting point from which your eye can take in the whole space with ease.

FEATURE ATTRACTIONS

■ **DO IT YOURSELF.** If your home's builder left out architectural character, add some yourself. An antique fireplace mantel, a large-scale furniture piece, or a grand painting underlined with a cabinet or a bench can anchor a seating group. Or, center seating with a hunt board or sideboard teamed with an oversize mirror.

■ **GRAB THE EYE WITH COLOR AND PATTERN.** Use bright or bold hues to create a focal point. A boldly colored and artfully shaped sofa or a brightly painted armoire can grab the eye in an otherwise bland living room. Or, use a beautifully patterned area rug to draw the eye and anchor seating pieces.

■ **TURN TO THE VIEW.** If you have a great window or view, arrange seating to take advantage of it. Paint the window trim an accent color or add curtain panels that capture the eye without competing with the view.

OPPOSITE: Embellishing this plain window with rustic shutters transforms a plain wall into a focal point for living room seating. The expanded window is more in scale with the sideboard beneath it. Colorful wall art draws the eye to the new focus. **RIGHT:** Why choose when you have two views that are worth savoring? By arranging upholstered seating at a right angle and tucking a chaise under the window, the family and their guests can enjoy the rocky hearth in this seaside living room and still watch for passing boats. A large area rug and a slim sofa table help set the seating group apart from the adjacent dining area.

More Grace Than Space

Your living room can be small or midsize and still offer big style and comfort.

How you design a small, featureless space is more important than its square footage. With the right furnishings and creative arrangements, small spaces can be as gracious as larger ones—and offer even more coziness and intimacy too.

LESS CAN BE MORE

■ **RESHAPE THE BOX.** Put the sofa on a casual, room-widening angle and enhance the effect with a diagonal area rug. Hang a window valance on a rod mounted on the wall above the window so the fabric clears the glass completely. Add tall items, such as a lofty secretary or a ceiling-high ficus tree, to make an 8-foot ceiling seem higher.

■ **MAKE COLOR A PLAYER.** White walls and sparkling mirrors make a room look bigger, but if you love color, use bolder hues for a cozier feel. Forge a space-expanding link with the outdoors by bringing in the colors seen outside your windows—desert neutrals, forest greens, or garden-flower brights, for instance.

■ **PUT WALLS TO WORK.** Give a small space grand architectural character with built-in shelves or bookcases. Such storage creates a focal point and corrals clutter. A bookcase built to stretch from wall to wall and floor to ceiling expands space by pushing the walls out and the ceiling up. Balance furniture groupings with wall displays of art or collections.

■ **PARE FURNISHINGS.** Use fewer, bigger furniture pieces and include some light-scale and dual-purpose items. A drop-leaf sofa table expands for dining and entertaining. An over-size ottoman offers extra seating.

■ **LIGHTEN UP.** Light fabrics and wall finishes and simple window treatments, such as trim, light-hued draperies, curtains, or shades, give rooms an expansive and open feeling by keeping things bright and airy.

■ **STRETCH YOUR SPACE.** To create long sight lines, link adjacent spaces with the same colors and flooring.

ABOVE: Ample seating plumped with floral cushions snugs up to one wall, allowing space to move through the room to the terrace beyond. Simple drapery panels frame the atrium door without blocking precious light. Artwork turns a blank wall into a secondary focal point. OPPOSITE: A sofa and armchair are angled to break up boxiness in this living room. Flanking the window with shelves turns the entire wall into a focal point. New canvas slipcovers, light pattern-free walls, and a light rug bordered in flowers also give the room a gracious, expansive look.

Make a Large Space Inviting

Variety is the decorating solution for large living rooms. By dividing your rambling space into several intimate seating and activity areas, you can create islands for relaxing, reading, enjoying a garden view from a window seat, or letter writing at a corner desk. Instead of arranging a single, overly large conversation area, divide up the seating. Two smaller sitting areas for guests to gather around are friendlier for entertaining too.

■ **DEFINE WITH FURNITURE.** To subtly separate two sitting areas, arrange a pair of seating pieces with their backs to each other. Include some lightweight chairs that can be moved from one group to another as needed. Use the room's narrow ends for tall case goods or a desk. Tuck functional tea or console tables for serving and display into alcoves and corners.

■ **UNIFY YOUR SPACE.** Even when you've subdivided its functions, treat the room as a whole, weaving it together with the same window treatments, the same wall color or wallcovering pattern, and the same sweep of carpet or hardwood flooring. Define separate conversation spots by using area rugs.

■ **FIND FOCAL POINTS BEYOND THE FIREPLACE.** Pull up a chaise lounge, a desk, or a couple of chairs to a window with a great view. Adding a window seat creates seating, storage, and architectural interest.

LEFT: The original, early-1900s hearth in this art-filled home is a natural focal point for one seating group. A chair by the tall window takes advantage of the view. A movable ottoman provides extra seating. OPPOSITE: Back-to-back leather sofas define two conversation areas in this oversize living room. In a large space like this, one focal point isn't enough. The fireplace, a tall grouping of artwork between the windows, and an alcove accented with a console table and decorative mirror attract the eye and balance each other.

Changing Seasons

When falling temperatures and snowflakes
make cocooning indoors so appealing, warm body and soul by redecorating with slip-
covers in rich colors and a seasonal change of accessories. In the living room of this 1920s Arts and Crafts-style home,
the French settee and windows dress in cut velvet, and fireside seating dons chenille cover-ups and textured pillows
in winter. Even lampshades change to dark-hued silk. Iron masks of the North Wind and clay pots of winterberries
accent the fireplace and mantel. Turn the page to see how this cozy room cools off when summer arrives.

Changing Seasons

It's summertime, and the livin' really is easy—
and easy care. The living room sheds the warm winter wear shown on the previous pages and slips into something cooler and more comfortable. White is the unifier, making the space feel and look airy and expansive. Tapestry slipper chairs pop on white canvas slipcovers, windows dress in crisp linen, and the settee and fireside seating shrug off their extra layer. Pillows are brighter, lampshades are lighter, and the mantel is "seascaped" with beachcomber shells and sea glass. Displaying art on an easel makes it easy to change the scene to fit the season.

family rooms

Your home is your haven, and for many families, the family room is the heart of it.

No wonder you have great expectations for that great All-American space where you log lots of family time, relaxing together, dining, entertaining, and being entertained. Whatever the size of your gathering spot, it can be as great-looking as this easygoing space. Good design will make your space work and play as stylishly as the family rooms in this chapter.

Success in the Family Business

Once the family's retreat to avoid messing up the "good" furniture in the formal living room, family rooms and great-rooms are today's casual but stylish hub for everybody, including guests. To design for comfort, flexibility, convenience, and, of course, your personal style, consider the four Ws: Who's using the family room? What's going on? Where are the activity areas? When is it used most?

■ **PICK YOUR FOCAL POINT(S).** Yes, there may be more than one. In family rooms, seating often must focus on a fireplace and a media center—a problem often solved with a diagonal furniture arrangement that can focus on two walls at once. Let your focal point anchor your furniture arrangement.

■ **USE FURNITURE WISELY.** Break a large great-room into two or more seating areas to increase versatility and provide solo spots for reading, watching television, or playing video games. A table can double as a desk and a crafts or games spot. Let furniture direct traffic around, not through, activity areas.

■ **DESIGN FOR COMFORT.** Durable, easy-clean upholstery, natural-fiber rugs, and cotton, denim, and other no-fuss fabrics relax the mood.

■ **INCREASE STORAGE.** Built-ins and free-standing storage organize an active room filled with books, magazines, electronics, toys, and more.

OPPOSITE: Sharing neutral hues, natural materials, and a fireplace view, the great-room's living and dining areas flow seamlessly into the kitchen. The limestone island incorporates shaded lamps—an especially warm touch for any kitchen that is part of a larger great-room. A cloud painting draws the eye to the sky. The bright yet mellow scheme of warm woods, warm whites, and dashes of black is punctuated by tangy lemon and lime accents. The kitchen's focal point wall presents an uncluttered face on the family room side, but turn the page and you'll see the storage bonus it holds.

BELOW: Grab the remote, a good book, or the kids for cuddling and sink back among the citrus and white pillows on this spacious daybed that serves as the great-room sofa. Its shapely legs end in wheels, giving it the flexibility to move anywhere in the room. The seating piece is pulled away from the wall, so traffic glides behind it and not through the seating area.

GREAT-ROOM, GREAT IDEAS

Cares of the day melt away when family and friends gather in this simply dramatic great-room where sail-white backdrops, snuggle-in seating, and a mix of warm, natural textures create its getaway mood. Every detail in this talented three-in-one space was thoughtfully designed to enhance family living.

1 Refreshments, anyone? Convenience inspired the features at this handy intersection, where you can grab a log for the fire, make a snack on the stone-slab island or a cappuccino in the beverage center, and plop down on one of the dining table's leather chairs. To keep the mood airy and expansive, cabinetry is a pale maple, and glass doors are lined with rice paper for a frosty, textured look. **2** Remember the kitchen's focal point wall on page 198? It turns a clean-and-pretty face toward the living space, but it works hard behind the scenes too. Step behind it into the "butler's pantry" with built-in freezer, refrigerator, bar sink, food prep counter, and storage for table linens, serving pieces, and great-room "stuff." (Clutter doesn't play in this contemporary scheme.) At the end, the built-in desk keeps the household organized. **3** Not in the mood to cook on a sultry summer night? Try take-out—without leaving home to fetch the food. With a circle of cheery chairs under backyard oaks, impromptu picnicking on the shore is just steps away. Creating access to the outdoors, be it a big yard or a sliver of garden, makes any family room live bigger and adds the fun option of fresh-air dining.

ABOVE: This room offers fun for all ages. Ask the kids what activities would turn your family room into a great-room. Here, it's a child-size table and chairs for art projects, a soft wool rug for floor games, and nearby, a TV on a bench that lies low so it doesn't obscure the view. Remote-controlled blinds temper the sun, clerestory windows all around invite natural light, and uplight sconces, such as the one on the wall high above the TV, handle general lighting.

New Look
Smarter Storage

BEFORE

Well-loved family rooms have a way of becoming well-worn family rooms, overstuffed with accumulated treasures—and, yes, clutter. Still, updating your family room doesn't mean out with everything old and in with all new. It means dressing up that broken-in sofa, arranging for more function, and putting lazy walls to work. Here's how this family room kept its best and changed the rest:

■ **TWO UNFINISHED PINE CORNER HUTCHES,** simply stained, make a powerful addition to the fireplace wall. They expand storage and display space, introduce needed vertical interest, and widen the room by carrying the eye from wall to wall—and around the corner. Remember: With the right cabinetry, 12 to 24 inches of floor space along a wall yields a lot of storage between the floor and ceiling.

■ **THE DECADE-OLD YET STILL-COMFY SOFA** was spiffed up with a washable slipcover in multicolor paisley that disguises spills. Accent pillows in coordinating fabrics link the "new" sofa and "old" woven chair.

■ **TWO SMALL TRUNKS** replace the ho-hum coffee table. They add character, are handy for stashing toys before company arrives, and they're easily moved aside when the kids play floor games.

■ **A NEW WOOD-LOOK LAMINATE FLOOR** accented with an inexpensive sisal rug replaces the old beige carpet, underscoring the room's traditional character in fuss-free style.

■ **CHECKED FABRIC** on the window's pleated valance and side panels complements the paisley sofa. Full-length shades control sun more effectively than the half-shutters did.

RIGHT: With extra storage and easy-clean fabrics and flooring, this family room is now more kid-friendly and more carefree for parents too. Rearranged seating and a versatile two-trunk "coffee table" open up the space, making it more inviting. Corner hutches add storage and architectural impact.

Link with Color and Style

Today's most popular floor plan, the great-room
with kitchen, dining, and living space

flowing together, poses some tricky
decorating challenges. Forge links
with design elements and you can
blend those rambling spaces into
an inviting, unified whole.

MARRYING SPACES

■ **CREATE FLOW WITH FLOORS.** Use the
same flooring throughout, especially
in smaller spaces. If you do change
flooring materials between adjacent
areas, it's wise to stay in the same
color family to avoid jarring contrast. Use area rugs to define and
anchor groupings.

■ **LET WALLS AND WINDOWS CARRY YOUR EYE.**
In this French Country-inspired
room, the walls are drenched in yellow paint, and topiary-print fabric
carries the hue to Roman shades
and draperies. Window treatments
don't have to match, but, like
floors, should be color-related.

■ **REPEAT FABRICS,** accent colors, and
surface materials, varying intensi-
ties and patterns. Here, stripes,
prints, and miniflorals spin off the
sofa's dominant blue-and-yellow
fabric. The same tile tops the dining area built-ins and the
kitchen counters—a shade of blue echoed in the sofa.

■ **USE EASY GO-BETWEENS.** Work in mixable naturals, such as wicker and mellow woods. Punch up your scheme with painted
pieces. Here the dining chairs and antique table base were
painted blue to pull the hue through to the dining area.

■ **SHARE COLLECTIONS AND ACCENTS.** Blue and white ware, displayed
on kitchen soffits, walls, and tabletops, inspired this palette.

■ **KEY COLORS** to the natural light. Add "sun" to a north-facing
room or a room used mainly at night by including touches of
yellow or red; cool a sunny room with green or blue. *(For more
color tips, check the "Color" chapter, beginning on page 24.)*

ABOVE: A parade of blue and white plates
sets off in the kitchen and then marches
around the great-room. Tile on the
peninsula and fabric on the stool cushions
repeat in the dining area. **OPPOSITE:** Terra-
cotta flooring, birch cabinetry built in as a
buffet, and fabrics in golden yellow and
blue carry the flavor of the kitchen to the
living and dining areas where this family
likes to entertain.

Add to the Fun

What would it take to make your family room more family-friendly? Is seating a tight squeeze when you entertain? Would you stay more organized or homework get done faster if the computer were handy? Small changes may be a better solution than extra square footage.

FAMILY-FRIENDLY ZONE

■ **CATER TO YOUR CROWD.** Add an oversize coffee table or a drop-leaf sofa table for playing board games. (Have little ones? Pull some child-size chairs around it.) Tuck a desk or computer center into a wall of built-ins. Add a comfy chair for the book lover and build in a window seat for extra seating with bonus storage below.

■ **PROVIDE FLEXIBLE LIGHTING** and spread it around. Include general lighting for kids' play, task lights for reading, and over-the-table lighting—a pendant, recessed fixtures, or a strip of track—on a dimmer so it can be turned up for reading and down for dining.

■ **MAKE IT PERSONAL.** This is where you display and enjoy belongings that reflect your family at its happiest. Create a portrait of your loved ones by displaying family treasures and just-for-fun finds. Items such as vacation souvenirs, handcrafted textiles, and children's artwork make great conversation starters when guests arrive.

■ **ACCENT ARTFULLY.** Consider larger artwork or groupings that can hold their own in typically large or vaulted great-room spaces. Artwork should be hung at eye level; in plop-down family rooms, hang artwork lower so you can better view the art while seated.

ABOVE: Too small for even a sofa, this den wasn't very entertaining until this sofa-sized window seat was built in. Now there's room for a few guests and a place to store games and other gear below the cushioned seat. RIGHT: Togetherness in this family room starts with a wall of built-ins where Mom or Dad can read or pay bills and the kids can do their homework on the computer. Wrapping built-ins like these around two walls creates work space on one wall and home entertainment space on the other. OPPOSITE: With a dining table, an oversize coffee table for board games and casual meals, and gather-around seating, this family room is ready for action. Distressed woods and easy-care fabrics relax the mood.

TO FIND OUT MORE ONLINE, VISIT US
@ www.bhg.com/bkdecoratingcenter

Living in the Library

With a little ingenuity, you can transform an infrequently used space into a book-lined retreat that welcomes family activities and entertaining. Do you walk past a standoffish formal dining room every day? Could you turn that often-idle guest room into an evening retreat for the family? A little-used room and a lot of shelves can perform this decorating trick.

CREATE DO-IT-ALL SPACES

Wrapped in floor-to-ceiling shelves that hold a collection of books, this ambitious library added a few more tasks to its job description. With the addition of a desk and round game table at one end, a set-for-eight dining table, and leather chairs and sofa, the library also serves as an office, game room, dining space, and den. Even in smaller spaces, you can pull off this kind of practical room transformation. Start with shelves to set the mood, then follow these tips:

■ **MAKE MULTIFUNCTIONAL ARRANGEMENTS.** Move the dining table to one side to make way for a deep love seat and an armchair. Dining chairs can pull around for dining or conversation as needed.

■ **LIGHTEN UP.** Make lighting less formal by swapping the typical dining chandelier for dimmable recessed lights or track lights that can illuminate the table, spotlight artwork, and bounce light off walls for an indirect, general glow. Add lamps for reading, hobbies, and homework and accent lights for art.

■ **EXPAND STORAGE.** For almost every activity that goes on in a family room, there's a corresponding set of items and equipment to be neatly housed nearby. Use shelves and storage furniture, from armoires to chests and trunk tables, to neatly corral electronics, games, dishes, and table linens.

ABOVE: Lightweight faux-bamboo stools upholstered in fluttery "eyelash" fabric serve the desk at the library's sunny office end and provide extra seating at the round game table nearby. Behind the desk, an English fishing box on a new base holds the phone. **OPPOSITE:** Family-friendly activity areas defined by vintage Oriental rugs break up the long, narrow shape of this Arts and Crafts library. Bentwood chairs wearing dressmaker-style slipcovers edge the crackle-finish table that hosts everything from casual everyday meals to elegant dinners for guests, who love dining in the library.

At Your Service

Your rooms don't have to be small to benefit from the talents of flexible and double-duty furnishings.

In spaces large and small, these clever, well-designed pieces always add a dimension of comfort and function. Family rooms are inherently spontaneous spaces, and they're more fun if lightweight seating scoots where it's needed, if tables expand for dining and impromptu games, and if practical storage adds character to the space.

ADDING FLEXIBILITY

■ **LET OTTOMANS RULE.** Because these talented pieces can be used for dining, storage, seating, and resting tired feet, they've taken over for coffee tables,

which once stood in front of every sofa. Group seating around an over-size ottoman, or for flexibility, pair two smaller ottomans that can serve or seat. Add a tray to protect the fabric and hold drinks and snacks.

■ **TURN THE TABLES.** Versatile drop-leaf, gateleg, extendable, or flip-top tables are ideal for any family room. Drop-leaf tables can serve as everyday sofa tables, then quickly flip up into company dining spots.

■ **SHOP FOR FURNITURE THAT CAN DO TWO JOBS.** Chests or trunks work well as coffee tables and end tables—and hold games, work files, and guest linens if your sofa hides a bed inside. Dressed-up daybeds make inviting settees when piled with enough pillows for back support.

■ **RECAST COLLECTIBLE FURNITURE.** Antique armoires, painted cupboards, dry sinks, and pie safes can stow entertainment gear. An old bench or a flea market chest makes a perfect surface for a TV—and an instant focal point when you hang eyecatching artwork above it.

■ **CUSTOMIZE WITH MODULARS.** From upholstered seating to stackable chests and wall storage units, flexible modular furniture lets you tailor—and re-tailor—the configuration to suit changing needs. Modulars come in styles from clean-lined contemporary to traditional; some are scaled down to fit compact spaces.

OPPOSITE LEFT: Casters make this artful trio of diamond-shaped ottomans a functional gem. Clad in synthetic suede fabric, these soft seats roll around individually, but when they are lined up in front of the sofa, they become a colorful server for snacks. CENTER: Classically detailed with shapely wood legs, this oversize ottoman makes a modern design statement. An inviting feet-up spot, the ottoman also serves as a handy table when a large tray is placed on top of it. BELOW: A small living room yields grand comfort when a table-size ottoman pulls up to the sofa. In addition to its regular footrest duties, the ottoman offers a spot for hors d'oeuvres and casual dinners.

TelevisionSpots

Whether your family room boasts a home theater
or an old-but-reliable 20-inch portable, living in this media age means the TV is
never far from view. Of course, there are times when you wish it weren't so visually demanding, especially when
friends are gathered for lively conversation or the family converges to catch up on each other's news. Creative
storage and customized furniture pieces can solve the "big black eye" problem by corralling and camouflaging
the television and other electronics. Before building or buying storage, measure your TV and electronics compo-
nents; not all storage units are deep enough to hold big TVs. If you're considering a home theater, ask an electronics expert's advice on selecting and placing speakers in your family room and install window treatments that
block sunlight and glare.

OPPOSITE: Over an antique limestone mantel, a flat-screen "plasma" television keeps a low profile in this elegant family room of mixed-century classics, including the Le Corbusier leather lounge. A French pine cupboard stows more entertainment gear. **1** Instead of competing as focal points, the fireplace and built-in media center are packaged side by side in this family room. The two are linked with moldings, and they're set at an angle to preserve the see-through views

in this home. **2** This big screen gets a media room of its own with comfy chairs for watching the latest box-office hits. The carpet has an inset decorative "filmstrip," and the round tabletop provides soft lighting during movies. **3** Expansive windows and French doors leave this family room with precious little wall space, so the pop-up television is set in built-in cabinetry. At the push of a button, the television raises for viewing. **4** To keep this room's two favorite features in line, the television is stacked atop the fireplace. The built-in media cabinet has doors that close when the TV is not in use.

Dining rooms

At your home, are mealtimes a leisurely taste of gourmet fare, served family style for a crowd, or something quick and simple before everyone scatters? No matter who's at the table or what's on the menu, you deserve a dining area that's as inviting as this New England classic—one that reflects your decorating taste and your lifestyle. In this chapter, you'll find ideas for creating attractive dining spaces—even in unlikely places.

Formal or Casual?

You know how awkward it feels to dress formally if you're a jeans-and-T-shirt person.

but proper dining to you may mean the works—fine china, crystal, and silver. To relax yourself and your guests, define your dining style and design for it.

A CIVILIZED TWIST

Formal dining can be a getaway activity in itself—a civilized, unhurried sharing of your best, from manners to food and wines. The design principles for creating a formal look work equally well in contemporary and traditional spaces.

■ **USE SYMMETRY** (mirror images on either side of an imaginary centerline) for wall and furniture arrangements.

■ **DRESS UP** with gleaming mirrors, gilt frames on artwork, lacquered finishes, polished veneers, and crystal stemware and candlesticks.

■ **FORGO FUSSINESS.** Nothing makes a stronger formal statement than furniture with pure, classic lines, be it 18th-century antiques or contemporary classics, and lustrous fabrics—from silks and taffetas to brocades.

RELAX IN STYLE

Whether your style is cottage-casual or urban-sleek, your own unique mix of fabrics and furnishings will give guests a warm and welcoming taste of your personality.

■ **RELAX WITH TEXTURES.** As a general rule, choose rough textures instead of smooth; wicker, rattan, pine, and iron are less formal than polished woods and glass.

■ **MIX THINGS UP.** Consider a collection of unmatched vintage chairs around the table. Even one unmatched chair at the end breaks up formal uniformity. Or pair matching chairs with a table of a different material. Team wood chairs with an iron-base table or wicker chairs with distressed wood or stone. Mixing stained and painted wood finishes also adds an informal air.

■ **BRING FABRIC TO THE TABLE.** Choose casual, coarse weaves over shiny silk or damask. Easy-care cottons and wrinkle-resistant fabrics make a casual dining room more approachable. Dress down formal chairs with slipcovers and a formal table with a floor-length cotton skirt.

ABOVE: Is this dining room in a European villa or in the suburbs? It's the latter, but with an aged paint treatment on the walls and ceiling, elegant fabrics, and a graceful mix of furnishings, home entertaining here has "new" old-world flavor. OPPOSITE: Relaxed yet sophisticated in its juxtaposition of natural textures, this dining room has an oversize soapstone-top table to match its hospitality. Antique fabric on the woven chairs' cushions, charming folk art on the wall, and a painted chest as sideboard reflect the homeowners' travels and collections.

Plan to Dine

Dining rooms are among the easiest spaces to plan. Their dimensions dictate what's needed. Use common sense, a tape measure, and these tips to pull your dining room together. *(For more help with space planning, turn to the room-arranging kit on page 410–415.)*

DESIGN FOR DINING

■ **CHOOSE A DINING TABLE** to suit the area's shape. Long tables—formal banquet or casual farm tables—fit long, narrow spaces. A square or oblong table—teamed with a bench that can tuck under the table to save space when not in use—can suit small spaces. A round table softens the angles of a square room.

■ **KEEP ROOM SCALE AND BALANCE IN MIND.** You can squeeze a large table into a tiny room or place a table for two in a cavernous space, but proportionally neither will look right. If you must use a large table in a smallish room, consider a glass top to consume less visual space. Evaluate vertical space too; a room with a soaring ceiling may require high-back chairs and perhaps a weighty patterned area rug to anchor dining pieces. Plan for a mix of high and low pieces, adding a tall hutch or sideboard topped with a wall-hung painting.

■ **POSITION THE TABLE SO TRAFFIC FLOWS** smoothly around it—usually near the room's center. To turn a dining room into a multiuse space, push the table to one side to make room for lounge chairs or a sofa. Plan at least 8 square feet for a table for four, plus about 36 inches so chairs can be pulled out. To make the dining table a focal point, set it atop a colorful area rug.

■ **ALLOW ELBOW ROOM.** To determine how many can dine at a table, allow a space of 20 to 24 inches wide and 15 inches deep for each place setting. Ideally, reserve a 12-inch-wide strip down the table's center for centerpieces and serving dishes.

RIGHT: Raspberry walls set a cheery and gracious stage for formal or family dining. Relaxed and casual, the well-worn farm table gets an unexpected sophisticated touch from faux-bamboo chairs and a wrought-iron console. The console, a pine hutch, and slim built-ins on one wall handle storage, display, and serving.

TO FIND OUT MORE ONLINE, VISIT US
@ www.bhg.com/bkarrangearoom

Dining-In Personality

Beyond the scrumptious menu at your favorite restaurant, what is it about the decor and ambience that keeps you coming back for more? Do aged walls and old-world furnishings transport you to a Mediterranean villa—if only for an evening? Does colorful art make you feel as if you're dining in a gallery? Or do you love to look at the collections? Borrow some decorating ideas and turn your own space into the hot spot to dine.

■ **FRESHEN UP WITH PAINT.** Consider the time of day the dining room is most frequently used. Depending on your lighting, wall color in a bold apple

green may be dramatic for dinner but overbearing at brunch. Pretty by day, soft pastels may wash out by night. Create special effects—aged plaster, stone, or fabric—with painted wall finishes.

■ **SLIPCOVER IN STYLE.** It's an easy way to change the look of your chairs and the entire room. Bold colors and busy patterns are best when window treatments and walls are pattern-free. For a quick change, make or buy simple seat cushions to add color and texture without concealing the chair design. Or pop fabric "cozies" over chair backs and miniskirts over seats. Floor-length slipcovers give wood chairs an upholstered look and provide visual relief in a room full of exposed-leg pieces.

■ **SHARE YOUR PASSIONS.** Set the style stage with your era-evoking antiques, quirky collections, art, and artful lighting. Pick personality-packed furnishings and accessories to add a bit of unexpected visual

spice and color. Instead of the predictable hutch, a French baker's rack can serve as a sideboard while also showcasing collections.

OPPOSITE LEFT: This gracious dining room, with its faux-aged walls, arched windows, and antique French table, is like a Tuscan getaway for guests. Dining chairs are slipcovered in burlap with monograms on the chair backs. The wall finish was achieved with bronze and gold-tone glazes. CENTER: Enclosing a terrace created this lively dining space, which celebrates a collector's love of art, whimsical art glass, and contemporary style. The sculptural bent-maple table and chairs host casual meals; diners enjoy the view and, on the brick wall, a painting done by the homeowner. BELOW RIGHT: A tulle-dressed mannequin is a glamorous and unexpected guest at this fete. Slipcovered wing chairs and an oak server anchor the setting, illuminated by a tulle-draped chandelier. Color punch comes from art that's actually gift wrap from Germany, hanging from a curtain tieback.

Dining Out at Home
Today many of us dine all around the house.

Tonight it might be dinner for eight in the dining room. Tomorrow morning? Coffee and a bagel in the kitchen. And on Sunday—if you're lucky—it might be a leisurely brunch in the master suite. All that variety demands creative space planning. Start with a good understanding of your special lifestyle needs.

DOUBLE-DUTY DINING

■ **ARRANGE A DINNER DATE.** As home building costs soar and square footage shrinks, a formal dining room may not be your priority. If you require an everyday den and rarely a formal dining room, plan one room to do both. Let the table double as a desk. A hutch can hold books and dishes. Or push the table to one side and add a small love seat or easy chairs that can double as dining seating. (Just be sure the seats of such pieces are close to the 18-inch seat height needed for dining.)

■ **SQUEEZE A TABLE** into unexpected places. A half-round (demilune) or drop-leaf table in a wide hallway can be a lunch-for-two spot. Or set a modest rectangular dining table behind a sofa or against a wall in the family room or living room. Even a slim sofa table can serve dinner when you pull up a couple of chairs. To give B&B-style romance to a master bedroom, snug a slim dining table or sofa table against the foot of the bed or in front of a window, or replace a nightstand with a larger table that can serve for cozy, late-night snacks.

LEFT: Designed to look like an English garden folly on the outside but serving up Swedish cottage charm inside, this poolside pavilion gives elegant new meaning to backyard dining. This steps-away getaway is also a garden room and library. OPPOSITE: No reservations are needed for this romantic table for two. The library fireside makes an inviting spot for tea and casual dinners. An armchair in sunny yellow toile and a scoot-anywhere ottoman for extra seating at the bistro table add comfort and convenience.

Dining in the Kitchen

A staple of older homes and a selling point for new ones, the big, eat-in kitchen beckons family and friends with its casual, back-door air, bringing back heartwarming memories of gathering around that icon of the American home—the kitchen table. Give your kitchen's informal eating area special decorating attention and make some memories of your own.

KEEP IT CASUAL

■ **USE EASY-CARE FABRICS** and finishes for fuss-free kitchen dining. Use hard-wearing stain- and water-resistant fabrics, add chair pads with zippered covers for easy removal for washing, or have your kitchen's signature fabric laminated and fashioned

into wipe-clean chair pads. Tabletops finished with paint or polyurethane are easier to clean than those that have an oil-base finish.

■ **CONSIDER EFFICIENT BUILT-INS.** Pull a table up to a window seat for dining. Built-in banquettes make efficient use of floor space and corners and give the kitchen a cozy look. New freestanding booths that tuck into corners offer similar space efficiency.

■ **KEEP TRAFFIC IN MIND.** Position the dining table and chairs so they're out of the everyday flow of traffic.

■ **LIGHT THE SCENE.** Replace the ceiling light switch with a mood-setting dimmer. If the kitchen lacks an over-the-table light, use a plug-in swag light or wire in a hanging fixture, recessed lights, or a strip of track lighting so diners aren't kept in the dark.

LEFT: A walk-through space between the den and kitchen now stops traffic. Reupholstered garage-sale chairs and a discount-store wicker table funnel traffic around this new breakfast spot. The chandelier both lights and defines the space. ABOVE: Beaded-board paneling and a built-in banquette make for cozy corner dining. Shelves above the seating create space for the owner's cookbook library and collectibles. OPPOSITE: An all-in-one cabinetry-and-table unit transforms a blank wall into a dining spot and focal point. Wrapped around an early-1900s French poster, the shelves hold books, pottery, and collectibles.

ServeUp Style

Dining rooms don't require as much storage

as kitchens, but mealtimes are easier when linens, dishes, and serving pieces are close at hand. Dining rooms also benefit style-wise from open storage that allows you to show off your favorite collectibles. Use these tips to expand storage.

■ **PULL IN A HUTCH,** buffet, or cupboard. A low sideboard is ideal if you have a large painting, a mirror, or a plate rack to hang above it. If not, maximize vertical storage

space with an armoire, a hutch, or a Welsh dresser.

■ **HANG IT ON THE WALL.** A small wall rack, wall-mounted shelves above a table, or a unifying shelf encircling the room can add style and stow your dishes too.

■ **BUILD IT IN.** Built-in china cabinets or shelf-lined niches turn blank walls into storage assets. Put dead corner space to work with corner cupboards. For formal symmetry, treat corners identically.

OPPOSITE: A pretty mix of fancy and Irish country, this garden-style room relaxes a classic pedestal table and ornate chandelier by mating them with cottage-white chairs, a primitive cupboard, and a shelf above the wainscot. **1** Found at a flea market, this focal-point buffet was primed and painted before toile wallpaper was applied with adhesive, then aged with a tea-hued glaze. **2** Built-ins that served this space when it was a library adapt beautifully to the room's

new dining role. Although the table is an antique Biedermeier, seating is a casual mix of nothing-fancy, Italian-style chairs and a wicker settee. **3** Two dining room classics—a hand-me-down sideboard and new Swedish-style plate rack—add up to one dramatic focal point with linen storage below and display for china and pewter servers above. Fresh paint blends old chairs with the new table. **4** An old storage piece gains new life when treated to a fresh coat of paint. Blue accents inspired the choice of blue rod-back dining chairs. Table linens and patterned chandelier shades pull the new color scheme together.

Bedrooms

Busy lives have turned bedrooms into round-the-clock retreats. New-home master suites are packed with amenities from entertainment centers to mini refrigerators—details you can add to any bedroom if you employ some decorating ingenuity. Even a small bedroom needs a spot to tuck in a TV and maybe a computer. What little luxury does your bedroom need? A sitting spot? A fresh mood? Filmy curtains on pegged rods sparked a new romance for this four-poster. Whatever you add, put your comfort first.

Sleep Styles

For sweet dreams, do a little decorating matchmaking. Although it applies to every room, decorating with what you love is most important in the bedroom. What colors and materials relax you most at bedtime? What sights—and even scents—would you love waking up to each day? Play matchmaker—put colors, furnishings, and accessories together in a way that reflects your tastes and comfort needs—to create a bedroom that serves as your ultimate time-out spot. For starters, are you formal or casual? Do you lean toward cozy clutter or artful displays of a few select objects?

ANALYZE YOUR DREAM SPACE

Forget style labels and instead use these tips as a guide for gathering

accessories and choosing and arranging major bedroom furnishings to serve your practical needs and make you feel utterly at ease.

■ **IF YOU PREFER FORMALITY**, you won't feel quite right unless you center the bed along a wall or between two windows and then flank it with matched lamps and nightstands. Balance accessories such as wall art and collections on the mantel in a similar orderly way.

■ **IF YOU EQUATE RELAXING** with casual ambience, you may lean toward looser, asymmetrical room arrangements. Move the bed to one side of the room or angle it headfirst into a corner. Placing furniture on the diagonal can make rooms look larger and free up floor space for a desk or love seat. Balance an off-center bed with a weighty armoire or other storage piece, a reading chair and lamp, or bold artwork.

■ **IF YOU LEAN TOWARD CLEAN-AND-SIMPLE** minimalism, comfort may mean paring down to the beautiful, clutter-free basics. Start with an eye-grabbing bed, then add a few well-designed accents. Provide plenty of closed storage to keep your retreat free of visual clutter.

■ **IF YOUR TASTES ARE ECLECTIC** and don't fit neatly into one style category or degree of formality but you aren't sure how to create your own mix, clip magazine photos of rooms you love. Before you decorate, study the clippings for hints of your true style and mood preferences. Then use the photos as a guide to creating your own perfect blend of design styles and approaches.

OPPOSITE LEFT: An antique Victorian settee and handsome secretary team with a classic canopy bed to hint at formality, but checked fabric, the angled placement of the settee, and the gathered canopy and chair skirt lend a touch of casual ambience. OPPOSITE RIGHT: Simplicity reigns in this clean-lined retreat. Textures and rich woods turn up the heat while a sleek bed dressed for comfort softens hard edges. BELOW LEFT: Bold colors echoed in the velvety duvet, accent fabrics, and dramatic rug unify this personal mix of the modern and the unexpected. BELOW RIGHT: Symmetrically placed lamps and nightstands please formal sensibilities, but soft textures and feel-good fabrics, including a quilted headboard, create a comfortably casual air.

Bedroom Essentials

Only you can define what's "essential" in your personal retreat. To do so, first determine the role your space plays. Is it for sleeping only? Does it work part-time as a den or office? How you use your room determines your essential furnishings.

■ **LIST THE BASICS**—sleeping, storage, seating, work space. What size bed fits your room and the way you live? Do you need a king-size bed, or a queen-size with space left over for a lounge chair and ottoman? What are your storage needs? If you have a large walk-in closet with built-in shelves and drawers, can you forgo a dresser and free up space for the writing table or chaise you long for? If you take newspapers and stacks of books to bed, use a larger bedside table. Dimmers and lamps with three-way switches let you control light levels for reading and relaxing. Sculpt space with accent lights and art lights; use strip lights to illuminate collectibles or books. *(For more help, see "Arranging," pages 410-415.)*

■ **DRESS THE BED FOR COMFORT.** Cotton sheets soften with washing and let the body breathe; cotton-polyester blends wrinkle less but aren't as soft. Pima and Egyptian cottons are silky to the touch. Thread count, the number of threads per square inch, indicates sheet quality—180 to 200 is standard; 350 means luxury. Do you want a spread or a plump duvet? (A duvet is a comforter, usually down-filled, with a removable cover; it serves as top sheet, blanket, and bedcover all in one.) Duvet covers can be pricey, but you can make one by sewing two flat sheets together on three sides and adding buttons or snaps to close the end. (Update an old comforter the same way.) A feather bed atop the mattress adds luxury.

LEFT: Stargazing over the ocean and waking up to the waves were "essentials" in this seaside cottage bedroom, so the owners used double box springs to raise the duvet-covered bed for a better view. A freestanding armoire handles storage, and a roomy built-in seat for lounging stretches across the bay window.

> **TO FIND OUT MORE ONLINE, VISIT US**
> @ www.bhg.com/bkarrangearoom

Customize Your Retreat

Whether your sleep space is large or small, careful floor planning can help you make the most of it. Measure your room and major furnishings, then sketch it all out on paper using our room-arranging kit on pages 410-415, or pop floor-planning software into your computer. Use these design tips as you plan.

A PERFECT FIT

■ **CONSIDER THE SIZE OF THE BED.** Treat yourself to a larger bed if you have a large closet or built-ins and can forgo freestanding storage. Also remember that the bed's visual size is determined by more than its mere dimensions. A tall scrolled-metal headboard consumes less visual space than a carved-wood headboard of similar size and shape; visually, dark woods and finishes consume more space than light ones. Size bedside tables to mattress height.

■ **CREATE EASY ACCESS.** Avoid placing the bed so close to a door that the bed becomes a speed bump. For easy bed making, allow at least 2 feet on both sides. In front of the closet allow about 3 feet for dressing (or more if door swing demands it). Allow at least 36 to 40 inches in front of chests and dressers for using drawers.

■ **TUCK IN STORAGE.** Add a highboy or armoire or a dresser-mirror combination to a wall of built-ins. If you have space for freestanding storage, consider turning the closet into a home office with a built-in desk and shelves.

■ **THINK BIG IN SMALL ROOMS.** Scale up furnishings. Fewer but larger high-function pieces can handle practical needs and help you avoid the visual clutter created by a scattering of small furniture pieces. Stick with an arrangement of major pieces parallel or perpendicular to walls; a diagonal bed may steal too much floor space in a small room.

LEFT: An upholstered bed with an ocean view serves as an island of comfort in this whitewashed master suite addition. A long desk, a comfy chair, and a computer turn a windowed alcove into a convenient home office spot. OPPOSITE: Across from the bed, upholstered armchairs with high backs that invite settling in pull up to a cast-concrete fireplace. A built-in conceals a pop-up television. Wall-to-wall sea-grass carpet and neutral hues are naturally relaxing touches.

ABOVE: Walls in this luxurious master suite look as if they're draped in elegant fabric, but it's actually wallcovering that flows into the bath. Fabric in a neoclassic floral print—used for the coverlet, the graceful window treatments, and the roll-arm bench at the foot of the bed—inspired the soft rose-and-green palette.
OPPOSITE: In the tranquil bath, the wallcovering teams with crisp white trim and pale marble floors. The green-checked fabric on the chair cushions reinforces the green stripes on the wall. Plantation shutters afford the focal-point tub a river view. An Oriental rug pulls in the traditional mood set in the bedroom.

SuiteInspiration
Decorating a master suite presents special creative challenges.

Let your bedroom and bath share style and mood so they flow together into a retreat where you can relax and rejuvenate. Why settle for a chrome-and-mirrors bath if your sleep space is swathed in country French fabrics? Why live with a bathroom's aging floral wallpaper or busy tiles if you've gone clean and modern in your bedroom? Forge links between the two spaces with color, pattern, finishes, and decorative accessories.

SUITE REWARDS

■ **COUNT ON COLOR** to make this marriage of spaces work. Start with the same palette for bed and bath, perhaps changing the color emphasis in each room for design interest.

■ **UNIFY WITH FABRICS, PATTERNS, AND MOTIFS.** In the bath, you won't use as much fabric as you do in your comfy bedroom, but carry fabrics and pattern through in bath window treatments, chair cushions, and wall coverings.

■ **PICK FINISHES THAT FIT YOUR STYLE.** If your bedroom sets a classic mood with a marble fireplace, use marble or a stone-look material on the vanity top or the bathroom floor. If rich natural wood is your bedroom look, add an antique cupboard to the bath—you'll appreciate the extra storage.

■ **SHARE THE ACCESSORIES.** An Oriental rug or Japanese bench at the side of the tub, well-edited collections, and framed wall art can bring the bedroom mood to the bath. If your vanity is long enough, top it with a mood-enhancing lamp for soft light.

Redo
With A New View

BEFORE

A big helping
of illusion
brings the mood
and the magic
to many beautifully decorated
rooms. Plain closet doors may
be the last place you'd look
for help in coaxing your bedroom out of its sleepy style
rut, but the wall of clutter-
shutters is exactly where this
space started to capture
French country flavor. On the
new "French door" closets, the mirrored panes are subtle—not glitzy—
and hardworking, reflecting space and light. These elegant doors are
custom-made and open beneath a top row of fixed panes. Running mirrors to the soffit visually raises the roof and coaxes the eye to gable
windows. Here are less expensive ways to get the look:

■ **GLUE LIGHTWEIGHT MIRRORS** to closet doors; then top them with glued-on
batten strips or country lattice. Paint or stain the strips or lattice before
applying to the doors.

■ **HAVE MIRRORS CUT TO FIT DOORS,** leaving a border all around about one-sixth
of each door's width and length. Attach them to the doors with mirror
clips. Top mirrors with pop-in window muntins secured to the mirrors
with pieces of cushioned, double-stick tape.

In the lighten-up spirit of this redo, fresh fabrics and a floral carpet
moved in. A graceful pencil-post bed more in scale with the space
replaced an old brass one. But the roomy antique linen press, stowing
the television, stayed put.

RIGHT: Inspired by the garden air of new "French door" closets, this bedroom—
once a garage—gets both its palette and its alfresco look from the floral
patterns of the needlepoint carpet and the bed skirt. The blue quilt not only
echoes the blue in the carpet, it also provides welcome, cool contrast to the
room's golden woods and warm accent colors.

Make It Personal

If you yearn to let your design fantasies take flight, the best place to launch them is your bedroom. By surrounding yourself with favorite things, you'll create a truly personal refuge that soothes the body and delights the eye—and the soul. Treasures such as antique quilts, pretty plates, and heirloom furniture may be too fragile for a high-traffic family room, but they're perfect in the bedroom where you can display them to enjoy every day.

ACCENT YOUR SIGNATURE STYLE

■ **SHOW YOUR STUFF.** No matter how quirky your collections, if you love them, let them show. Grouping objects adds impact; arrange flea market teacups on a wall-hung shelf or enameled boxes on a tabletop; you'll recall the fun of the hunt every time you pass by. Is art your passion? Turn a wall into a gallery. To display family photos, frame them to match; have some enlarged to make displays more interesting.

■ **PLAY WITH FABRICS.** Give the bed an unexpected twist: Instead of the typical spread, use a tablecloth, a vintage throw, a lightweight kilim rug, or your grandmother's quilt that you've had packed away. Dress your bed in a mix of prints, breaking up florals with snappy stripes, gingham checks, and colorful solids. Mix up the pillows too, blending new ones with those covered in vintage fabrics.

■ **SET YOUR PRIORITIES.** What makes you feel pampered? Eyelet-edged sheets? A sound system for the music lover? A library full of favorite books? Plants from your garden? Even a sleeping spot for a pet may top the priority list in your domain.

LEFT: The English plant-drying rack and the 19th-century transferware that inspired the bedroom's fabrics are clues that the room belongs to a gardener and collector. A French silk-taffeta remnant accents the creamy silk draperies, the garden bench wears original paint, and the lamp is an electrified pitcher. OPPOSITE: Giving this country bedroom colorful personality was child's play: The homeowner pulled out 1940s and 1950s sandbox toys and tin dishes from her own childhood to display on a hand-painted shelf above the bed. Fabrics with farmhouse spirit mix it up on the iron bed, a family heirloom.

HeadboardClass
Making your bed the focal point of your sleep space often means giving that expanse

of empty wall above the headboard some creative attention. For an easy solution, hang one great piece of artwork or perhaps a trio of favorite prints in frames faux-finished in your bedroom colors. Here are more finishing touches to make your bed a standout:

■ **SOFTEN THE SCENE WITH FABRIC.** Canopies and flowing bed curtains guarantee a feeling of luxury and privacy. Or treat the wall like a window: Wall-mount two rods at ceiling height behind the headboard; shirr a curtain on one, a valance on the other, and add tiebacks on both sides of the bed. Kits for wall-mounted coronas are available at home centers—all you add are the fabric and trims. Even

a big quilting hoop, suspended from the ceiling and draped in mosquito netting or a gauzy sari, can conjure an exotic mood. Replace a ho-hum headboard with a screen made of louvered panels hinged together or plain panels upholstered in fabric.

■ **ADD ARCHITECTURAL CHARACTER.** Salvaged gingerbread trim from old porches, aged ironwork brackets, or lacy garden lattice add interest and texture to the headboard wall.

■ **STORE AND DISPLAY.** Wall-mount a carved antique shelf or a new antique-style one above the bed to highlight the headboard, display accessories, and keep bedtime books close at hand.

RIGHT: This collector's retreat accents the heirloom bed with an arc of blue and white plates echoing the headboard's curve. The window treatments and accessories, including the lampshades, pull the crisp colors around the entire room. **OPPOSITE:** Floral fabric drapes from a gilded, wrought-iron crown, marking the French fruitwood bed as the place of honor in this elegant bedroom. Two sets of portieres in the same fabric define a vestibule and a sitting spot in the bay window.

A Place for Everything

First comes the television, then the home office, and before you know it,

the bedroom is getting a bit crowded. A threat in so many other living spaces, clutter can be downright disastrous in a bedroom where serenity is the goal. Cast a creative eye around your bedroom. Could you outfit that sliver of wall with shelves to hold tidy wicker baskets for "stuff"? Could you scoot fabric-covered storage boxes and baskets under the bed? With such pretty storage, you might want to shed the bed skirt. Whether it stores a little or a lot, any freestanding piece is welcome if you have room.

■ **OUTFIT THE FOOT OF THE BED.** Bed linens and sweaters can hide inside a chest; on top, display collectibles and books. Slide an antique bench or an oblong cocktail table against the foot of the bed to hold books and magazines.

■ **LOOK FOR STORAGE FURNITURE.** Consider beds with headboard caches or drawers built in below the mattress and nightstands with drawers or shelves. A vertical stack or a horizontal lineup of slick storage cubes can hold TV and video gear on top and corral folded clothes below. Always practical, an armoire also can house a TV and clothing.

■ **EXPLORE FOR CLOSET-DEPTH SPACE.** By bumping out a wall between windows or on both sides of the bed, you can add architectural interest to a square space and gain a new spot to hang your hat.

OPPOSITE: Built-ins outwit angled attic walls, providing this redone bedroom with storage in the end wall and dividing the bed and bath with a headboard "wall." **1** Instead of letting this bedroom's spacious bay window sit idle, built-in, sill-high shelving organizes bedtime reading, displays accessories, and adds warmth and texture. **2** This compact master suite makes all the right moves to live big. Neutral colors open it up, glass-panel walls invite light, and the bed has built-

in drawers and pullout nightstands. **3** Just a few feet of space at the end of the bed works wonders when it's this well planned. A chest hugs a side wall, freeing up under-window space for a small but efficient desk and storage pieces. Note how the leggy desk and the airy, cantilevered chair consume little visual space and allow the eye to follow the floor all the way to the wall—a fool-the-eye space expander. **4** Working vintage doors into a newly crafted armoire brings unrivaled character, plus great storage, to a serene bedroom, romanced with a mix of fabrics and flea market finds.

Guest rooms

To create a welcoming retreat for your overnight guests, think about what made your last getaway memorable. Maybe a quaint bed-and-breakfast pampered you with the same luxurious linens, fresh flowers, and thoughtful amenities that beckon from this serene guest room. Even though your guest space may do double duty and work every day as a family room or home office, you can make it inviting and comfortable with a few well-planned decorative touches.

Welcoming Amenities

Decorating a room especially for overnight visitors is the ultimate in hospitality.

It's great if you have a spare room to redo, but you may find guest space in unexpected places. For starters, consider last year's overnight-guest list and plan accordingly.

DEFINE GUEST NEEDS

Choose a bed that fits the space and the needs of your most frequent guests. One or two twin beds or a queen-size bed are good choices. For extra company or visiting children, supplement sleep space by renting a crib or a rollaway bed. Offer guests a choice of synthetic or natural fillings in fluffy pillows. Dress the bed in charming linens, a sink-in feather bed, and a down-filled duvet, and provide bedside reading lamps that hold 75- to 100-watt bulbs.

SHOP FOR SPACE

Take a tour of your home, and assess each room, alcove, walk-in closet, and hallway as possible guest quarters. Tuck a daybed or sleep sofa into an alcove, put up an antique screen for privacy, and you have an instant guest spot. Or turn that spacious closet into a snug sleeper with built-in bunk beds. Add a futon sofa to a finished attic or reserve a top-of-the-stairs loft for guests. If you don't have a full-time guest room with a closet, find ways to help your visitors stay organized.

■ CLEAN OUT A HALL CLOSET near the guest space and add plenty of hangers, including custom hangers for suits and skirts.

■ STOW GUESTS' clothes on an over-the-door hanger, a decorative Shaker-style peg rack mounted on the wall, or a corner coat tree.

■ WICKER BASKETS and colorful bins and boxes can corral bath and personal items. Size them to fit on bookshelves or under a lamp table, coffee table, or bed. Use a trunk or hamper as an end table.

■ A LUGGAGE RACK makes a thoughtful addition that eases unpacking chores, and it can double as a tea-tray table.

OPPOSITE: A Midas touch with pattern and color pulls this classically furnished space together, imbuing it with a sense of luxury that guests are sure to appreciate. Striped walls blend with a mini-check fabric that dresses the bed and lines silk-taffeta curtains. BELOW: Whether guests use it for a laptop, writing postcards, or morning coffee, a desk is always a thoughtful amenity to tuck into any guest room, and in this small space, it expands storage. A sunburst mirror adds graphic energy.

Double Up on Comfort

In many homes, the guest "room" is a sofa bed, but the chunky heavyweights of yesterday

have slimmed down and prettied up. Today, however, sofa beds aren't your only option for creating dual-purpose guest quarters.

■ **THINK DOUBLE DUTY.** Let a sofa bed turn a family room or den into guest quarters. Position a sofa bed so guests can walk around the open bed safely and easily. Choose chairs and tables that move easily when the bed is opened. Dual purpose applies to accessories too, so decorate with day and night uses in mind. A cozy quilt doubles as a daytime throw and a footstool as a bedside table. A three-way lamp provides mood or reading light.

■ **SHOP FOR OPTIONS.** Consider daybeds (piled with pillows, they double for lounging when guests leave), futon sofas, flip-open chairs, and wall beds that tuck away into cabinets and wall units. New wall beds bolt to the wall studs and have a safety mechanism for raising and lowering slowly.

■ **GIVE GUESTS PRIVACY.** If windows are covered only in sheers or cafe curtains, add opaque shades or blinds to give guests privacy. Portieres—curtains hung across doorways—can turn even a living room into a guest spot. (Hint: Hang portieres on tension rods; remove them when guests leave.)

ABOVE: Curtains flow from ceiling-hung rods, and a twin bed dresses up in mixed-pattern linens in this home office. The bed serves as seating by day; at night, it becomes a private sleeping spot for guests. Projects in progress stow beneath the draped table. **RIGHT:** With the beach steps away, this cottage welcomes its fair share of guests, but the den is ready to accommodate them with a foldout sofa and a diminutive coffee table that scoots easily out of the bed's way.

TO FIND OUT MORE ONLINE, VISIT US
☞ @ www.bhg.com/bkarrangearoom

ABOVE: Usually it's a comfy chair in the family room, but when a guest arrives it folds out into a twin-size bed. Chinese chests serve as nightstands, and Asian wedding baskets double as tables that offer hidden storage.

Create B&B Ambience

What was it about that charming inn that won your heart in a weekend? A rustic pine bed piled with quilts? The romantic mood set by linens and lace? Collections of antiques inviting you to step back in time? Make the space you provide for guests a true getaway by taking cues from your favorite bed-and-breakfast.

■ **SCOUR YOUR HOME, FLEA MARKETS,** and antiques shops for accessories and furniture you can refinish or paint. Beware of antique beds; measure carefully to be sure the one you're considering can handle a modern-day mattress. Sort through collections and linens you've had tucked away; they could inspire a guest room palette and add character.

■ **MAKE GUESTS FEEL AT HOME** by designing comfort and convenience into your guest space. Is there a reading lamp, a cozy chair and ottoman for relaxing, a writing desk, mirror, alarm clock, radio, television, closet space, an empty drawer or two, a phone, and an outlet to plug in a laptop? Thoughtful touches such as scented, padded hangers; a unisex terry robe; a hair dryer; thick towels; and a basket of shampoos, soaps, and lotions are always appreciated.

■ **BE YOUR OWN GUEST.** Before your official guests arrive, invite yourself to spend the night in the guest space. You'll quickly find out if the mattress is comfortable, if the room temperature is OK, if the lighting is practical and inviting, and if the furniture placement is safe and easy to navigate at night.

LEFT: Old wood paneling painted sage green gets this guest room off to a fresh start. Between the handcrafted four-poster beds dressed in floral and striped linens, a circa-1800 tiger maple chest holds an antique shaving mirror, and bird prints nest above each bed. **OPPOSITE:** The world's fast pace slows instantly when guests enter this simply romantic guest room in an 1800s home. Twin beds have a new-old mix of linens—fuzzy white blankets, floral coverlets, and lace-edged pillows—and the rusty nightstand has a new glass top.

Bring the Baby

To provide safe, comfy sleeping space for your littlest guests, do you end up renting a crib?

Although that's a practical solution, the owners of this airy guest room came up with a different plan, turning a seating nook into optional crib space. Slide on the crib rail and the nook turns into a nursery, with sleep space roomy enough for even a toddler. The custom mattress/cushion fits snugly, and other than adding baby linens, the only accessory change is removing the painting. What makes this nook a quick-change artist is a pair of wooden brackets on each side of the opening. The wooden crib rail, with 1¾ inches between the slats, slides securely into upper and lower brackets. Pullout drawers below

keep baby linens and toys handy. When they want to switch the nook back to a sitting spot, the owners slide out the crib rail and pile on pillows so guests can snuggle into the lighted nook with a good book.

With antique French-style beds dressed in new striped quilts and crisp linens, this space is a treat for other guests too. (Twin beds offer the ultimate in flexibility for guest rooms.) Swing-arm lamps for reading serve each of the antique beds, and the nightstand is a circa-1880 faux-bamboo bed cupboard. Access to a porch also makes this room a guest favorite.

Guest-Ready
In a Weekend

BEFORE

Feathering a luxurious guest nest doesn't demand a big budget

or a lot of time. With ready-made linens and curtains, simple projects, and savvy shopping, this "leftovers" bedroom now welcomes weary travelers in charming style. Adapt these strategies to rediscover the art of pampering.

■ **GET INSPIRATION.** Remember the children's story about the princess and the pea and the princess's high-rise bed? The homeowner who decorated this room did. The existing iron bed gained elevated focus and comfort with a second set of box springs. Each box spring wears its own matelassé bed skirt.

■ **WARM IT UP.** Walls painted corn-silk yellow take the chill off the north-facing room. Crisp green accents add cool contrast.

■ **TREAT THE WINDOWS.** Provide window treatments that create privacy and block unwanted early-morning sun. If using sheers, add a blind or shade behind them.

■ **DO SOME "HOME SHOPPING."** This owner scavenged other rooms for the vintage armoire and the silver, wrought-iron, and ceramic accents. The armoire packs entertainment gear and baskets of books, magazines, candles, stationery, CDs, bottled water, bath scents, and even raffia slippers and a jar of peppermint candies.

OPPOSITE PAGE: An apple green checked duvet, pristine linens, and an architectural headboard accent make both the bed and pure comfort the focus of this room scheme. **1** This low iron table stands ready to hold a suitcase for unpacking or a tray for afternoon tea. **2** Bow closures—daisy trim glued onto sheer wired

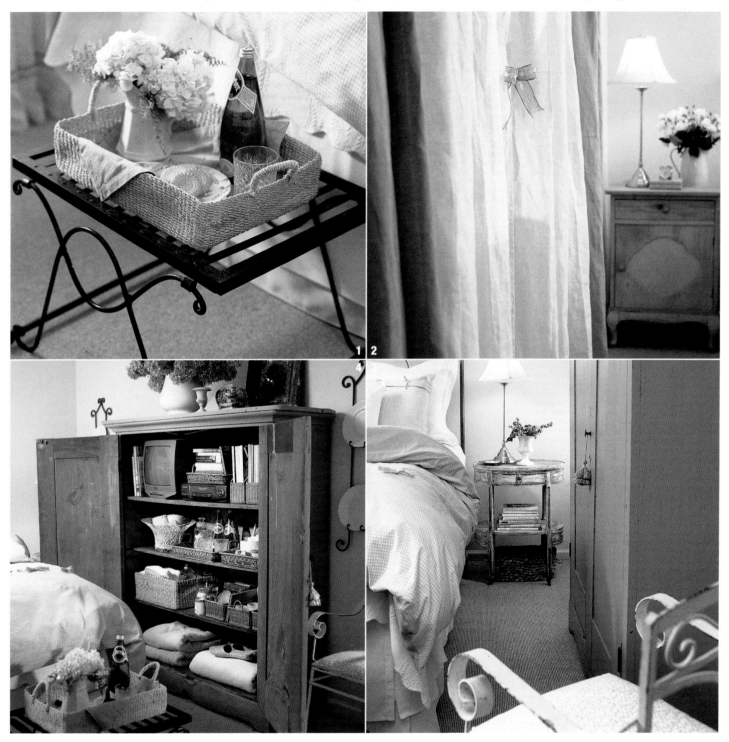

ribbon—add custom detailing to plain, ready-made curtains. **3** An old garden chair—its cushion re-covered in a fabric remnant—joins the inexpensive iron table at the foot of the bed for casual dining and relaxing. **4** Borrowed from another room, the painted armoire delivers the storage, display space, and character that every guest room needs. Here, it holds blankets, robes, bottled water, toiletries, and even a TV.

Kids' rooms

Delightful children's rooms are the stuff of dreams. That's why they're fun to decorate.

This little boy's blue room is fit for a prince, and his pillow proclaims "The Prince Sleeps Here." A storybook canopy and antique daybed could make the space regal enough for a little princess. Creating spaces where little ones learn, explore, and dream takes imagination, but unlike forever-young Peter Pan, this chapter's charmers grow with your child.

Rooms Grow Too

With bold colors and playful touches, kids' rooms are among the most fun spaces

to decorate. Plan on reworking your child's room three times during the growing years: baby-to-toddler transition, the early school years, and adolescence. Careful planning and wise furniture choices can reduce the extent (and cost) of that inevitable redecorating.

DESIGN TOGETHER

Fortunately, you have an in-house expert—your child—for decorating inspiration. It's important to get a child involved in choosing colors, themes, and accents. Starting at age 3 or 4, kids can help choose wall coverings, paints, and fabrics; however, resist the temptation to overembellish. In addition, always retain veto power; if a child wants a color you truly abhor, compromise by using it for easy-to-change accents.

FURNITURE WITH A FUTURE

Opt for sturdiness and easy care over style. Laminates, plastics, and painted surfaces are ideal. Look for on-the-grow cribs that convert to youth beds, changing-table chests that can store items beyond the diaper stage, and modular storage with adjustable shelves. For a child's first big bed, consider a full size; it will allow growing room and space for parent–child talks and stories. In major furniture pieces, avoid themes. Winnie the Pooh may suit a child today, not tomorrow.

KID-FRIENDLY SCHEMES

Children naturally head for the brightest hues in the crayon box. Bold, primary colors and defined shapes stimulate learning. Cast those bright hues in accents; for backdrops, pick enduring neutrals and classic wall coverings in stripes, checks, or florals. Use a neutral-plus-one scheme—for example, white walls and red curtains, bed linens, cushions, and area rug. If a child's favorite color changes from red to, say, blue, you can switch accessories without repainting. Other quick-change accents include drawer knobs and pulls, lampshades, wall and bulletin board art, reversible rugs, colorful storage bins, and, of course, bed linens.

TO FIND OUT MORE ONLINE, VISIT US @ www.bhg.com/bkarrangearoom

OPPOSITE: Nary a cartoon character can be found in this nursery. It's wisely designed for the baby-to-toddler transition, with a neutral backdrop, bright primary accents, and a convertible crib. The gingham and vintage-print fabrics are sweet but not too babyish. BELOW: When it's toddler time, the wall color and nautical theme still work. The crib converts to a daybed with the removal of a side rail, and colorful toy bins and a child-size armchair slipcovered in chenille move in.

Planning a Nursery

A baby is coming! It's cause for celebrating—and decorating. The list of nursery necessities is long. When you consider the hours you'll spend in your baby's nursery, you'll understand why nursery schemes must please you as well as your baby.

NURSERY STARTERS

■ **A CRIB THAT MEETS TODAY'S SAFETY STANDARDS.** Only use pre-1992 cribs if they are in good repair and have slats no more than 2⅜ inches apart and a drop-side that, when lowered, is at least 9 inches above the mattress. Two-stage, drop-side catches are best. Avoid vintage cribs; check secondhand cribs for lead paint, shaky construction, missing slats, or removable knobs and decorations. If in doubt, buy a new crib. Place the crib away from the window to

prevent falls against the glass or tampering with the window blinds, curtains, and cords.

- **A STANDARD CRIB MATTRESS,** $27\frac{1}{2}\times51\frac{7}{8}$ inches. For baby's safety, no more than two of your fingers should fit between the mattress and crib.
- **ROCK-A-BYE SEATING.** A rocking chair or glider with flat arms and an ottoman make feedings comfy. How about a daybed, a futon sofa, or a twin-size bed for your own naps too?
- **A DOUBLE-DUTY CHANGING TABLE** with a high top rail and open shelves for diapers now and toys and books later. Some styles double as dressers to adapt to changing storage needs.
- **ADJUSTABLE LIGHTING.** Dimmers allow brighter light for changing baby and softer illumination for feedings. Add a night-light too.

COLOR AND PATTERN

- **TRY A SOFT-TOUCH PALETTE.** Infants respond to contrast, bright colors, and patterns, but avoid going overboard. White or pastel backdrops may be more soothing; add brighter colors and patterns with accessories.
- **DRESS UP WALLS** with scrubbable wallcoverings in simple prints that aren't too babyish. On painted walls, use decorations you can remove and change when your child outgrows them. If walls have pattern, keep rugs neutral or a solid color.
- **ADD A MOTIF** to painted walls at crib height for your baby to see. A graphic wallpaper border, even if only on one wall, provides definition and charm—and is easy to change in the future.

OPPOSITE: A sophisticated scheme of bright pastels and a ragged paint finish on the walls will welcome changing accessories later. CENTER: Playful and bilingual, this nursery underlines the walls' hand-painted stripes with a border of words and kid-pleasing images that were traced onto the wall, then painted. BELOW: Stripes and mini prints add depth and interest to the Peter Rabbit print hopping around this room. The cornice's freehand flowers and checkerboard trim match the changing-table chest.

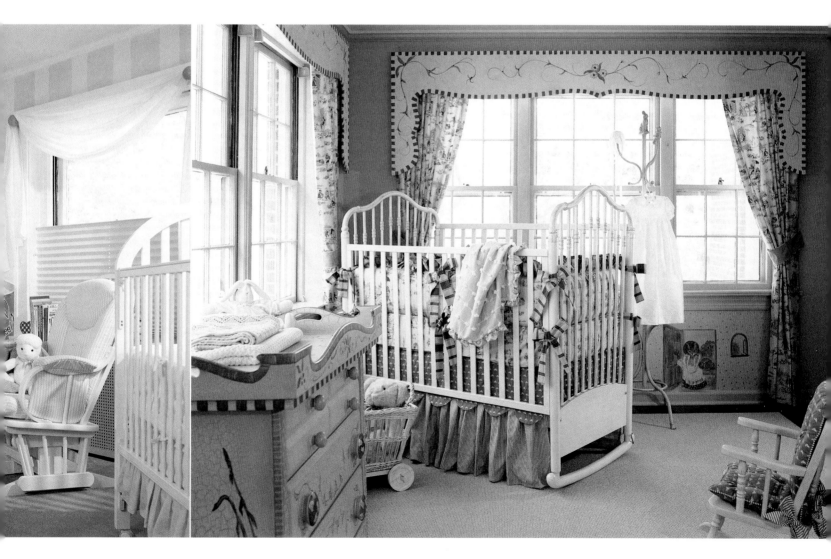

Looks to Last

Think of kids' rooms as whimsical canvases for their ever-changing dreams and creations.

The trick is choosing versatile design elements and timeless themes that make your child's room inviting now and for years to come.

PAINT ON MAGIC

Painting is a quick and low-cost way to splash on a child's favorite colors. Shop for low-VOC (volatile organic compound) latex paints; they're less toxic and nearly odor-free. Paint a thrift store chest color-block style, or let the kids help with simple paint techniques such as sponging, stamping, or stenciling on walls and unfinished furniture. Frame a wall section with molding and brush on blackboard paint so kids can do all the doodling they want.

SPACE AND STORAGE

With double-duty furnishings—beds with drawers and wall units with pull-down desks—even a small space can play, study, sleep, and grow. For crafts and homework, fit a triangular desk into a tight corner; skirt an old table for today's little-girl vanity and tomorrow's computer station. Check that all drawers have stoppers for safety. Bolt tall chests or bookcases to studs so kids can't accidentally pull them over. For shelves, use ¾-inch plywood spanning no longer than 30 to 36 inches between supports. Need sleepover space? Don't forget trundle beds or air beds plopped on the floor.

DETAILS COUNT

Low-pile carpet and wood floors offer good floor play space. Tailored Roman shades, valances, cafe curtains, and shutters stay out of a groping toddler's way. For safety, cut all cord pulls short so toddlers can't grab them. New blinds have split cords so kids can't get caught in them; on older blinds, cut loop-style cords to create split cords.

OPPOSITE LEFT: In this little pet-lover's retreat, stuffed toy dogs scamper over the plaid duvet. Attached with hook-and-loop tape, they're easily removed for washing. Dog art is hand-painted on linens and the toy chest, and the dog bed doubles as floor seating. OPPOSITE RIGHT: Fun fish accent the coverlet, pillows, and wall border in this boy's room. The coverlet's fitted corners convey nautical style with cording laced through brass grommets. Peg racks turn walls into efficient storage for nautical accents, keepsakes, clothes, and play gear. ABOVE: Thanks to Mom's passion for collecting vintage fabrics and on-sale remnants, this room includes fun colors and lively prints designed to last well into high school. The daybed for sleeping and lounging is draped in a chenille spread that inspired the palette.

ABOVE: Two-toned, painted walls and rope create a pinstriped wainscoting effect in this teenage equestrian's bedroom. Spaced 15 inches apart, the rope pieces were glued on, secured with finish nails, and coated with polyurethane. Heavy fringe on the pillows and plaid fabric on the bedskirt echo the room's English riding theme. OPPOSITE: Brothers share this bedroom; its crisp red, black, and white scheme is lively without seeming juvenile. Featuring an upholstered headboard with piping detail, the bed is one of a pair, each featuring a pullout trundle for overnight guests.

Teen Pleasers

Eager to establish their own identities, teens want to personalize

their rooms, so give them space. Letting them express their creativity—with reasonable guidance from you—is a great opportunity to help them develop good design and budget sense.

PLAN TOGETHER

How does your teen want the room to function? Do you need more storage for collections, electronics, books, or sports gear? Does your teen need a bigger desk for a computer or spots for grooming or exercising? For visiting friends, use oversize floor pillows, a daybed, or an upholstered chair. Does the closet need a do-it-yourself organizing system? Now is the time to strike compromises. Instead of taping posters to newly painted walls, consider a corkboard wall or an oversize bulletin board for changing displays.

FIX UP FURNITURE

Whether it's from your attic, a yard sale, or the secondhand shop, hand-me-down furniture can become fun, funky, and functional with a fresh coat of paint and new hardware. Also consider modular, unfinished furniture for lining a wall with bookshelves and a computer desk. Slipcovers are easy-care coverups for seating.

FIT IN HOMEWORK

Writing desks have a standard height of 30 inches; computer desks are about 26 inches high. Are file cabinets and drawers adequate and within easy reach? Create a quick-and-easy study spot by placing a door atop two file cabinets. Your teen can personalize the desk top with decoupage or paint.

LIGHT WITH CARE

Choose desk lamps that place the bulb about 15 inches above the desk top. Bedside reading lamps need to be 28 to 32 inches tall, or use wall-mounted swing-arm lamps. Choose lamps with stable, weighted bases. Because they produce extreme heat and can be a fire hazard, avoid halogen lamps in younger kids' rooms. For daytime computer use, control glare but preserve light with miniblinds or sheer curtains.

Suite Sharing

When siblings bunk together, make their room a cozy sleep space

and a fun place to play and study. Sharing works best if children are the same sex and close in age. Don't put a toddler with a 9-year-old whose tiny toys could pose a choking hazard for the little one. When well planned, a shared room can nurture each child's individuality with spaces for hobbies and separate lockable storage for treasures.

DOUBLE-UP STYLE

■ **EXPLORE FOR SPACE.** Underused rooms and attics, such as this top-of-the-stairs redo, offer plenty of privacy for siblings. Built-in shelves, back-to-back chests or bookcases, or a ceiling-hung blind can define territories. Avoid top-heavy floor screens unless they are safely anchored at the ceiling.

■ **MIX, DON'T MATCH.** Let children pick accessories and bed linens in their favorite colors. Then separate beds by hanging two back-to-back curtains, each of a different color or pattern.

■ **SLEEP SAFE.** Choose twin, trundle, or bunk beds that meet American Society of Testing Materials standards. Children younger than 6 years are too young to sleep on top bunks. Beds should be made of strong, durable materials with smooth, rounded edges. Look for securely attached posts; bolted-on side rails; guardrails with a fastening device; and sturdy, securely attached ladders with steps 10 inches wide and 12-inch vertical spaces between steps. Mattresses must lie at least 5 inches below the guardrail top, and there should be no more than 1 inch between the mattress and frame.

ABOVE: Removing interior walls and adding new drywall, dormers, and windows opened up this once-dark attic into a sunny sleep-and-play suite with easy-care fabrics and a minimalist Scandinavian spirit. Now the family cuddles up on the canvas-covered sofa for bedtime stories. OPPOSITE LEFT: Creating the children's suite was a family affair. Dad crafted the beds and the toy and sports gear chests out of cypress. Mom upholstered the headboards and stitched bed linens, and "Grandmom" created the quilts beneath the duvets. OPPOSITE RIGHT: Recycled one more time, this flea market chest was once the children's changing table, but with a new sink, it's now the vanity in their shared bath. The muted red, white, and blue tile is from a tile salvage company.

Home offices

Whether you're the CEO of a home-based business, in charge of keeping a busy family organized,

or both, going to work can be a pleasure when you put the "home" into your home office. With efficient furnishings, thoughtful space planning, and bonus personality, your home office can be much more than a landing pad for your laptop. This bright and breezy writer's retreat headed upstairs for peace and quiet and tree-house views.

WorkStyle Make It Cozy

Every day can be casual day when you work at home. There's no morning rush, no freeway commute, and no dress code, so take that conference call in your jeans and fuzzy slippers. And why not make your work space as personal as the rest of your home? After all, it doesn't have to look like a conventional office; it only has to work like one. To select the right space for a home office, consider how you plan to use it.

■ **IS IT STRICTLY FOR BUSINESS?** Is it a research library, a hobby room, or a multipurpose hobby and home management center? Is it strictly for desk work or will it double as a guest room?

■ **HOW IMPORTANT IS PRIVACY?** The family room may be a perfect spot for a bill-paying desk, but if you're writing the great American novel, the area may be too distracting. Will other family members use the office? If you hold client meetings, you'll need privacy and maybe a separate entrance.

■ **WHAT WILL YOU STORE?** Do you need space for research materials, sample books, blueprints, a computer and office equipment, a drafting table, or crafts items?

PERSONALITY PLUS FUNCTION

If you want to wallpaper your "corporate suite" in raspberry red toile and add a comfy chaise for stretching out to ponder a project, go ahead. An author did exactly that in turning a spare bedroom into this creative haven. From the closet's quick-and-easy desk—two filing cabinets and a three-board top—to handsome cabinetry, every inch works beautifully. Open shelves keep photos, reference books, collections, baskets, and fabric-covered boxes in view; doored storage hides messy projects. Fabric-covered foam-core panels turn closet doors into a message board/photo gallery crisscrossed with ribbon.

LEFT: This clever closet office gets to work with soft touches, such as the chenille-clad slipper chair and lots of family photos on display, even under desktop glass. The laptop may be high tech, but the accents—an old-fashioned phone and fresh flowers—are pure home.

TO FIND OUT MORE ONLINE, VISIT US
@ www.bhg.com/bkarrangearoom

ABOVE: Upholstered in a luscious plaid that spins off the room's cheery palette, the sink-in chaise works double duty as a spot to relax and read and as "guest" seating when the family drops in to check on Mom's projects.

WorkStyle Make It Sleek

Designing a home office that truly helps you succeed requires careful planning. How do you work? Do you like cozy clutter and leaving projects and paperwork spread out? Or does neatness count? Know your needs; then use these tips for setting up shop:

■ **CONSIDER BUILT-IN** or modular shelves, desks, and storage to optimize space. Custom built-ins are pricey, so check out stock kitchen cabinetry for its custom look and storage options.

■ **UTILIZE TALL STORAGE UNITS** that add vertical interest without gobbling up floor space. For an expansive look, combine open shelves and doored storage.

■ **WHAT'S YOUR REACH RADIUS?** You'll need everything within a comfortable arm's reach, so arrange your work area in an efficient L- or U-shape.

■ **LIGHT YOUR WAY.** To cut glare on computer monitors, use adjustable desk lamps, general lighting on dimmers, and lamps or sconces that bounce light off the ceiling.

PARTNERS BY DESIGN

Wrapped in rich woods from beams to built-ins, this home office doubles up on workstations for the couple who works here. Colorful pottery, collectibles, and family photos add the personality these home workers and their clients enjoy. The items also contribute to the textural mix that makes this space warm and welcoming. For client comfort, oversize chairs were reupholstered in plush mohair fabric, and breezes and natural light flood in from a lineup of transom windows. With room for supplies and files below decks in clean-lined cabinetry, workday clutter disappears after business hours, so the couple can pluck a good book from their office library, settle back, and relax.

OPPOSITE: Designed to flow seamlessly from the home's light-filled living spaces, this workplace-for-two opted for warmth and personality and left the heavy metals and austerity of conventional offices behind. Each workstation is designed in an efficient U-shape, and both share back-wall storage. **ABOVE:** Although this desk turns its back on the inner office, it still has a view of a colorful accent wall and art in the hallway. The hall functions as an annex, including custom storage to help the main space maintain its sleek good looks.

A Do-It-All Office

Many homes—including this one—have precious little space
to cast separately as a home office, a guest room, and a hobby spot. To ease its space crunch, this home called
on clever cabinetry, flexible comfort, and warm, round-the-clock color to triple the function of a spare bedroom. Granite countertop wraps the office area, which has sitting and legroom for adults to use laptops on the side while the kids work at the computer angled into the corner. When guests are due, projects stow away behind doors and in ample drawers and wicker baskets
and the countertop is swept clean so guests have room to spread out. Then out of the cabinetry comes the queen-size wall bed,

OPPOSITE LEFT: With a warm palette and three walls wrapped in action-packed cabinetry, this ambitious home office has turned into a family hub where everybody can do homework or pursue their hobbies. The vintage rocker invites settling in for a chat or a good read. BELOW CENTER: The everyday space makes quick work of changing into a guest room that has all the comforts of home. When the bed is in the open position, it reveals niches for nightstands on either side with rear outlets for reading lights and a clock. BELOW RIGHT: For safety, the fold-down sewing table has a lock inside the upper cabinet so it can't fall or be pulled down accidentally. The cabinet is outfitted with an adjustable light and has plenty of specialized storage for sewing supplies.

lightweight and well balanced so it raises and lowers easily and safely. With dressed-up touches such as crown molding that gives cabinetry a furniture look, faux-finished aubergine walls, and a cheery floral-fabric window treatment, the space is always ready for a quick and smooth transition from work to relaxation. The cabinetry holds one more surprise—a fold-down table for sewing projects and gift wrapping. The sewing machine slides out and plugs in inside the cabinet, and there's plenty of adjacent storage for fabrics, wrapping papers, ribbons, and the stitcher's library.

Make Room for Homework

When it comes to squeezing in a home office,

your bedroom can handle desk work with a slim sofa table at the foot of the bed or with a farm table in place of a night-stand. But if you like to burn late-night oil while your part-ner tries to sleep, it may not work as a full-service office.

WHERE TO WORK?

■ **FOR QUIET,** forget busy kitchens. Spare rooms away from household hubbub are obvious winners. Can you tuck a vintage secretary into a corner of a little-used living room?

■ **FOR FAMILIES WHO SURF** the Internet, the family room or din-ing room may be the answer.

■ **CONVERTED GARAGES OR WALK-OUT** basements with streetside access are ideal if you need privacy and receive clients.

■ **WALK-IN CLOSETS,** under-the-stairs nooks, and corners make cozy work spaces.

■ **KNOW YOUR MEASUREMENTS.** Desks are 30 inches high; com-puter tables about 26 inches high—important to know if you are converting an antique table to office use.

■ **KNOW YOUR FILE NEEDS.** File cabinets offer letter-size or legal-size drawers. Hanging-file and specialized drawer inserts can convert ordinary chests into officeware.

■ **SQUEEZE IN THE FUNCTION.** Laptops fit the smallest office, and flat-screen monitors free up desktop space.

■ **CUSTOMIZE VERTICALLY** with prebuilt shelves; open-bookcase sizes begin at about 18×30 inches, with shelf depths starting at 12 or 13 inches.

■ **CONSIDER CLOSET ORGANIZER SYSTEMS.** Freestanding units offer good looks and storage.

■ **MODULAR STORAGE** comes in varying dimensions, from stack-able cubes to shelf units with optional drop lids, shelves, doors, and drawers.

ABOVE LEFT: Scooting the sofa out from the wall frees up a living room corner for an antique secretary that's convenient for writing, reading, and paying bills. With doors open to showcase collectibles, it adds charm and focus plus function. **ABOVE RIGHT:** Crisp white cabinetry and a split-level counter put this tiny top-of-the-stairs room to work as a home office. An antique weaver's chair serves the high counter—handy for gift wrapping and projects—and baskets keep supplies organized on open shelves. **OPPOSITE:** This airy home office features beaded-board paneling—a remnant from its past life as a porch. A cushioned window seat nestles into new built-in shelves. An antique desk handles correspondence. Sentimental collections abound in this book-lover's retreat.

ABOVE: With antique woods, natural textures, and a tranquil neutral backdrop, this busy office stays user-friendly around the clock. The soft leather chair swivels easily from the English pine desk to the computer, which takes a backseat on a metal stand. LEFT: To emphasize the "home" in this home office and make it an inviting space for after-hours entertaining, cold metal file cabinets are camouflaged with pull-back slipcovers in a linen-cotton fabric.

Working the Swing Shift
Home offices don't have to be all work and no play.

Linked in color and style with other living spaces, they can move gracefully from day job to nighttime relaxing and entertaining when you choose anything-but-corporate furnishings and plenty of clever storage.

AFTER-HOURS ELEMENTS

■ **A SPACE THAT'S AN OFFICE BY DAY** and a den by night needs decidedly homey furnishings, such as graceful round tables instead of massive, hard-edged desks. Add comfortable seating—even a dining table—and the space can host after-work cocktails or dinners for two.

■ **USE COLOR TO FORGE** visual links between your home and office if the work spot is open for entertaining. Choose hues for office walls and other design elements from your home's palette. As guests flow in and out, a drastic color change won't jar the senses.

■ **MAKE CLUTTER DISAPPEAR.** Files, books, and projects in progress need to stay organized but out of sight. If romance is your style, pop slipcovers over your metal file cabinets. Rolling metal shelves can hide in closets.

■ **TO PUT THE OFFICE** in an after-hours mood, supplement desk lamps with reading lamps, accent lights, candles, and recessed lights. Put general lighting on dimmers.

■ **FLEXIBLE WINDOW TREATMENTS** can bridge the gap between day and night. Shutters and blinds, perhaps softened with fabric curtains, modulate natural light to control glare on work surfaces; then they add privacy when the sun goes down.

BELOW LEFT: Travel souvenirs and books gather on this "table," which is actually hardworking storage made of metal file cabinets covered in fabric. The louvered office door is always open and accented with art. BELOW RIGHT: Open shelves that served this former bedroom now hold books and collections. The homeowner annexed the adjacent closet for storage by rolling in a freestanding wire unit to keep magazines organized behind doors.

Special spaces

Your home's quirky spaces—entries, hallways, attics, landings, odd nooks and crannies—often get second-class decorating treatment or none at all. Instead of letting them sit idle, make every square inch contribute personality and function to your home's overall design. A slim bench and painted walls turned this entry into a welcoming woodland bower. Here's how to put the bloom on your own "leftover" spaces.

FirstImpressions

When guests cross your threshold, what's their instant opinion of your home? Is the entry inviting? Does it reflect your personality? If it's just a pass-through, coax it into living up to its design potential with a few warming touches.

INTRODUCE PERSONALITY

■ **CHANGE THE SCENE WITH PAINT** and wallcovering. In a tiny entry, stencil on a checkerboard for impact. In small entries, use a wallpaper border instead of a busy all-over pattern.

■ **CONSIDER THE FRONT DOOR** as a potential design element, whether you faux-finish it, paint it one bright hue, or leave it natural.

■ **SELECT FAVORITES.** If art, collections, or plants are part of your home's charm, introduce them in the entry. Greetings will be leisurely because guests will linger for a look.

■ **ADD COMFORT.** Choose functional furniture pieces such as a bench, small chairs, or a console table to hold keys and packages and to display collections.

■ **REFLECT THE GLORY.** Mirrors visually enlarge small entries and create a spot for last-minute primping before leaving the house.

■ **MAKE AN ENTRANCE.** If your front door opens right into your living room, create an entryway with a floor screen, a fabric panel, or a tall bookcase placed perpendicular to the door.

■ **LIGHT CREATIVELY.** Focus accent lights on art or collections. Stack sconces to dramatize a corner. Direct uplights on plants to cast dappled shadows on a wall.

■ **ADD A KILIM OR COLORFUL RAG RUG** to casual or contemporary entries. Consider an Oriental rug or needlepoint rug in more traditional spaces. Secure rugs with no-slip liners.

ABOVE: Size doesn't stop this small cottage entry from showing off the homeowner's creativity and love of antiques, such as the Victorian Eastlake table paired with a Victorian chair. Stair risers were wallpapered in scenic toile, then sealed with polyurethane for cleanability. **RIGHT:** Porch-style wicker pieces and an old love-seat-size settee piled with pillows transform this tiny kitchen laundry area into a pleasant and functional entry, handy for slipping on shoes, reading cookbooks, setting down grocery bags, or chatting with the neighbors.

ABOVE: Guests can't wait to see the next act once they step into the drama of this romantic entry. A 19th-century mirror provides a space-expanding backdrop for the painted table, accented with the home's hallmark—intriguing collections.

PassingPleasures

Anyone who thinks hallways should function as elevator music, in the background and hardly noticed, is missing a major decorating opportunity. Even the smallest home has some kind of hallway connection, so why not turn those ho-hum passageways into places worth enjoying?

MAKE IT WORTH THE TRIP

■ **DISPLAY FAVORITES.** Walls decorated in gallery fashion convey style without taking up square footage. If you don't have a collection of art or prints, gather framed family photos; frame posters, hobby or sports mementos, textiles, or other collectibles for wall art. For uniformity, keep framing treatments similar in style—no sleek metal frames mixed with ornate carved and gilded ones.

■ **ADD FUNCTION.** When the hallway offers ample space, consider subtracting a foot or more from its width for an antique chest or floor-to-ceiling shelves, either built-in or freestanding. Add shelves at the short end where a hallway terminates. Because hallways are transition spaces between living areas, group two chairs and a small table for a conversation and afternoon tea spot.

■ **GET DOWN TO BUSINESS.** Dead-end hallways are prime spots for home offices. If there isn't a window, you can build in desk and storage space from floor to ceiling. If you want to preserve light from a window, consider a variety of modular pieces that will allow you to customize and organize even the smallest spaces.

OPPOSITE: A long, 5-foot-wide hallway turns into a library with the addition of sleek built-in bookcases. Mixed in with the floor-to-ceiling volumes, framed photos tell the family's story. **FAR LEFT:** Linking a new family-room addition with the kitchen, this breezeway invites passersby to linger for a look at collections. Blue Willow dishes fill a handcrafted child's cupboard, and wall-hung platters and a striped wall covering create vertical interest in this narrow space. **LEFT:** Once a screened-in dumping ground for boots, shoes, and outdoor gear, this breezeway gained year-round solarium appeal with the addition of new windows and French doors, whitewashed board-and-batten cedar panel-ing, and casual seating for reading and enjoying the view.

ABOVE: Attics can be dark and boxy, but this suite lightens up with neutral hues and a recessed wall of new windows. Slim blinds allow privacy and sun control. Built-ins combine drawers for clothes and shelves for books and the television. **OPPOSITE:** The low-flying beams in this attic bedroom were imposing until a space-expanding brush of white over all turned them into architectural assets. Skylights on the angled wall above the bed brighten the space by day and frame the stars at night.

Retreat to the Attic

If you've considered adding a new room to your home, think vertical, not horizontal. Transforming an old-house attic or a new-house bonus room above a garage into living space makes economic sense. The storybook charm of a treetop hideout or quirky sloped ceiling is romantic reason enough to put such underused spaces to work. With these ideas, attics and bonus rooms can become idyllic playrooms, children's bedrooms, adult sitting rooms, home offices, or master suites.

BRIGHTEN BONUS SPACES

■ **BRIGHTEN WITH SKYLIGHTS.** Without tampering with the roofline, skylights increase natural light and add head room. Opt for energy-saving glass; control light with blinds or shades.

■ **STREAMLINE YOUR FURNITURE.** Built-ins make the most of knee-wall space. Sleek freestanding chests can line a hallway. Tuck low-slung seating and shorter chests under the eaves.

■ **CONTOUR YOUR SPACE.** Visually shorten and square up a tunnel-like attic with a fireplace or a bookcase built in across one end. Widen the space with diagonal rugs and furniture groupings. Raise the ceiling with vertically striped wallcovering. Or square it up with paint. Darker hues on end walls visually shorten the room; lighter hues on the sidewalls make it look wider.

TO FIND OUT MORE ONLINE, VISIT US
@ www.bhg.com/bkdecoratingcenter

A Place for Hobbies

How can you find space for hobbies without adding a room?

Here's where a home's out-of-the-way places—a laundry, basement dead space, or even a walk-in closet—can save the day. Not every space will work for every hobby. Only you know the demands of your favorite pastime, so analyze your needs before designing your space.

CRAFTING CRAFTY SPACES

■ **STEAL SOME SPACE.** Have a laundry or utility room waiting to do double duty? Great! If not, check out a main room—even a living or family room—for a corner that can cater to your passion. How messy is your activity? Will it be a maintenance nightmare on a polished wood floor? Will clutter quickly stow away, or do you need to conceal the hobby corner with a folding screen? Is quiet important? If creative writing is your avocation, find an out-of-the-way space with a door, even if that means refitting a guest room closet with a desk or replacing your nightstand with a writing table.

■ **CHOOSE HARDWORKING FURNISHINGS** that play along with your leisure pursuits. How important is storage? What kind do you need—deep drawers for bulky items, wide flat drawers for artwork? Do you or other household members prefer open or closed storage for your hobby gear? For work space, will a portable folding table suffice, or do you need to leave projects spread out? Will you need special task lighting for sewing or tying fishing flies? Or is natural light from windows better for, say, oil painting?

ABOVE: To get a railroad buff's retreat on track, walls were painted a deep coral to showcase a prized collection of O-gauge Lionel trains dating from 1946 to 1956. Display racks accent dormer angles in this over-the-garage bonus room furnished with comfy seating for reading and researching railroad history. **RIGHT:** Plunked down in a lush garden, this studio/shed doubles as a nap-time getaway and a quiet work place for the home's artist in residence. Casual open shelves and humble containers keep painting supplies within easy reach.

ABOVE: Although this storage-packed studio was designed for a potter, it could be adapted for sewing or painting by switching the potter's wheel for a center worktable. A hammered-copper sink handles cleanup, and the floor gets double protection with vinyl-coated grass matting and a floorcloth.

Landing a Job

Call them leftovers, those spaces in your home you pass by every day without a second glance. Next time you walk past, consider whether you might be passing up a good thing. That landing, the corner beneath the eaves, the sliver of wall space at the top of the stairs, or the odd, good-for-nothing nook or cranny could be just the extra space you need. Just put them to work one by one.

OLD SPACES, NEW ROLES

■ **TO FIND THESE HIDDEN TREASURES,** do your own space exploration. Tour your home as if viewing it for the first time. Look for blank walls, dead-end nooks, or little junk rooms or pantries with doors that are always closed. Then recast them to expand your storage, sitting, or display space.

■ **ARE YOUR STAIRWAY LANDINGS UNDERACHIEVERS?** Is there room for a desk, storage chest, or bookshelves? Adding a small lamp table, a chair, and wall art can brighten the journey up and down. Turn a wide landing with a window into a mini retreat by adding a window seat and wall-hung reading light.

■ **CORNERS,** especially those with low-flying or angled ceilings, can become especially snug getaways with the addition of a chair and ottoman for reading. You could even wrap the corner in low, built-in bookshelves to keep best-sellers within easy reach.

OPPOSITE LEFT: Although the dramatic, two-story entry with an overlook landing is a typical feature of many new homes, it's often underused space. A desk, a comfy chair, and personal accessories transform this overlook into a sunny home office with a bird's-eye view. CENTER: Crafted in France almost a century ago, the hall bench with bonus under-seat storage stars on this cottage landing. The tall mirror expands space and adds vertical interest. BELOW: This roomy landing offers bonus display space. Flanked by Hitchcock chairs, the pine chest is the stage for miniature pine furniture, Cole pottery, and silhouettes of the family's children.

Kitchens

Be it galley or open-plan, today's kitchen has become a true "living" room, a hub for family gatherings, entertaining, cooking, and dining.

No wonder it's so important to outfit and decorate a kitchen to reflect your personality and suit the way you live. What's your goal? Energizing your room with spunky colors like the ones here? Banishing clutter with efficient storage? How about an easy-does-it redo with paint, fabric, and a few of your favorite things? This chapter helps you plan and pick design elements for a kitchen that will delight your eye and your taste buds.

Spice with Color

Wood or white? Kitchen trends come and go, but the crisp appeal of white

cabinets and appliances never dates. White sets a timeless mood and makes the room seem more spacious. It also makes the most of natural or artificial light—a real plus in small kitchens or those with few windows. If you adore color—and your white kitchen—count yourself lucky: White makes the perfect backdrop for colorful, downright happy accents.

White exists in myriad variations, so carefully choose wall paint that matches your cabinets. Some whites have undertones of blue, pink, yellow, gray, or brown. Lighting and surrounding surface materials can make a tint look different. Take home paint chips in different tones to see how natural and artificial light changes the look of them throughout the day and evening.

WARM UP A WHITE KITCHEN WITH COLORS AND TEXTURES

When versatile white dominates your kitchen, the accent colors, wallcoverings, fabrics, artwork, and accessories that make kitchens friendly and comfortable can vary with your tastes.

■ **PAINTED FURNITURE,** stenciled borders, and decorative paint finishes on walls introduce color to help personalize a white kitchen.

■ **SOLID COLORS**—a sky blue ceiling, delicious peach-hued walls, or forest green stain on the island—add contrast. Again, consider the effects of natural and artificial light when making color choices.

■ **SURFACES ADD WARM-UP TEXTURE** and color too. To cut the monotony of an open kitchen with lots of white storage, vary countertop materials and cabinet hardware; introduce color, motifs, and texture in backsplash tile; and accent with rich woods and more color.

OPPOSITE: White cabinetry pops against chartreuse walls, bold-patterned vinyl flooring, and mixed textures in this remodeled Victorian-era home. A trio of leather-and-chrome barstools conjures a retro feeling, and dishes in glass-front cabinets echo the wall color. LEFT: Inspired by its coastal setting, this cottage brought the colors of sun and sea into its kitchen with a lemon yellow countertop and backsplash. Chandelier shades, ceramic accents, and the coffeemaker and teakettle fit the yellow and blue scheme.

Choosing Cabinetry

Every kitchen needs it, but beyond its obvious function, cabinetry is your kitchen's main style-
setter, whether you are buying new or updating the old. Crisp white cabinetry with beaded-board doors and open shelves sets a well-scrubbed cottage mood. Natural woods and chrome hardware convey modern style. Antiqued, raised-panel doors and features such as plate racks convey classic style. Dark-stained woods with stone countertops feel warmly rustic, and clean-

lined laminates are beautifully contemporary. To restyle existing cabinets, replace door panels with glass, punched tin, or beaded board, create a raised-panel effect by applying molding to door fronts, or remove some doors to create open shelves.

OPEN OR SHUT CASE

Do you want open or closed storage, or a mix of both? Open storage lets you show off bright-hued pottery and collections and

gives a kitchen an airy look, but neatness counts when cabinets are open to view. Opt for the best of both worlds and remove only a few upper doors, then paint the cabinet interiors in the wall color. Or have sections of solid doors cut out and replaced with glass for a fresh, airy look.

SHOW YOUR COLORS

Stock and custom cabinetry comes in a range of hues: solids, two-toned or antiqued, glazed pastels and naturals, and opaque color over wood grains. Colors can be as dramatic as barn red, French blue, and black or as classic as glazed yellow or creamy white. Transform old cabinets with paint, colored semitransparent stains, or decorative paint techniques such as sponging, antiquing, or stenciling. Choose durable enamel paints.

OPPOSITE: The alabaster light fixture helped set the color scheme in this new kitchen with old-world flavor. Tuscan yellow cabinets with a rubbed, painted finish and the distressed, russet-hued hutch feature furniture details, such as columns and bun feet. CENTER: Against a deep-green granite wall, two inexpensive wooden étagères— a sculptural and functional alternative to upper cabinets in the kitchen—keep everyday dishes handy by the range. Wall cabinets with lead-glass doors are recessed to free up counter space. BELOW: Cubbyhole-style upper cabinets, made of plywood and maple veneer to match the stock maple ones below, give this modest-size kitchen breathing room. The stacks of dishes and the baskets for holding smaller essentials provide a "view" that is all color and texture.

TO FIND OUT MORE ONLINE, VISIT US
@ www.bhg.com/bkkitchenguide

One Great Piece

Like other living spaces, every kitchen needs a focal point,

and if it boosts function, character, and style, so much the better. In open-plan kitchen/family rooms, create focal points for special areas, such as the breakfast spot. For example, dress the range in a hearth-style hood for a dramatic view from the family room. A handsome piece of furniture brings instant distinction to a bare wall. By mixing old design sensibilities with modern function, some kitchens today achieve a warm "unfitted" look with furniture-style cabinets that temper the typical sweep of utilitarian cabinetry.

PAST-PERFECT GALLEYS

In past centuries—before cookie-cutter cabinetry—furniture pieces formed the kitchen. A dresser or hutch held dishes and utensils. Ingredients lined the countertop, other freestanding cabinets, and wall-hung shelves. The ancestor of today's islands was an old table for food prep and dining. Buy new cabinet designs to replicate the look or use these tips:

■ **USE FREESTANDING HUTCHES** to add vertical interest and display space. If you can't squeeze in a big wood piece, use a slim wrought-iron baker's rack for charm in small spaces.

■ **IF WALL SPACE IS AT A PREMIUM,** look for antique corner cupboards, wall-hung shelves, or plate racks. Beneath windows, tuck a small chest for linens or a table for baskets of apples, potatoes, and onions. Don't forget pot racks for storage and character.

■ **INCLUDE FUNCTIONAL ACCENTS.** Old spice and tea caddies, distressed wood boxes, small iron shelves, and even antique glass milk bottles add character while stowing kitchen necessities.

OPPOSITE: Measuring 9 feet long, this 18th-century French pastry table made such a spectacular addition to the kitchen that the homeowners extended a wall several inches to fit it in. It stores and displays various items and holds casual buffets on its marble top. **ABOVE LEFT:** Some of a collector's favorites roost on this enchanting antique hutch that's a focal point for the kitchen and dining spot. The transferware is vintage 1830s. Rare Staffordshire casseroles featuring chicken, duck, and egg-basket covers also are on display. **ABOVE RIGHT:** A hutch doesn't have to be a massive piece of pine and centuries old. This red stair-step beauty is right at home with the lively colors and playful mobiles that a professional chef mixed up for this kitchen redesign.

Cooking Light and Bright

BEFORE

Bringing a new attitude to an aging kitchen doesn't always translate into a to-the-studs remodeling. Decide which elements to change to make your kitchen more efficient and fun; then pour on the color. With mauve walls, a sheet vinyl floor, and dark-stained cabinets, this kitchen was a 1980s fossil. Now—with a few cosmetic additions and subtractions—it's a lively family hub.

■ DELETING A RAILING and three upper cabinets over a peninsula opened the kitchen to the dining spot and family room. The peninsula is now an eating bar with a new green granite countertop. A reproduction hutch moved into the dining area to take up storage slack and add character.

■ WALLS WERE PAINTED SUNNY YELLOW, and for about one-fifth the cost of new cabinets, old ones were painted a delicious lemon chiffon hue. Artfully painted pulls and traditional moldings on the cabinetry capture a French Country look.

■ THE DECADE-OLD DINING SET spiffed up with new cushions, and overhead, the cast-iron chandelier has hand-painted linen shades.

■ NEW TERRA-COTTA TILE in 17×17-inch squares covers the backsplash and the floor. The ceiling and eating bar wear farmhouse-style beaded-board paneling.

■ A DESK BESIDE THE REFRIGERATOR keeps counters free of clutter. A magnetized message board on the refrigerator and a wall-hung cabinet use vertical surfaces for storage and display.

RIGHT: The refresher course for this once-dark kitchen started with lively colors, some new surfaces and lighting, and gallons of paint. But the country charm of the space comes from the thoughtful details, such as new moldings on cabinetry, hand-painted motifs on new lampshades, and inexpensive ceramic cabinet pulls.

Soft Touches

Instead of a total redesign, give your kitchen a facelift

and a beautiful new future. Paint, fresh fabrics, and a change of accents may be all you need. Updating color and design elements creates an instant change of mood—and guarantees big decorating impact on a small budget.

PAINT IT

Nothing renews a kitchen faster than fresh color on the backdrop, cabinetry, and even the floor. A broad brush of the same crisp white or light hue over cabinetry and walls makes a small kitchen seem bigger. In large kitchens, conjure coziness and intimacy with darker colors. Decorative paint finishes and special effects such as stenciled borders add depth and texture to walls and unify space. Before you paint, sand and use a deglazer to remove all the old finish so the final look will be as fresh as the new hue you choose.

TRY NEW "SOFTWARE"

Fabric softens the hard-edged look of appliances; it also absorbs sound. New curtains, softly shirred valances, sink skirts, seat cushions, rugs, table linens, and other fabric accents may provide the soft style statement your kitchen needs. Use fabric to carry color and pattern around the kitchen and link the kitchen with a breakfast area or adjacent family room. In addition to the softness that billowy fabric itself provides, look for romantic or curvilinear patterns that will break up the boxy look of a wall of cabinets. Florals, botanicals, or modern graphic designs with soft shapes will do the job.

OPPOSITE: Garden-fresh fabric and artful painting infuse this lighthearted kitchen with New England charm. There's no need to wash the dishes in these upper cabinets because they're painted-on "trompe l'oeil"—French for "fool the eye"—designs. The floor's diamonds are done in paint and stain.

BELOW: Childhood memories of a family's 1950s beach cottage inspired this kitchen's easy-does-it update. Beneath a salvaged countertop, drawer fronts on the laminate cabinets are clad in galvanized tin secured with construction adhesive, and washable linen skirts replace doors for a softer look.

Collected Works

The best kitchen warm-ups come right from your heart when you decorate with what you love.

Display your favorite collections in your kitchen to turn on a little design charm—and to tell your personal story.

COLLECTOR'S PARADISE

■ **EXPAND DISPLAY SPACE** by replacing cabinet door panels with glass or by simply removing doors on one or two upper cabinets. Paint, wallpaper, or add beaded board to cabinet interiors before arranging Grandmother's china or boldly colored Fiestaware.

■ **LOOK HIGH AND LOW** for display space. Glass shelves attached to a kitchen window frame become a showcase for bright-hued bottles sparkling in the sun or a fragrant array of herbs in terra-cotta pots. Turn wall space under upper cabinets into your own art gallery.

■ **ADD COLOR, TEXTURE,** and more storage with wicker baskets, fabric-covered boxes, hand-painted tins, and interesting old jars. Allot open-shelf space for colorful cookbooks. Instead of lining objects at the back of the countertop, group them in artful vignettes.

ABOVE: When a big new refrigerator moved into this older-home kitchen, it yelled "modern" and stood out awkwardly until the wall was built out around it and shelves were added for more display space and practical storage. **RIGHT:** Things don't get lost behind doors in the deep corner cabinet in this collector's kitchen. Rounded pitchers called "ball jugs," made by Hall Pottery in the early 1900s, join funky salt and pepper shakers in the colorful, open-shelf display.

■ **DISPLAY THE UNEXPECTED.** Bring out your quirky flea market finds or heirlooms—art, framed letters, dishes, old or kitschy kitchenware, and other treasures. If it's fragile or especially valuable, place it on a high shelf or under glass. Use a sliver of wall to hang a small antique shelf for display.

ABOVE: Boring no more, the painted backsplash in this small kitchen is cast in a new role as a gallery. On exhibit, a mix of old prints, photos, and flea market finds delivers color, texture, and charm.

InstantIslands

In newer kitchens, built-in islands often take center stage. Jam-packed with appliances, storage, and counter space for efficiency, they also reroute traffic and shorten distances within the work core. No island? Take heart. In many small to midsize kitchens, you still can add function with a freestanding island. That is especially true in some U-shape kitchens, which can offer too much open area in the center of the room. A small table or a butcher block 18 to 24 inches across can make all the difference when you need extra counter space. An antique baker's table or a farm table in the center of a kitchen also can handle food preparation, buffet service, and even informal dining in warm style. For comfortable movement, plan on at least 3 feet around all sides of an island.

■ **IN SMALL KITCHENS,** draft a console or drop-leaf table, a roll-away cart, or a freestanding butcher block on legs.

■ **PICK A TABLE,** old or new, that's sturdy enough for daily use. Even a chunky old sideboard can be customized to work as an island.

■ **AGE A NEW ISLAND** with vintage-look hardware and crown moldings. New cabinetry lets you customize the height and features, such as eating counters and inset cutting boards.

ABOVE: Reminiscent of old trestle tables, this charming new island is a functional addition to a small kitchen. It's a quick turn from island food prep to the range; when it's time for reading cookbooks or paying bills, pull up a stool. **CENTER:** Cutting travel time from one side of the kitchen

to the other, this trim console table directs the kids around the work core when cooking is under way. It's roomy enough for a lineup of ingredients; rings keep dish towels within reach. RIGHT: Two roll-out toolboxes, one topped with a butcher block for chopping and the other with granite for rolling dough, give this island ample storage. The island top is made from a solid-core door wrapped in copper sheeting.

Decorate with a pamper-yourself attitude, and getting away can be as easy as walking into your bathroom.

Where better to soothe away the stress of the day and rejuvenate your spirits? But what takes a bath beyond practical and makes it luxurious? A sparkling crystal chandelier and sconces and an artist's mural, copied from real landscape photographs, transform this Victorian-era bath into an elegant retreat. This chapter offers more decorating and pampering ideas.

Bath Basics

A well-organized, well-appointed, and well-lit bath can jump-start your day

and become your round-the-clock oasis. Whether you are designing a new bath or updating an old one, turn up the comfort and convenience by paying attention to the bath's design elements and fixtures.

■ **FIXTURES COME FIRST.** For sinks, tub, and shower, buy high-quality faucets—the most frequently used device in the bath. If the bath layout works well, upgrade to a whirlpool or oversize tub or steam shower without moving plumbing lines. Add a double-sink vanity to cut traffic jams in a shared bath.

■ **MAKE A BIG SPLASH WITH SURFACES.** Set the mood with dramatic hand-painted tile, a run of colorful cabinetry, marble or granite vanity counters, elegant wallcoverings, or painted faux finishes. Let your bare feet choose flooring—water-loving tile or stone can be softened with warm carpet or nonskid area rugs.

■ **BANISH SHADOWS.** Warm incandescent lighting provides true and flattering bath light. For a shadow-free makeup spot, flank a vanity mirror with lights; for mirrors wider than 36 inches, a strip-light fixture over the mirror works best. For better general lighting, substitute track or recessed lights for a single, glaring ceiling fixture. Add a dimmer for leisurely after-work soaks.

■ **PRIVACY PANES.** Soften lines of a utilitarian bath and guard privacy with window treatments. Choose Roman shades, decorative valances teamed with blinds or shutters, or drapery panels fashioned from easy-care fabrics. Honeycomb shades that rise from the sill up can provide privacy while admitting a treetop view or exposing a decorative round-top or transom window.

■ **THINK WASHABLE.** So you don't have to perch on the tub to put your socks on, bring in a cushy upholstered chair or ottoman. Dress it in a quick-dry and easy-wash slipcover stitched from prewashed terry cloth toweling or lightweight cotton fabric.

■ **MAKE IT SAFE.** Add a telephone, childproof latches on cabinets and medicine chests, tub-and-shower grab bars, and ground fault circuit interrupter (GFCI) plugs on outlets.

LEFT: Designed around a sleek center island for storing clothes and accessories, this dramatic bath is a natural beauty with limestone flooring and white oak cabinetry, a lush view, and an oversize skylight. The yellow hue of the stone tile mimics the sun, and walls are painted and glazed in pale periwinkle blue for a sky-and-clouds effect.

ABOVE: Warmed by a clever interplay of textures, this master bath juxtaposes the unexpected old with the minimalist new. Sculptural glass sinks and expansive sconce-topped mirrors create the vanity wall. A circa-1920 French chair upholstered in skin-pleasing velvet in an Oriental warrior pattern carves out a nearby sitting spot.

Add a Little Luxe

Your aging bath may be short on square footage, but you can indulge it— and yourself—with style, quality fixtures, and touches of luxury.

■ **SPLURGE ON MATERIALS.** A small bath is an advantage here. It takes fewer marble floor tiles to add luxury to a diminutive bath. A new countertop does wonders for an older vanity.

■ **FREE UP SPACE WITH FIXTURES.** Replace a boxy vanity with a pedestal sink. Or, if you need lots of countertop space, shop for a slim

18-inch-deep vanity instead of a standard 24-inch-deep model.

■ **PAINT IT.** Visually expand space by keeping everything in the same light color family. Add depth to walls with finishes such as combing or sponging, and use semigloss or gloss paints instead of flat paints. Bathroom facelift specialists can repaint wall tile.

■ **REFLECT THE GLORY.** Mirrors work magic in small baths, reflecting space and light. Run mirrors from wall to wall and countertop to

ceiling, or for vintage character, frame a large mirror to hang like art over the vanity.

■ **ADD PERSONALITY WITH FABRIC** and pattern. For romance, consider gathered curtains and replace undersink doors on a newer vanity with a softly shirred sink skirt on a tension rod. Consider scrubbable vinyl wallcoverings, or for just a touch of pattern, add a border at the ceiling or chair-rail line. Use a ready-made wallpaper border or be playful and stencil or stamp on your own painted designs in the colors that you love.

■ **DELIGHT THE SENSES.** Create a personal paradise—inexpensively—with scented candles, sachets, small bouquets of fresh flowers, and an over-the-tub rack or tubside basket filled with soaps, oils, and loofahs.

OPPOSITE LEFT: Trailing ivy, fresh blooms, and a trompe l'oeil garland painted on the wall turn this romantic bath into a garden spot for primping. The vanity's vintage linen accents and a distressed mirror propped in the window turn back time. OPPOSITE RIGHT: A comfy upholstered chaise and a timeworn table and chair add the relaxed ambience that this simple bath needs. Flower-strewn fabric links the Roman shade and chaise pillow. The dressing table displays antiqueware. BELOW LEFT: Blue ticking and a floral sheet were fashioned into this charming shower curtain; a false beam with molding defines the tub area and hides the curtain rod. Paint-grade, beaded-board wainscoting delivers farmhouse flavor. BELOW RIGHT: This powder room had two things going for it—a strip of black-and-white checkerboard tile that inspired a new palette and a charming corner sink. The sink skirt's toile repeats on the wall. The black-painted mirrored medicine cabinet enhances the crisp color scheme.

Getaway Baths

The decorating options for a grand-size master bath can make you feel like royalty.

A steam shower, sauna, exercise area, whirlpool tub, audio/video systems, and other amenities can add up to a true bather's utopia if you have the space.

LUXURY ON TAP

■ **WARM UP AN OVERSIZE BATH.** Add decorative touches so sweeps of porcelain, tile, stone, metals, and mirrors don't make a large space feel cold or cavernous. Break up a large bath into zones for bathing, grooming, dressing, exercising, and relaxing. Fresh color, textured fabrics and accents, and rich woods (in a vanity, a chaise longue or chair, or cabinetry) will turn up the heat in a chilly bath. If your countertop is large enough, plug in a shaded lamp to add a warm, mood-enhancing glow.

■ **GO ALL OUT.** How about replacing a window with French-door access to a terrace or deck so that you can lounge with the morning newspaper and a cup of coffee? How about adding an overstuffed chair and ottoman for après-bath relaxing? If lounging in the whirlpool is your thing, why not set the scene with a master-bath fireplace?

■ **INDULGE.** Treat your bath to heated bars for toasty towels, lighted makeup mirrors, a television, or a massage table. Wire in speakers and let yourself get carried away by music. For safety, position a television, a radio, or a sound system away from any water source.

RIGHT: Adding a shapely slipcovered chair (or a chaise if you have room) makes a big bath feel more like a cozy sitting room. Scented with candles and flowers, this relaxing spot has a garden view and a table handy for a teacup. **OPPOSITE:** Bathed in sunbeams and stay-awhile comforts, this serene yet upbeat master bath marries vintage elements, such as the claw-foot tub, with a contemporary marble-clad shower that has a sleek, frameless glass door. Linen Roman shades mounted at the ceiling line visually heighten the windows.

Splash
On Color

BEFORE

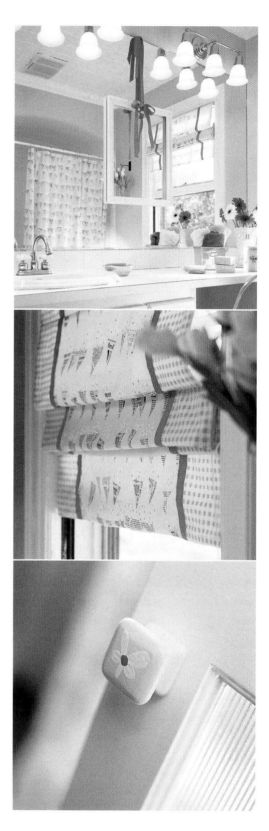

If your bath is aging, but not gracefully, apply the lipstick principle—without the lipstick. Revitalize it with clever cover-ups and splashes of color. Here, an old saccharin pink wallcovering, which no longer suited the owner's style, disappeared, and inexpensive fixes stepped in to provide fresh style. Adapt these ideas to your bath.

■ **PAINT THE WALLS.** Here, a soft lavender soothes the mood and provides contrast that makes the mosaic floor tile come to life. Painting the tub nook green accents the arch over the tub and adds a punch of unexpected color.

■ **GIVE THE CABINETRY A FACELIFT.** Replace metal door inserts with ribbed glass panels to allow colorful towels and toiletries to shine through. It's a less expensive option than having new glass-front doors made. A stained-glass store cut the panels to fit.

■ **DECORATE WITH SHEETS.** Print and gingham sheets provided fabric for the shower curtain, studded with grommets at the top, and the Roman shade that's easy to make with a kit or patterns from the fabrics store. The big surprise? The cushy bath mat is actually made from a pillow sham stuffed with thin batting. All are trimmed in red grosgrain ribbon.

■ **DON'T FORGET THE KNOBS.** Daisies were painted onto these wooden knobs, but you could stamp or stencil yours instead. Changing hardware is one of the quickest and easiest ways to update an old vanity.

TOP RIGHT: For a new view without removing the expansive vanity mirror, a smaller framed mirror hangs on grosgrain ribbon. Twin light fixtures over the sit-down makeup spot and the sink make the bath bright enough for two. CENTER RIGHT: A custom Roman shade, sewn from print and gingham sheets and trimmed in ribbon, underscores the new palette. BOTTOM RIGHT: A brush of fresh paint, textured glass door panels, and hand-painted knobs give outdated cabinetry a bright new look. OPPOSITE: Despite its natural resources—ample cabinetry, a charming bathtub nook, and a sunny window—this bath needed a punch of color. Paint and sheets, sewn into accents, filled the bill.

> **TO FIND OUT MORE ONLINE, VISIT US**
> @ www.bhg.com/bkbathguide

Accent Personality

Surround yourself with things you love. It's a decorating maxim that applies in the bath too. Favorite colors, motifs, and objects on display soften the bath's utilitarian elements and take the edge off cold tile and metal fixtures.

■ **CREATE EYE-CATCHING GALLERIES** of favorite photos or framed art, but consider the humidity. With no tub or shower to add humidity, a half bath makes a wonderful showcase for a treasured painting or limited-edition print. In a full bath where steam could damage fine art, however, it's best to stick with lower-cost prints.

■ **ADD COLLECTIBLE CHARACTER** with wall-hung displays or arrange treasures on shelves or atop the vanity.

■ **WARM UP WITH CONTRASTING TEXTURES.** Weathered flea market finds and antiques in rich woods play off beautifully against slick porcelain, ceramic, and glass.

■ **LOOK FOR SHAPELY VARIETY.** Soften a bath's hard edges with rounded accents: curvy hampers, plant stands, and softly gathered curtains.

■ **DECORATE IN UNEXPECTED AREAS.** Put framed prints and good-looking racks, shelves, and small cabinets above toilets, between windows, over doors, or on neglected walls.

OPPOSITE: Outfitted with modern-day spa amenities such as the whirlpool tub, this bath honors its farmhouse roots too with timeless botanical prints in antique frames. A medley of textures—wicker baskets, an old wood shelf, and a pail for sponges—warm this comfort zone. BELOW LEFT: Although its dimensions are small, this powder room squeezes in personality with a gallery of black and white photos above the boxcar wainscoting. Attached to the wall with brass upholstery tacks, family portraits mix with "ancestors" adopted at flea markets and antiques malls. BELOW RIGHT: Dramatic against the high-contrast backdrop of red walls and cream trim, the display of antique tole trays adds folk art punch and pattern to this cozy powder bath without taking up much space. Highly collectible, the elaborately decorated metalware dates from the late 1800s.

Character Vanities

All vanities are not created equal. They all do the job, but some do it with personality—and an admirable dash of the unexpected. As long as there's room to nestle in a sink, a vanity can be anything from a pair of chunky corbels to an elegant antique sideboard. Even adding stylish new hardware to a ho-hum vanity can boost its character. These one-of-a-kind vanities are the personal masterpieces of homeowners who wouldn't settle for the ordinary.

LEFT: The distressed finish on this old dresser gives it more character and charm as it assumes its new role as a vanity. Instead of occupying the usual middle position, the sink is set to one side so the drawers can open. **BELOW:** Stylewise, these movable wooden storage towers are a perfect fit for this bath in an open, contemporary attic space. In addition, they provide invaluable stashing space beneath the concrete countertop. If more storage is needed in the future, there's room to add another tower or two.

ABOVE: Gracefully carved pine corbels from France were attached to the wall to create the base for this vanity, as artistic as the gilt-framed gallery in this master bath. The corbels are topped with an all-in-one sink and counter and a mirror in a fittingly old-world frame.

OrganizeYourBath

If you've ever rummaged under the sink to find the hair dryer or lost tweezers in a cluttered drawer, you know that efficient bathroom storage belongs on the luxury list with whirlpool tubs and scented candles. First, take an inventory of the items you frequently use in the bath; then consider these ideas for getting organized.

■ **USE VERTICAL SPACE.** Stack a corner with wedge-shape glass shelves or stow grooming supplies on a trim étagère. Install shelves above the toilet, stow rolled towels in a wall-mounted wine rack, or wall-mount the hair dryer.

■ **RETROFIT CABINETRY** with pullout hampers, tilt-out waste cans, and drawer organizers for cosmetics. Beneath the vanity, add stacked pullout trays.

■ **ADD A NARROW LEDGE** to the wall behind the sink if yours is a sleek new wall-hung or pedestal sink. (Before opting for pedestal sinks, decide if you can sacrifice under-vanity storage.)

■ **TAKE ADVANTAGE OF SPACE** between wall studs; carve out shallow recesses for shelves to hold toiletries and makeup.

■ **FILL A TUBSIDE WICKER BASKET** with rolled towels, sponges, bubble baths and oils, and fragrant candles.

■ **ADD A WINDOW SEAT** with storage below and a cushion on top for relaxing.

■ **STEAL SPACE.** Consider sneaking a few extra square feet for your bathroom by annexing space from an adjoining closet, hallway, or room.

OPPOSITE: The star of this bath is a multitalented antique dresser that is recast as a charming vanity; the sink was inset in a cabinet to the right. To expand storage, lower doors were removed and shelves added. New lighting replicates the beauty of the past. BELOW LEFT: Adding to the character of this bath with thick wainscoting and a salvaged tub, the green medical supply cabinet was purchased for $5—a storage bargain for towels and necessities. BELOW RIGHT: With trim styling and a mix of glass-front cabinets and colorful cubbyholes, this bath built-in has an open, airy feel. Hidden hinges enhance the slick design. Before hiring a craftsman to make built-ins, list and measure what you want to store so you can size the storage to suit your needs.

Americans love to live in the great outdoors on sunny porches, decks, patios, and patches of garden barely big enough to slip in a chaise. With a city view beckoning, the owner of this Manhattan home created a top-of-the-world retreat with a lush rooftop garden that's ready for alfresco dinner parties and hours of leisure. The inspiring garden "rooms" in this chapter also welcome with furnishings as comfortable and beautiful as those found inside the house.

Living on the Porch

Decorate your railed Victorian porch, screened gazebo, or corner-of-the-yard retreat like any indoor living space.

First, decide how you will use it. Think beyond just relaxing and barbecuing, because whatever activities you include can determine the furnishings and arrangement. Is it an entertaining spot with a table and chairs for sit-down dinners and buffets? How about hobby space? Outdoors, nobody frets about paint fumes or spills. If you like model building or decoupage, set up a worktable on a covered porch. Transform an upper deck into an observatory with patio chairs and a telescope for stargazing. Whatever's on your porch agenda, plan for privacy. Consider folding screens, container plants, and even draperies, roll-down shades, or shutters.

ARRANGE FOR FUN

■ **CREATE SEPARATE BUT EQUAL HALVES.** A central door often divides two porch groupings. For balance, anchor one half with a single large piece, such as a porch swing or settee. On the other half, group lounge chairs or place a dining table with similar visual weight. Link the halves with a center rug or runner, or define the separate groupings with individual area rugs.

■ **RESCULPT THE TUNNEL.** Add a look of width to long, narrow porches by placing a sofa or settee cross-wise or on the diagonal; if possible, squeeze in a chair at one or both ends. Arrange three or four chairs in an on-the-bias cloverleaf for increased width, and lay rugs on an angle to play up the space-widening diagonal.

■ **LEAVE ROOM TO MOVE.** Arrange seating close enough for easy conversation and allow a minimum of 3 feet between furniture for the path from the steps to the front door.

OPPOSITE: New weatherproof wicker seating, cushioned in bright hues, teams with an easy-care natural sisal rug to bring living room style and comfort out to the front porch. An artisan-crafted pierced-metal screen and plants add touches of needed privacy and block the view to the neighboring house.

BELOW: On the porch of this 1930s cottage, new and vintage fabrics cover a daybed. A cup rack—hung upside down—holds garden tools. Look for water-resistant fabrics and pillow fillings, but plan to take cushions and pillows inside and cover larger upholstery with plastic when the rain comes.

Weather the Elements

Neither gentle rain, nor gusty winds, nor blazing sun will keep you and your guests

from enjoying your porch, patio, or deck as long as you plan cover-ups. Awnings, umbrellas, tented roofs, and big shade trees can keep capricious weather from spoiling your day in the great outdoors. Plan ahead to protect your open-air space.

THE RIGHT LOCATION

Build an outdoor structure where it will get indirect light or shade for at least part of the day. A grove of trees makes the perfect spot for a gazebo or a detached pavilion. Look for a spot that's shaded by the house, by a detached garage, or even by a garden shed for part of the afternoon. To add bistro charm, shade your patio with an adjustable market umbrella, the kind used for years to shade vendors' stalls in Europe. (With an umbrella stand that does not require a dining table for support, you can create instant shade virtually anywhere.) Deflect sun and rain with a retractable awning or stitch simple curtains or roll-up blinds from new, weather-resistant fabrics.

OUTDOORSY FABRICS

Newer synthetic materials simulate the look and feel of natural fibers, but they weather the elements beautifully.

■ WOVEN VINYL-COATED POLYESTER—a popular material for cushions, slings, and colorful umbrellas—is waterproof and resists fading.

■ ACRYLICS sew up easily into soft furnishings and curtains. They dry quickly, don't mildew, and look and feel like indoor fabrics. Check tent, awning, and fabric stores for acrylics.

■ LAMINATED COTTON yard goods are made for outdoor use. Or waterproof your own fabrics with iron-on vinyl available at fabric stores. Natural fabrics fade and mildew with time, so reserve them for sheltered areas.

LEFT: Defined by columns and protected from rain and sun by a covered pergola, this off-the-kitchen patio encourages after-dinner relaxing on cushioned teak and wicker seating; it can host dinner itself on a table that winters indoors. OPPOSITE: Most of the bad weather comes from the south here, so the clever builders of this home added a south-facing "window" to the covered porch to protect wicker seating—dressed in country-print fabrics—from wind and rain.

ABOVE: Cool green with crisp white trim, this cottage porch has roll-down shades to fend off glare and comfortably slipcovered chairs for settle-back ease. The inviting grouping is anchored by a leafy area rug and a round oak dining table that was cut down to tea-table height and painted white. Lamps invite lingering long after the sun has gone down—on mosquito-free spring and fall evenings, that is.

Fresh-Air Style

Once you've settled on how you want your outdoor room to function,

translate the "how" into what furnishings you'll need. If you want to sink into a lazy afternoon, a cushioned chaise is a must. Conjure simpler times with an old-fashioned porch swing or glider; or create a sleeping porch with a daybed or futon sofa that doubles as daytime seating. Even little luxuries—a fan for sultry summer nights, a quilt for crisp fall evenings, a waterproof lamp for reading—add up to a peaceful oasis.

PICK PORCH-FRIENDLY FURNISHINGS

Consider indoor furniture for protected outdoor areas. An extra coat of paint or varnish and fresh slipcovers and cushions made of washable, mildew-resistant fabrics and fillings can make these pieces weather-hardy. If your furniture is a jumble of flea market finds, paint all the pieces in a single hue to create unity. Keep accent colors flowing with fabrics on cushions, pillows, shades, table linens, rugs, and also on collectible accessories.

THE GREAT INDOORS

Put porch-friendly furnishings and nature-inspired accents in reverse, and create a garden room indoors. When cold weather chases you off your real porch, you'll still have your place in the sun. Well, almost. Set the indoor mood with outdoor standards, such as Adirondack chairs, wrought-iron tables, and wicker pieces. Add slipcovers and cushions with washable covers so you—and Rover—won't be afraid to put your feet up. Choose bright accents and botanical-print fabrics for summery color and style, rugged textures that speak of wild places, and painted woods with comfortably worn surfaces.

ABOVE: An iron bed sets the scene for this romantic sleeping porch. Piled with comforters and set on a painted wood floor, the bed makes an irresistible fair-weather sleeping or lounging spot. A great temporary guest room as is, the porch would need roll-down shades to fend off rain and a waterproof cover for the mattress and box spring if the bed was to be left out all summer.

GetAway to the Garden
Whether you head for the deck or create an outdoor room

for relaxing in your lush shade garden, you'll naturally want to bring along the comforts of home—at least cushioned seating and a table for books and the lemonade pitcher. A fireplace, fire pit, or chimenea warms guests on cool nights, and burbling fountains always add a relaxing touch.

A LASTING OASIS

Outdoor furniture can be as big an investment as indoor pieces, so here are some tips to help you choose wisely.

■ **ALUMINUM** is lightweight, durable, and rustproof. It comes in wrought or cast forms with a baked-on enamel or textured finish. Cast-aluminum pieces are more expensive. Look for thick, heavy-gauge alloys and smooth seams on welded parts.

■ **IRON** is good for windy climates. Made from cast or wrought steel, it's heavier and less expensive than aluminum, but it rusts and may need more upkeep.

■ **WICKER** must go under cover unless it's synthetic all-weather wicker. On new wicker, look for aluminum frames and baked-on polyester finish.

■ **MOST WOODS** require at least a yearly coat of paint or varnish.

■ **PLASTIC** lasts for years. PVC (polyvinyl chloride) furniture is made of plastic piping joined together. Resin furniture can be molded into various shapes.

■ **CUSHIONS** need to weather the elements. Pick waterproof and mildew-resistant fabric covers; covers and fillings should allow water drainage. It's always best to take cushions indoors during storms.

■ **PAINT** designed for outdoors protects furniture. Exterior enamel paints last longer than flat finishes. Industrial paints contain more binders to adhere paint to surfaces, and they're more fade-resistant. For bright colors, ask for industrial safety paints.

ABOVE: Stepping into this outdoor "family room," created with salvaged brick and cement-walled planters, is like taking a quick trip to Provence. The garage is dressed in lattice to improve the view. The flea market table and metal chairs serve up dinner. **OPPOSITE:** This 700-square-foot home grabbed extra living space from the garden, where inexpensive lattice creates privacy for an intimate sitting spot. Weathered collections and salvaged finds such as the marble slab atop the console accent the space.

Home
Tours

Inspiration by the houseful

Decorating tends to happen one room at a time, but you and your family live in the whole house all the time. Creating a whole-house decorating plan and, eventually, fulfilling it can make your home a more functional and beautiful place. By looking at your entire house as you plan, you'll find new ways to accommodate everyone's needs and understand how the rooms relate to each other. You're sure to find some surprises in the process. Be inspired by the stories these eight homeowners and their commitment to creating a unique home.

Home Sweet Seattle

Home Sweet Seattle

JANET AND SHELLY JONES OF SEATTLE, WASHINGTON

PREVIOUS PAGES: Overlooking the backyard and garden, a covered patio has old-fashioned porch appeal for relaxing and entertaining, rain or shine. The blue-gray shingle siding and architectural details capture classic Cape Cod spirit. The galley kitchen may be small, but it's bright and efficient with glass cabinets that match panes in the new bay window. The built-in dining nook is dressed in crisp navy blue fabric, from the cushions to the chandelier shades. **BELOW LEFT:** Tradition lightens up and comfort rules in Janet Jones's home, where Emmett, the family's golden retriever, happily volunteers as the sofa-tester. **OPPOSITE:** Warm red on the walls of the family room is the perfect antidote to Seattle's frequent rainy days. Translucent lamp shades also impart a soft glow. Fabrics with color in common link the reupholstered sofa with the new wing chair and club chairs. In this dog-lover's retreat, the couple's four-legged favorites pop up in mantel art, coffee-table books, and accent pillows that Janet mixes with her own needlepoint creations.

"Down, boy!" isn't in Emmett's vocabulary. Neither is the word "metaphor." But the golden boy—retriever, that is— who shares this cozy Cape Cod-style home with Janet Jones and her husband, Shelly, is a tail-wagging symbol of its fetching personality. "We didn't want an all-white home that looks like people visit from time to time," Janet says. "Emmett's the kind of dog you saddle, so it's definitely his house."

TRADITION ON THE FUN SIDE

Keeping up with the Joneses means showing the world what you love, in a casual yet elegant context. They define "home" with lots of family photos, books, nature art, Janet's needlepoint, and the French and English antiques and accessories they've accumulated. It's the details, from hand-pleated lampshades to red animal-print upholstery, that takes the starch out of a proper wing chair. It's dreaming of butterflies in the bedroom, then searching high and low for that perfectly fanciful fabric. And it's color, always warm and bright in Seattle's rainy climate.

Dogs, however, rule the day. "I collect anything that's got a dog motif—dog books, dog art, dog dishes," Janet says. Etchings and prized Wedgwood plates on the sideboard display canine portraits by British artist Marguerite Kirmse, who illustrated

1940s *Lassie* books. Guests have favorite antique, dog-theme napkin rings they expect to see by their plates.

Janet would rather reupholster furniture than buy all-new pieces. "There's no such thing as a furniture graveyard." she says. Because the family room sofa is a favorite lounging spot for Emmett and Phoebe, the couple's elderly collie, it's reupholstered in $10-a-yard cotton duck. Two sets of cushions, one set for daily use and one for company, make it dog- and guest-friendly.

On evening strolls with Emmett, Janet found that she was drawn to one special Georgian colonial home. "There were beautiful lamps, beautiful oil paintings of the children and of dogs," she says. "It was the most inviting thing." It was also the home of British designer Bambi Goodhew, living temporarily in Seattle. Her warm, personalized style clicked with the couple's vision, and she guided the redesign of their home.

Originally a "mongrel, Cape Cod, ranch," the home underwent seven years of remodeling and decorating and has emerged with a fresh, easygoing take on classic style. "It's a lovely house," Janet says. "It's casual and cozy. I think we just made it what it wanted to become all along."

Let it rain. Inside, the mood is always cozy with a warm palette of reds and yellows.

To create the golden hue on living room walls, paint was mixed on-site and applied in test spots to view in changing light. Botanical-print pillows punch up the sofa, and Janet dipped into her collection of antique tea caddies and Battersea boxes for coffee-table accents.

ABOVE: Deep "military blue" walls create an intimate mood for entertaining in the dining room, where Janet mixes pieces new and old that share a noble pro-file, such as the reproduction table and shield-back chairs. **OPPOSITE:** A distinctive collection of transferware plates featuring drawings of dogs by British artist Marguerite Kirmse turns the sideboard into an art gallery that also displays antique figural napkin rings, most with a canine motif, from the late 1800s.

ABOVE: Designed for pampering visiting family and friends, the guest room is "a chameleon," Janet says, because light changes the stipple-look wallcovering from robin's-egg blue to soft green through the day. Fabrics link the suite, and the English rose pattern on the triple-fringed draperies repeats in the bath's shade.

Playful patterns and luxurious fabrics are the dream-weavers in everyday getaways.

ABOVE: Wallpapered from the ceiling to the baseboards in a soft yellow miniprint, the charming master bedroom layers English chintz onto the duvet-topped bed. Eton checks act as a crisp foil. Treating the cushioned window seat to an ottoman gives it extra comfort for reading or lounging.

Big Apple, Little Bite

Big Apple, Little Bite
CAROL MARYAN AND JOEL BERSTEIN OF NEW YORK, NEW YORK

Architect Carol Maryan is no Chicken Little. When her home's living room ceiling really was falling, she didn't panic. She designed an oasis. Far above the madding crowds, her family's 1,250-square-foot co-op is an airy whitescape awash in soul-soothing neutrals. Over that major hole in her "sky" caused by a leaky roof Carol built the most soothing space of all—a skylit bedroom loft with postcard vistas by day and city lights by night.

NURTURING NATURE
"When I'm in the city, it's very frantic, but up here, I'm in this pure space looking out at the city. It feels very cocoonish, very safe, like being in a womb almost," Carol says.

Carol bought two dinky, dingy apartments—"my trailer park in the sky"—with merger and renovation in mind. She removed the water-damaged ceiling and covered the 8×16-foot void by building a sky-light-topped loft bedroom over it. White scaffolding doubles as the loft floor and living room ceiling. "I wanted big light in here," she says, and sunshine pours down the spiral staircase.

The serenity of cool white walls and earthy hues is contagious the second you walk inside. Carol keeps her color options open with a wardrobe of slip-covers in browns, grays, and whites for a quick seasonal shift or mood change. "All white is when I've had too much of everything," she says. "Some people clean their closets. I just slipcover."

With relaxed neutrals, it's easy for this adept mixer of textures and treasures to add and subtract when new loves—worn leather chairs or a 1960s acrylic lamp—follow her home. Clean modern pieces settle in beautifully with retro, rustic, and functional finds, such as weathered wood panels from an old mansion that she hinged into a screen behind a sofa. The old-new mix is "like a family," she says. "You have grandparents, and you have children, and I think it's great when you watch them interact. That's life."

Carol made use of every inch and then some to create her live-big spaces. Floor-to-ceiling mirrors bounce light around to expand space. Floating bookshelves define "rooms." The supersize, glass coffee table keeps the eye flowing, and the kitchen sink and dining banquette scoot out mere inches into greenhouse windows.

You can take the girl out of the country—in Carol's case, Indiana—but she'll still crave that nature connection. To keep the river in view over a parapet, a platform elevates living spaces; glass doors with window-box gardens replace windows.

PREVIOUS PAGES: Carol Maryan layered on warm pattern, texture, and more sink-in comfort by substituting big, squashy pillows for back cushions on the petit point sofa. Satiny slipcovers on the chairs remind her of "old-fashioned quilted robes." For parties, the paneled screen folds back to open up the space even more. On casters for easy moving, a floating "wall" has a splash of bright yellow color that stops the eye but hints at space behind it. The leather chairs are from the 1930s or 1940s; the triangular nesting tables between them are space-savers that go anywhere.
RIGHT: From the rooftop terrace of their New York co-op, Carol Maryan, husband Joel Berstein, and sons Nathan (seated) and Lyle enjoy views of the Empire State Building and the Hudson River.
OPPOSITE: Behind the stretch-out sofa, built-ins with adjustable shelves add functional focus to the family room, which steps down to the original floor level. An ottoman scoots under the coffee table, angled to make the simple shape—and the room—more interesting.

ABOVE: Carol jokingly calls this space-saver counter "a Popeil pocketknife" because it's multifunctional. It handles food prep, casual meals, and party buffets, and the undercounter refrigerator opens on two sides so kids can get juice without squeezing into the kitchen. OPPOSITE: Contemporary wire chairs and an antique table pull up to the window box banquette for dining. When plumbing pipes spoiled the see-through view, Carol sandwiched them between a glass-door mahogany cupboard and matching shelves on the kitchen side. Checkerboard ceramic floor tiles set on the diagonal visually expand the space.

The serenity of cool white walls
and an earthy palette is contagious.

Postcard vistas by day;
by night, a planetarium view of the heavens.

As the sun sets and city lights blink on, the skyline view from the glass-loft bedroom is as magical as the stars. "It's like being in a tree house," Carol says. "It's a lot of fun, and at night, it's so pretty."

OPPOSITE: Yards and yards of white sheeting for sun control and privacy make the skylight bedroom a dreamy space at any time of day. Carol linked the tops of the sheets together by sewing on lengths of grosgrain ribbon; then she draped the fabric panels over cables so they slide back easily. The panels are rarely closed, because Carol loves her "postcard view." **1** After fitting in necessities, this tiny bath had nary an inch to spare for decoration, but Carol gave it a dramatic color shot with periwinkle blue wall tile. She then mixed textures, pairing a brushed-metal mirror with a $3.50 outdoor light fixture and a rustic towel bench. **2** By tucking an antique canvas-upholstered bed behind the living room's floating wall of bookshelves, Carol created a cozy guest room with all the requisite comforts, privacy, and even a view of terrace greenery. Guests can stow their stuff in the adjacent wall of built-ins. **3** For parents' and kids' homework, Carol set up a corner office in the family room. Instead of a utilitarian desk, she installed a round table to hold the computer. An old wrought-iron gate climbs the wall as a decorative yet space-efficient accent.

Relaxed Gulf Classic

Relaxed Gulf Classic

SUNNY AND JAMES ENDICOTT OF PASS-A-GRILLE, FLORIDA

PREVIOUS PAGES: A telescope in the "den" end of the living room brings the ocean view even closer. Rollaway chairs gather at the games table but can glide away easily for reading, relaxing, and entertaining. As construction began, James Endicott scaled scaffolding to check out the view, which proved so spectacular they perched the main living spaces and an expansive terrace on the third level. Everyday meals are alfresco, served up with vistas of dunes, breeze-ruffled sea oats, and boats plying Gulf waters. **BELOW:** Emptynesters Sunny and James Endicott take tea on the terrace of the beach home that they designed to be easy-going and elegant. **OPPOSITE:** The unexpected addition of a pair of roll-arm wicker chairs by the fireplace boosts living room comfort. On the mantel, Sunny displays an oversize poster that adds a bolt of dramatic color and graphic pattern and fits the room in scale.

When Sunny Endicott packed her beach bag, in went the gold-leaf demilune, the ormolu planter, and Chinese exportware from the 1700s. They're not exactly the typical take-alongs for fun in the sun, but Sunny and James were off to the beach—for good—and couldn't leave behind the classic furnishings, art, and antiques they love. Barefoot elegance was their goal.

"Everybody's so laid back at the beach. It's much slower paced," Sunny says. "We didn't want things too formal. We wanted to take that edge off." Relaxing the palette was easy enough: Open the doors and let snappy sail-whites, cool ocean-blues, and sunshine-yellows flow in.

TIME AND TIDES

"You've got to be comfortable in your home," Sunny says. "You go into it, and it picks you up. It should be constantly renewing." The icy white cottons on the mix of upholstered seating feel cool and refined, yet they're easy to clean. Friendly wicker chairs tone down the gilt and mirrors with warm natural texture. Comfort includes pleasing the eye, and white backdrops showcase works of American artists and the rich woods of heirloom furniture.

Hard decorating choices come with the territory when you down-scale, Sunny says. Beyond favorites, what made the cut? Double-duty pieces with inherent flexibility. Antique chests add character, storage, and visual weight in the high-ceiling spaces. The dining table is two pedestal tables that also can go solo. Chairs on casters and a French bench tucked under the sofa table provide extra seating.

"We do a lot of gathering up and entertaining, so this home is all about family and friends," says Sunny, who likes intimate dinner parties—no matter how long the guest list—with small tables spilling from inside onto the terrace. Tampa interior designer David van Ling tamed the rambling living room so it's as cozy for two as it is for a crowd. Towering built-in shelves make up for the library in their previous home, and the conversation area moves center stage to focus on the fireplace, leaving end zones for a mini observatory and the piano.

Sunny nurtures roses, perennials, and orchids to match the home's interior colors because the blooms end up inside. "I'm not a kitchen person. I'm a gardener. I'll spend all day in my garden," she says.

Filled with cherished heirlooms and grandchildren's laughter, "our home is all about family," Sunny says.

ABOVE: Wing and slipper chairs, in dress whites, gather around the twin dining tables that serve in tandem or separately. Chinese export pieces on the burled walnut sideboard echo the refreshing blue and white palette. **OPPOSITE:** A mirrored wall reflects the seascape outside and adds visual width and depth to the living room. Blue ceilings temper bright sunlight. Centering the sofa freed up space for a music "room," built-in bar, and more high-rise bookshelves.

ABOVE: Even if guests in the adjacent dining room are seated facing the kitchen, they enjoy a peek at the sea, thanks to a mirrored backsplash that reflects the view behind them. White cabinetry and a black granite countertop create a crisp backdrop for art. OPPOSITE: For high drama in the third-floor foyer off the living room, an 1800s gold-leaf demilune holds a marquetry planter with Sunny's homegrown orchids. Framed etchings of shells and shellfish accent striped walls.

Sun and sea colors flow through
the home, emphasizing a sense
of place and a feeling
of grace and ease.

Cool, calming comfort reflects the ocean's presence, and the palette is as romantic as a sunset.

ABOVE: An antique dressing screen fitted with sheers and mirrors reflects the master suite's soft peach hues, chosen because they're flattering to complexions and always soothing. The down-filled chaise is a relaxing spot for reading, writing, and watching the sunset beyond the French doors. OPPOSITE: Although Sunny loves antiques, she's not a purist, especially if comfort is at stake. Instead of reworking an old bed to fit a new mattress, she chose a new, reproduction bed with an ornate headboard to set a classic mood; then she layered on vintage, hand-embroidered linens and lacy shams collected from French fairs and street markets.

Finesse for Less

Finesse for Less

KATHY AND TOM SOHN OF SAN DIEGO, CALIFORNIA

PREVIOUS PAGES: Fresh paint turned Kathy's mom's old kitchen table into a new-generation occasional table pretty and functional enough to serve living room love seats. Paired with a trio of insect prints that Kathy framed, the vintage console table creates an "entry" for the tiny cottage. Accents are pared to a few favorite white and silver pieces. **BELOW:** After making their rooms warm and bright, Tom and Kathy Sohn took their style outside, flanking the front door with potted privet topiaries and perennials. **OPPOSITE:** Instead of a large sofa, twin love seats make friendlier, more flexible seating in the small living room; slipcovers guarantee easy care. The coffee table is a new wood bench that can double as extra seating when the couple entertains.

First came love. Then, for Kathy and Tom Sohn, came marriage and a few raids on her mother's garage to shop for cast-off furniture for their first home. They added a few secondhand and unfinished pieces, but the crucial stop was the paint store. Color by the gallon made the furnishings mix a family and their 1,200-square-foot beach cottage feel larger. "The big thing was lightening it up and making it airy," says Kathy, who takes cottage style beyond plain white. "I definitely have color, but it's a clean feeling, kind of refreshing."

EASY, BREEZY BEAUTY

After they whitewashed the original pine ceiling, removed wooden blinds, and rolled soft yellow color over the walls, the stage was set for their spray-painted oldies and a few functional splurges.

Decorating on a newlywed budget, Kathy and Tom prioritized for function, spending the biggest chunk of their dollars on a pair of small sofas. "I like that shabby chic kind of feel that's really comfortable," says Kathy. To fit the beachy look and lifestyle of the cottage, she intentionally picked slipcover fabrics in prints and solid hues that hide a little dirt. "My parents' house has everything white, and it was hard as a kid in a white-white house," she says.

The couple learned at least one major decorating lesson: Pick fabrics before the wall color. They didn't, and finding the perfect yellow for curtains took a while. Instead of pricey hardware, the curtain rods consist of two wood poles screwed together and painted white.

Restraint and patience are keys to accessorizing their small space. Kathy bought cheap framed pictures, then substituted fruit prints from an antiques store. An old metal magazine rack, a carved wooden tray, or any fitting accent is fair game for a shot of white paint. They buy bargain lamps separately, then have fun searching for cool shades.

"This is the perfect first house for us," Kathy says. "It's manageable, nothing too daunting." Tom says he's learned a lot about decorating: "It's a process, and I'm the mover. I love it. I'm such a believer in what she can do." Their next project? It's the rosebud-wallpaper bath.

ABOVE: The couple finds that the whites they love are a perfect foil for a tactile mix of weathered and natural woods, including the dining table and chairs. Whether new or old, character-rich light fixtures, such as the chandelier, are a priority. **OPPOSITE:** When they painted the old green cabinets white, they removed the doors to let open shelves visually expand the small kitchen. Simply designed pottery bowls, dishes, and glassware create artful displays.

Pale paints, pale fabrics, and a pure and simple touch turn the ordinary into extraordinary.

OPPOSITE: One great find from Kathy's mom's garage is this hand-me-down dressing table. With a little paint and a soft skirt, attached with hook-and-loop tape, it doubles as a guest room nightstand. **1** Kathy tacked inexpensive sheers at the guest room window, leaving the ties to flutter in the breeze. **2** Glass knobs

from an antiques store and spray paint give this basic chest from an unfinished furniture store a cottage look. The picture frame was a gift, but it's easy to make using spray paint and painter's tape to mask off stripes on a plain wood frame. **3** In the master bedroom, embroidered and eyelet-trim linens are a mix of old and new. The flower-filled garden window becomes the headboard. **4** Tucked between a new arbor and rose-covered wall, weathered secondhand furniture creates a private backyard spot for relaxing and entertaining friends and family.

Take the New off New

Take the New off New

SANDY HAYES AND DAUGHTER KIT OF TAMPA, FLORIDA

Sandy Hayes will always be a gardener at heart, but she's downscaled to a new townhome with no flower patch she can call her own. Her past homes overlooked water and woods, but her best "view" now is the patio where she's coaxing lush bougainvillea up the lattice. "With no yard or garden, I wasn't going to have Mother Nature to help me," she says. "The eye had to be entertained inside." That's where her garden grows with the color, fabrics, and art she loves.

CHARACTER ON CALL

Did she want walls painted white, eggshell, or cream, the builder asked. None of the above, she said. What about kitchen cabinets? Pop the door panels, and ship just the door frames, she said. "I had a relatively clean slate, and I was determined to put my mark on it," she explains.

Sandy and her daughter, Kit, were eager to get cheery color on the walls before moving in, but Tampa interior designer Debbie Perez advised them to wait and experiment after the furniture arrived. "We bought pint-size cans of greens and yellows and decorated our walls and looked at it morning, noon, and night," Sandy says. The winning green for their open-plan living room, kitchen, and breakfast spot reminds her of watermelons.

After living in "serious traditional homes," mother and daughter decided they'd go casual here. Purchasing a modular, twin-chaise sofa ended one dispute. "We had been fighting over who got the sofa for the Saturday afternoon snooze," says Sandy, who had the three pieces upholstered in two fabrics—a whimsical topiary-and-bumblebee print and a coordinating plaid to accent curves.

New crown moldings, a fireplace, and built-ins add architectural character. Sandy found ways to include touchstones of the outdoors, including a pantry screen door, screening on built-ins, chicken wire over fabric on kitchen cabinetry, sea-grass area rugs, and roosters and roses on the chandeliers. "The pantry door catches everybody's eye, and they love it," she says.

As you move through the home, the mood changes with color, toile wallcovering, and faux finishes, but there's always a touch of black. "It's my anchor for the other colors," Sandy says. She browses antiques shops and art fairs, looking for old French posters, original art, and pottery. She can't pass up a treasure, so she changes what she displays when new items catch her eye. "I have to work at editing," she says. "I'm still guilty of 'it's not done until it's overdone.' It's the sense of homeyness that gets me right to that edge."

PREVIOUS PAGES: Although the living room is small, sacrificing 3 feet for a new fireplace and furniture-look built-ins is a smart trade-off. Silver-screening inserts look airier than solid doors. Original artwork above the mantel features the colors used throughout her home. With scant gardening space outside, a weathered planter on the mantel satisfies the owner's green thumb. RIGHT: Decorating their new townhome was a team effort for Sandy Hayes and her daughter, Kit, who collaborated on a wish list and made casual, colorful comfort their priority. OPPOSITE: From the fresh green walls to plaid and topiary-print fabrics on the modular, double-chaise sofa, design elements draw the outdoors into the living room. Old painted shutters were out on the patio and waiting to be made into a coffee table when Sandy came up with a better idea: To give a blank wall in the living room more focus, she paired the shutters with one of the French advertising posters from her collection and then pulled in a 1700s pine hall bench to supplement seating.

By adding color to a plain-vanilla builder home, Sandy stamped her style all over it. Now it's a wow!

ABOVE: Clad in green paint and new copper screening, an old screen door replaces the pantry's solid door to give the breakfast room down-home appeal. The table has a junk shop base, repainted and topped with distressed maple. Down-filled cushions make seating extra soft. **OPPOSITE:** The original cabinet doors created a boring living room-to-kitchen view, so Sandy perked up the doors and the view with chicken wire inserts over checked fabric.

OPPOSITE: A peaceful neutral palette romances the master bedroom. A dramatic, hand-forged iron bed is dressed luxuriously in toile curtains and custom linens. Faux paint finishes age the new bed and give walls the look of aged plaster. ABOVE RIGHT: Others might have turned this off-the-foyer space into a living room, but Sandy and Kit wanted a homey home office they could share for business and homework. With plenty of pattern in this small room, they kept furniture, such as the pine desk and ladder bookshelves, leggy and light in scale. BELOW RIGHT: Portieres in gingham-trimmed cotton duck soften the entry. When the sofa couldn't squeeze up the stairs, it moved in and donned a slipcover. An heirloom blanket chest serves as the coffee table. The area rug is sea grass banded in black.

Inspired by Color

Inspired by Color

PAM PANIELLO OF TAMPA, FLORIDA

It's only natural that the bounty of cheerful hues inside this vintage home would spill out onto the terrace when it's time for entertaining. A quilt dresses the old iron table set with artisan-crafted dishes bearing fruit and vegetable motifs. Pam Paniello's collection of dishes includes designer pieces and art fair finds; all share vibrant blues, yellows, oranges, and greens. BELOW: Pam enjoys the tropical greens of her landscape, so she pulled those calming hues inside. The greens also provide a refreshingly cool counterpoint to the Florida sun, which floods the home. OPPOSITE: Generously sized and clad in fabric that is bold in color and scale, an array of sink-in seating pieces cozies up the oversize family room. For sit-down meals, chairs pull up to a farm table behind the sofa. The green ottoman is ample in size—just right for snacks when the family gathers to watch television.

Pam Paniello's palettes start in her tote bag, because she always takes color inspirations with her to the paint store. For the perfect purple, she pulled out an eggplant. For "grown-up primaries"? A piece of majolica. Banana-tree leaves inspired her home's peaceful greens. Melon hues came from hibiscus blossoms. "Find something you love—pottery, fabric, art, flowers—and there's a reason you love it, and it's usually color," Pam says.

COLOR STRAIGHT FROM THE HEART

With high, arched windows and French doors overlooking the terrace, the large family room and kitchen in Pam's 1930s home was a sun-catcher thirsty for a drink of cool color. The cool palette Pam chose also sets just the right relaxing mood for a room where friends inevitably congregate. Color inspiration came from the dishes in her cupboard. The refreshing green backdrop cozies the large space, plays up the windows' crisp trim and curves, and visually links the room to the backyard's leafy, tropical greens. On the sofa, the farmer's market print offers a hint of green in that restful blue hue.

Once Pam laid her family room foundation of cool blues and greens, she notched up the heat with lively accessories and fabrics in luscious yellow-greens, yellows, and oranges, from melon to pumpkin.

"I wanted it fun, colorful, and relaxing, not staid and stiff," says Pam, who mixes her greens to soothe and open up her home. "This is a pretty serious house, but I pushed it as far as I could push it."

Recalling that traditional homes of the past often sported bold colors of their own, Pam says "bold colors contemporize tradition and bring it back to its roots." She notes that George Washington is said to have found his small dining room's verdigris wall color "grateful to the eye."

In choosing colors for the rest of her home, Pam follows her heart. She carries the signature reds, blues, and yellows of her beloved majolica collection through the living room. In the master bedroom, chinoiserie on an antique armoire inspires colors and fabric. When in doubt about color choices, she says, "Nature provides the best inspiration. We couldn't come up with those gorgeous colors."

She understands the fear factor. "People are afraid of making mistakes and choosing colors they'll tire of," she says. "Look up and down the hues. You can make any color work in some way. You may think you don't like pink, but fuchsia can be dynamite." If not, repaint.

1 Inspired by the real thing just outside her windows, Pam chose a tropical banana-tree green for the walls and for the fabrics on the banquette and the windows in the kitchen eating area. **2** Rich, dark glazes over marigold yellow paint age this reproduction Welsh cupboard, which displays pottery and gives the kitchen a colorful, functional focal point. **3** Pam borrows the organic colors she loves from collections, such as the charming Limoges vegetable boxes arranged like fresh produce on the window sill. OPPOSITE: Pam's vintage home calls for traditional cabinetry; her personality calls for color. Green walls back up the French blue cabinetry and a yellow island. She favors glass-doored cabinets and plate racks so her old pottery and bright dishes can color every view.

OPPOSITE: The jewel tones of majolica inspired the wall color, new upholstery fabrics, and the hand-painted mirror in Pam's Florida living room. The tilt-top, gateleg table is an antique—a portable picnic table once used for lunching in the French vineyards. ◼ With regal purple walls, the dining room is an elegant

and intimate entertainer, especially in the evenings when the rich woods and crystal accents glow in the candlelight. ◪ Used to cover an antique bench in the dining room, this 18th-century French tapestry inspired the backdrop color. ◪ The mellowed hues and floral motif on this 18th-century French armoire launched the master bedroom palette. Crisp red and white linens and accessories tone down the all-over pattern. ◪ Extravagant use of the same floral fabric on the upholstered walls, seating, and window treatments diguises the master bedroom's asymmetrical features, such as an off-center fireplace.

Style by the Yard

Style by the Yard

JANE OSBORNE OF HOUSTON, TEXAS

Jane Osborne's search for "software" leads just about anywhere if she suspects the perfect fabric awaits in a forgotten attic, a farm-field flea market, or the discount store down the block. Never mind a few worn spots in that old paisley shawl; it will look smashing tossed over an easy chair. Never mind the sofa's elegant upholstery; a new bargain-priced tea towel will stitch up into a pretty pillow for it because the color's just right. "I love the hunt," Jane says. "I love to find that perfect thing."

FOR THE LOVE OF PATTERN

To Jane, fabrics are friends, so when she and her daughter, Eden, moved to their new home, some old "friends" naturally came along. "Refresh, not re-cover" was the plan when Jane hired Houston designer Daily Howard to pull things together.

From the stylized, landscape-print linen on club chairs, they pulled out snappy reds and friendly blues and yellows for new upholstery and pillows to perk up the checked sofa. "That chair fabric is so memorable," she says. "It has lots of colors, so it was easy to go from there."

Jane loves to mix heirlooms, antiques, and flea-market finds, so layering on more fabrics only adds to the homey, collected-over-time look. "You can have beautiful furniture and wonderful old pieces, but if you don't dress it up with fabrics, it goes unnoticed," she says. "This is a labor of love. So many things have come from different places—antiquing, flea markets—and they fit."

Threads of rosy red color and floral pattern run through the old and new fabrics from the living room to the kitchen and upstairs to the family room, tying the spaces together. With accents of green throughout, Jane says, "It's a wonderful house to decorate for Christmas."

Golden yellow pulled from the living room wing chair is the dining room star. "I needed lots of color because I have four different sets of china that I use in that dining room," Jane explains. As another color link, the dining room draperies are trimmed in floral bands cut from the same striped fabric used on the wing chair.

In a worn piece of paisley or a snippet of old needlepoint, Jane sees possibilities. Needlepoint embellishes a new pillow; paisley makes a handsome throw for the sofa. "Great old fabrics have such character," she says. "I wouldn't drape a new piece of fabric over a chair. It has to mean something to me."

PREVIOUS PAGES: Classic Chippendale chairs seemed too formal for the country French mood Jane wanted for the dining room, so she relaxed them with provincial print slipcovers in the golden yellow of the walls. Illustrations from an Italian calendar look like vintage botanicals in elegant new frames. Since the living room's checked sofa and print-upholstered chairs were keepers from a previous home, Jane added color, pattern, and character with an infusion of old and new accent fabrics. RIGHT: Jane Osborne and her daughter, Eden, feathered their new nest with furnishings of various vintages for easygoing comfort and a sense of history. OPPOSITE: With larger scale patterns on the sofa and club chairs, small-scale prints dress the other seating. An antique French Voltaire chair is clad in red, sprinkled with what Jane calls "tiny green Christmas trees." The new mantel has a faux-stone finish. The coffee table is a salvaged firescreen atop a new hand-forged base.

Creamy white walls create a refreshing playground for an earthy, rich palette of toile, gingham, paisley, stripes, and friendly florals here and there. Threads of personality and color weave it together.

ABOVE: Fragments of vintage needlepoint and paisley combine with new trims and fabric on an elegant, one-of-a-kind pillow in the family room. Mixing is a creative way to use old textiles that are often found in less than perfect condition. **OPPOSITE:** Red accent fabrics echo the toile Jane chose for the family room chaise; all of the toss pillows and cushions on the wicker seating are mix or match. After the table and ottoman skirts were stitched up, remnants of the checked fabric were used as trim for the window shades.

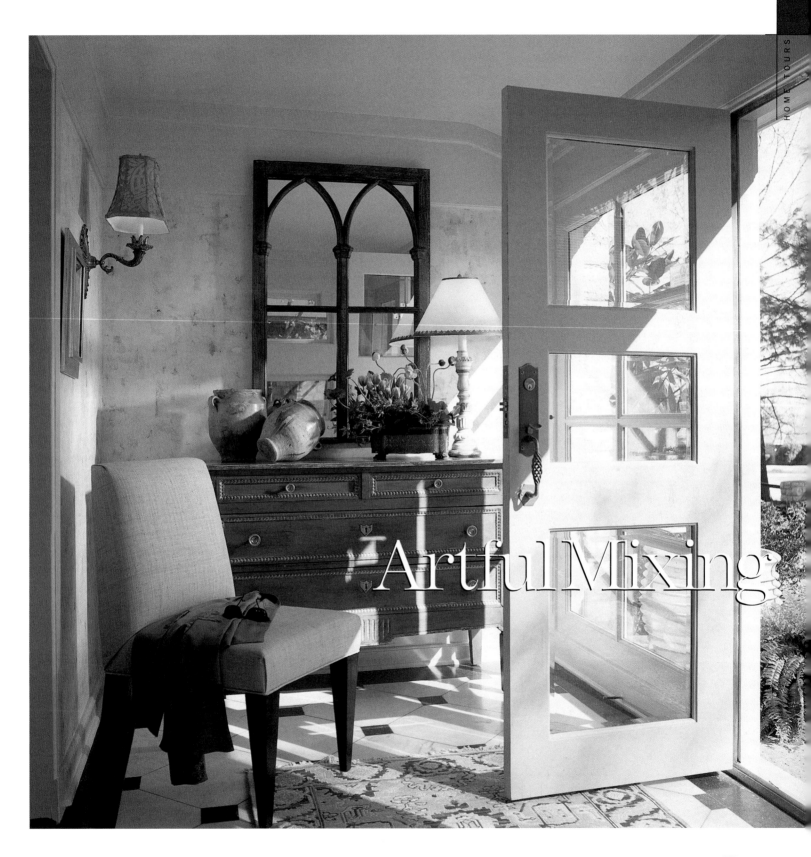

Artful Mixing

Artful Mixing

BETH AND ROBERT SACHSE OF TULSA, OKLAHOMA

PREVIOUS PAGES: Travel is a rich source of design inspiration for Beth, who admires the graphic drama of an African kuba cloth she hung in the breakfast room. The reproduction gateleg table is made from old wood. Decorative and functional, antique French doors hide a wet bar. The entry, set with a mirrored Gothic window, a contemporary chair, and an 1860 French chest, introduces her penchant for mixing styles and periods. **BELOW:** What makes a room homey? It's books and pets, says Beth, relaxing with her husband, Robert, and the family's boxers, Diego and Freda. **OPPOSITE:** This art lover honors a William Hook landscape painting by hanging it center stage. Colorful glass balls that catch the light echo the luminescence of the painting. Functional art, heirloom Imari porcelain, and vintage leather-bound books fill shelves.

If there's one constant in the elegant rooms of interior designer Beth Sachse, it's change, and she wisely designs for it. Static looks and labels don't last, she says. How can they when true personal style reflects one's changing life experience? To prove her point, Beth creates rooms that are movable feasts of furnishings and collections. "I really love moving things around, and you'll see positions changing year to year," she says. "That's something I grew up with. Moving furniture around was part of the entertainment when Dad was out of town, and he was always pleasantly surprised."

FINE LINES AND TIME LINES

Why do sleek, red leather chairs work as beautifully with a rustic table in the dining room as they do next to African art in the kitchen? If a piece is designed well, it mixes well, she says, so she picks each element to stand on its merits. "I like a layering mix of artistic influences. It makes more interesting design," Beth says. "The table looks kind of primitive and the chairs are real modern, and I love that combination."

Neutral backdrops set a flexible stage for the links of color that her furnishings and accessories carry from room to room. "I'm big on 'less is more.' I like to have a feeling of space...so your eye has time to focus on each thing as something important," she says. That requires editing when rooms start feeling too busy. She looks beyond the sentimental in assessing each element, asking: Why do I want to keep that? Her collection of antique Chinese and Japanese Imari porcelain always makes the cut. "I can't live without that Imari red color," she says. "There are certain colors I am always comfortable living with—those colors I use in the fabrics. And they can move around."

When it comes to rearranging elements, never fear, just experiment, she advises. In tabletop vignettes of metal or glass, she tucks in a wood element for warmth. If a grouping needs sparkle, she adds an object that catches light. "You've got to get personality in there. That's what accessorizing is all about," she says. "It's saying, 'I've got a sense of humor, I like an element of surprise, and I like certain colors'." What is the most important element in her rooms? It's artwork. "To me, it's like poetry," says Beth. "Make sure it means something to you. Never buy a piece of art to fill a hole because the wall is boring."

Pattern and color—always with a dash of Beth's favorite Imari red—flow throughout the home, creating harmony.

ABOVE: In the open-plan dining and living area, sleek Italian chairs clad in red leather present a striking contrast to the reproduction English table with its double gate legs. Flanking the French walnut buffet, 1930s chairs upholstered in a botanical print provide extra seating for the table. OPPOSITE: Sentimental objects give a room meaning, says Beth, who displays her mother's collection of tea caddies, miniature musical instruments, and tiny tortoiseshell pieces from the 1800s on the buffet. The lamp is fashioned from an antique hand-painted water jar. The circa-1820 chinoiserie clock is English.

OPPOSITE: Into her traditional-modern mix, Beth blends Oriental and Asian-inspired elements. The sofa's gold upholstery is sprinkled with scarlet Chinese characters, the bamboo bookcase is English, and the lamp is made from a tin Chinese jar. **1** On the terrace, neutral colors and natural finishes set a serene

mood for fireside dining and relaxing. **2** Antiqued cabinets and sleek stools echo the home's traditional-modern mix. Robert, a gourmet cook known for his pies, appreciates the efficiency of concrete countertops and high-tech cable lighting. **3** Botanical-print draperies, woven shades, and relaxed slipcovers enhance the master bedroom's casual "treehouse" ambience. The white Tizio lamp adds a stylish modern surprise. **4** Once a garage, the guest suite uses the textures of fabrics and primitive African stools (used as coffee tables) to warm sleek elements, including low-profile shelves and a modern LeCorbusier chair.

Workshops

Now that you've been inspired, it's time to create a plan for your new rooms. The information on these pages will help you make the best choices in materials, furnishings, and window treatments; refer to these helpful pages as you shop. Use the room arranging kit to try out different arrangements without the back-breaking effort of moving the sofa. And take the Decorating Taste Test for fun and to gain insight into your personal design preferences.

FurnitureBuymanship

Take your time when exploring the dizzying array of retailers, discount stores, custom shops, online businesses, and catalogs. Browse first; buy later. Peruse books and magazines to study styles and construction; then contrast items in all price ranges. Compare when buying high-ticket items. Here are tips for buying quality furniture:

UPHOLSTERY AND WOODS

■ **BE SURE YOUR FURNITURE WILL FIT.** When you shop, take along your to-scale floor plan, a tape measure, and fabric and color samples.

■ **TEST-DRIVE UPHOLSTERED SEATING.** Sit on it, lean on it, lift it up, and turn it over to check comfort and construction. Frames should be kiln-dried, seasoned hardwood joined by dowels or interlocking pieces, not butted together. Tempered-steel springs are coil or sagless; eight-way, hand-tied springs denote good quality. Polyurethane foam is the most common filling; down is softer and more costly. (Consult the "Fabric Basics" pages 416-417, before selecting upholstery fabrics.)

■ **KNOW YOUR WOODS.** When shopping for case goods, the industry term for chests and cabinets, check hangtags and labels to learn which woods or veneers are used in them. Look for strong construction where pieces bear the most weight—legs, shelves, braces, drawers. Check that doors and drawers open and shut easily and that finishes are hard and smooth with no visible imperfections.

■ **BONE UP ON HISTORY.** If you're buying reproductions, know period details and craftsmanship. Reproductions are exact copies of antiques, usually made with the same materials and detail; adaptations are loosely based on original pieces; visual reproductions are made with modern shortcuts to hold down costs.

OPPOSITE: When buying upholstered furniture, find the best value by balancing the quality of the fabric with the inside construction. Some furniture lines come with optional wardrobes of slipcovers, such as the cleanable cover-up on this chair.

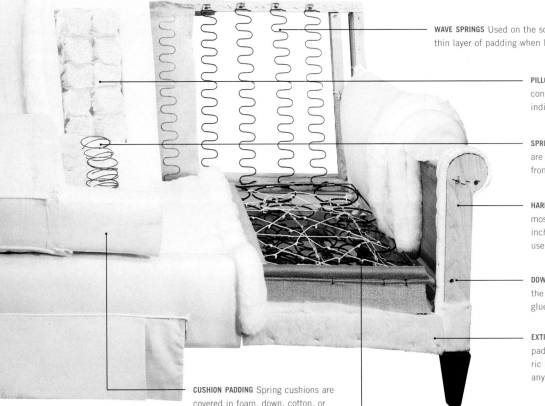

WAVE SPRINGS Used on the sofa back, they're covered with a thin layer of padding when loose back pillows will be used.

PILLOW BACK When the pillow is a part of the back construction, the wave springs are topped by individually pocketed coil springs or foam.

SPRING CUSHIONS In high-quality sofas, seat cushions are made from individually pocketed coil springs or from latex foam. Budget sofas use less dense foam.

HARDWOOD FRAME Hardwoods such as oak are the most durable, but semi-hardwoods in 1¼- to 1½-inch dimensions are good too. Low-quality frames use softwoods or plywood.

DOWEL AND SCREW JOINTS Good sofas use dowels at the joints; cheap ones don't. All frames should use glue, screws or staples, and corner blocks.

EXTRA PADDING Every surface of the sofa should be padded, including the front rail; padding makes fabric last longer. You shouldn't be able to feel wood anywhere—even on the outside back.

CUSHION PADDING Spring cushions are covered in foam, down, cotton, or polyester fiberfill.

EIGHT-WAY, HAND-TIED SPRINGS are the longest-lasting. Coil springs are each tied with cording to surrounding springs and the frame.

Room Arranging Kit

Creating an inviting room has less to do with what you have than with how you use it.

Following these guidelines will help you design a room from scratch or rearrange what you have to make the most of your furnishings and space. How would you like the room to function? Do you want places for desk work, hobbies, kids' games? Do you want to watch television, play the piano, dine, read? What about storage or display space? Look at your present furnishings and decide what pieces you'll have to add to meet your needs and which ones you can eliminate.

MAKING ARRANGEMENTS

Using the *Better Homes and Gardens®* floor-plan kit and templates, *opposite*, work through the following steps:

■ **MEASURE YOUR ROOM.** Plot your room on the kit grid—or graph paper—using one square for each square foot of floor space. Measure the length of each wall and draw it onto the floor plan. Mark windows with a double line; leave an opening for each doorway; and indicate door swings. Be sure to include architectural features, such as fireplaces, sliding glass doors, stairways, and bay windows.

■ **USE FURNITURE TEMPLATES.** Measure each furniture piece. Trace or photocopy the corresponding templates from the kit and cut them out with scissors or a crafts knife. **HINT:** If you need to make your own special templates, outline them on graph paper or cut them out of self-stick notes so you can reposition each furniture piece as needed.

■ **FIND A FOCAL POINT.** Physically, this is the cornerstone around which you build a grouping; visually, it's the dramatic element that draws you into a room. If your room doesn't have a natural focus—a fireplace, built-in bookcases, or an expansive window—substitute a large-scale or boldly hued accessory or use freestanding wall units.

GET MOVING

Once you've found the focus, arrange your furniture templates on the graph paper floor plan. Keep these tips in mind:

■ **DIRECT TRAFFIC.** If traffic passes through a room, it doesn't have to run through the center of it. Think of your furniture pieces as walls or guideposts that can easily funnel traffic around your conversation areas.

■ **FLOAT FURNISHINGS.** A lineup of furniture around a room is as uninviting as a waiting room. Pull pieces away from walls into close-knit groupings, with major seating no more than 8 feet apart.

■ **KEEP CONVENIENCE WITHIN REACH.** Set a handy resting place for drinks or books close to every seat. It can be a true end table, a stack of books, or a piece of glass atop a decorative basket or cube. Any such piece will work as long as the surface is roughly the same height as the arm of the chair or sofa next to it.

■ **DO A BALANCING ACT.** Use furnishings of different heights and hefts for interest. For balance, distribute tall or weighty pieces evenly around a room. Use large pieces to balance weighty architectural features.

■ **FORGET ROOM LABELS.** Use space creatively, letting your furniture determine the function of the room. Who says your L-shape dining area can't function as a TV spot? Why not dine in the living room?

■ **TRY A FRESH ANGLE.** Because a diagonal is the longest line through any room, an angled grouping creates an illusion of width in a narrow room. On-the-bias seating can also take advantage of more than one focal point—for example, a fireplace and a window view.

■ **COZY UP A BIG ROOM.** Break a large room into two or more groupings. Each grouping will feel more intimate and function better than the single large space.

■ **MAXIMIZE A SMALL ROOM.** Include a large-scale piece, such as a vintage armoire or a fat love seat, for a feeling of grandeur. Use vertical storage in tight spaces.

■ **FIX LOW OR HIGH CEILINGS.** Raise a low ceiling with floor-to-ceiling window treatments and tall furniture pieces that will guide the eye upwards. Lower a too-high ceiling with a colorful area rug and low-level lighting; play up the floor-hugging look by hanging artwork so that it's at eye level when you are seated.

Upholstered Furniture and Bedding Templates

Symbols

STAIR

DOUBLE DOOR

RADIATOR

COVERED RADIATOR

DOUBLE HUNG SASH

CASEMENT SASH OPENING IN OR OUT

DOOR SWINGING IN OR OUT

BIFOLD DOORS

SLIDING DOORS - 6 or 8 FT.

CASED OPENING (PASSAGE)

FIREPLACE WITH MANTEL

$ LIGHT OR OTHER SWITCH

LIGHT FIXTURE (Not Lamp)

SINGLE-POLE SWITCH

3-WAY SWITCH

DUPLEX OUTLET

TV ANTENNA OUTLET

AIR-CONDI-TIONING (20 amp.) OUTLET

FLOOR OUTLET

TELEPHONE

CEILING FAN

BELL

Incandescent Light Outlets

RECESSED CEILING

WALL BRACKET

CEILING

TRACK LIGHTING

To plan a room on paper, use the symbols above to indicate practical details. Photocopy or trace the templates that represent your furnishings, or cut your own custom-size templates; then experiment with different arrangements.

SOFA BED 35 x 75-92 — OPENS TO THIS SIZE

SOFA BED 35 x 70-82 — OPENS TO THIS SIZE

SOFA 32 x 72-78-84-90-96-102

SOFA 34 x 72-78-84-90-96-102

LOVE SEAT 32 x 50-55-60

LOVE SEAT 34 x 50-55-60

HEADREST | RECLINING CHAIR 30 x 29 (opens to 66) | FOOT REST

BARREL CHAIR 30 x 30

LOUNGE CHAIR 30 x 30

LOUNGE CHAIR 32 x 32

WING CHAIR 33 x 34

OTTOMAN 32 x 32

RIGHT-ARM MODULE 32 x 32

ARMLESS MODULE 32 x 32

LEFT-ARM MODULE 32 x 32

OTTOMAN 22 x 22

OTTOMAN 20 x 27

OTTOMAN 16 x 30

OCCASIONAL CHAIR 24 x 22

OCCASIONAL CHAIR 25 x 20

OCCASIONAL CHAIR 25 x 23

ARM-CHAIR 27 x 27

ARM-CHAIR 29 x 27

ROCKING CHAIR 22 x 24

32" ROUND OTTOMAN

CHAISE LONGUE 24 x 60

KING SIZE WITH HEADBOARD 80 x 83 | MATTRESS 80 x 78

QUEEN SIZE WITH HEADBOARD 80 x 64 | MATTRESS 80 x 60

DOUBLE BED WITH HEADBOARD 75 x 59 | MATTRESS 75 x 54

TWIN BED WITH HEADBOARD 75 x 44 | MATTRESS 75 x 39

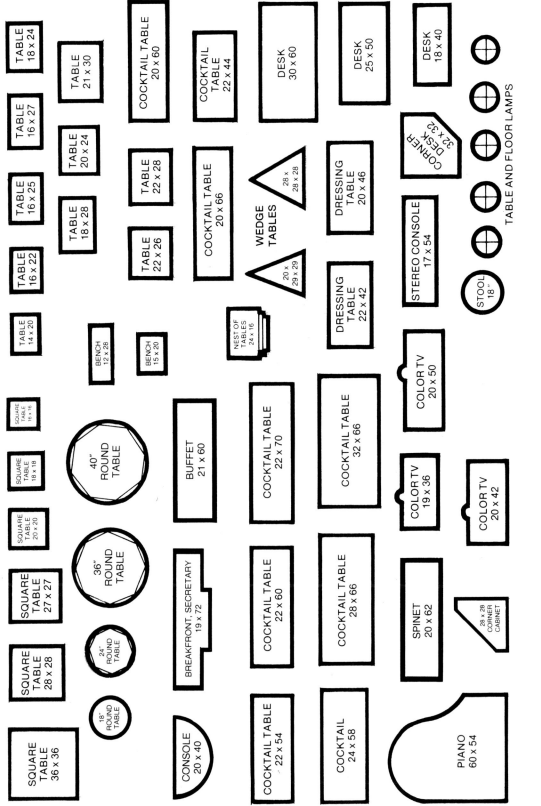

Occasional Tables and Special Pieces Templates

TABLE 18 x 24

TABLE 16 x 27

TABLE 16 x 25

TABLE 16 x 22

TABLE 21 x 30

TABLE 20 x 24

TABLE 18 x 28

COCKTAIL TABLE 20 x 60

COCKTAIL TABLE 22 x 44

DESK 30 x 60

DESK 25 x 50

DESK 18 x 40

CORNER DESK 32 x 32

TABLE AND FLOOR LAMPS

TABLE 22 x 28

TABLE 22 x 26

COCKTAIL TABLE 20 x 66

WEDGE TABLES

28 x 28 x 28

20 x 29 x 29

DRESSING TABLE 20 x 46

DRESSING TABLE 22 x 42

STEREO CONSOLE 17 x 54

STOOL 18"

TABLE 14 x 20

BENCH 12 x 28

BENCH 15 x 20

NEST OF TABLES 24 x 16

COLOR TV 20 x 50

SQUARE TABLE 16 x 16

40" ROUND TABLE

BUFFET 21 x 60

COCKTAIL TABLE 22 x 70

COCKTAIL TABLE 32 x 66

COLOR TV 19 x 36

COLOR TV 20 x 42

SQUARE TABLE 18 x 18

SQUARE TABLE 20 x 20

SQUARE TABLE 27 x 27

36" ROUND TABLE

BREAKFRONT, SECRETARY 19 x 72

COCKTAIL TABLE 22 x 60

COCKTAIL TABLE 28 x 66

SPINET 20 x 62

28 x 28 CORNER CABINET

SQUARE TABLE 28 x 28

24" ROUND TABLE

18" ROUND TABLE

SQUARE TABLE 36 x 36

CONSOLE 20 x 40

COCKTAIL TABLE 22 x 54

COCKTAIL 24 x 58

PIANO 60 x 54

Dining Tables and Chairs Templates

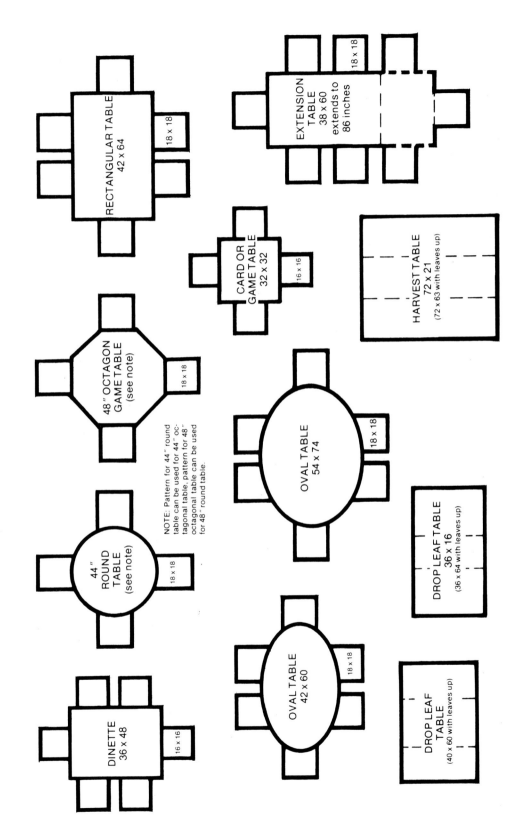

RECTANGULAR TABLE
42 x 64

18 x 18

EXTENSION TABLE
38 x 60
extends to
86 inches

18 x 18

CARD OR GAME TABLE
32 x 32

16 x 16

HARVEST TABLE
72 x 21
(72 x 63 with leaves up)

48" OCTAGON GAME TABLE
(see note)

18 x 18

OVAL TABLE
54 x 74

18 x 18

NOTE: Pattern for 44" round table can be used for 44" octagonal table, pattern for 48" octagonal table can be used for 48" round table.

44" ROUND TABLE
(see note)

18 x 18

DROP LEAF TABLE
36 x 16
(36 x 64 with leaves up)

DINETTE
36 x 48

16 x 16

OVAL TABLE
42 x 60

18 x 18

DROP LEAF TABLE
(40 x 60 with leaves up)

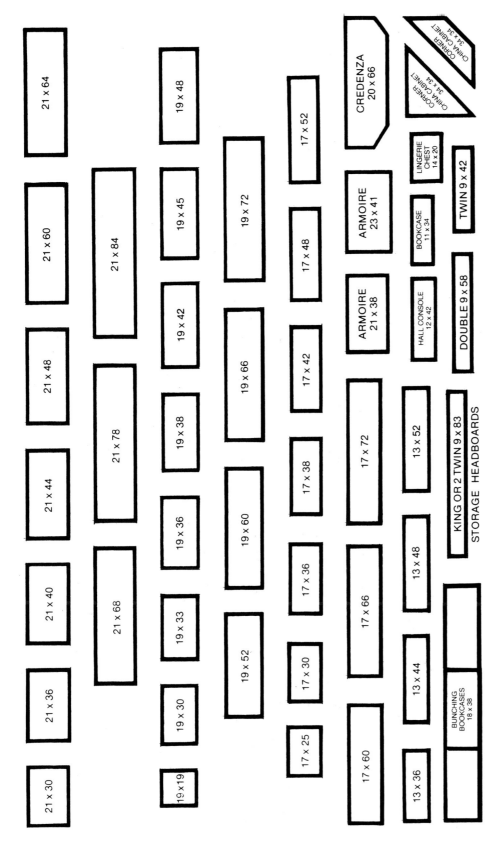

Interchangeable Storage and Special Pieces Templates

Room Arranging Graph Guide

1 square equals 1 square foot

21 x 64
21 x 60
21 x 48
21 x 44
21 x 40
21 x 36
21 x 30

21 x 84
21 x 78
21 x 68

19 x 48
19 x 45
19 x 42
19 x 38
19 x 36
19 x 33
19 x 30
19 x 19

19 x 72
19 x 66
19 x 60
19 x 52

17 x 52
17 x 48
17 x 42
17 x 38
17 x 36
17 x 30
17 x 25

17 x 72
17 x 66
17 x 60

CREDENZA 20 x 66

CORNER CHINA CABINET 34 x 34

CORNER CHINA CABINET 34 x 34

ARMOIRE 23 x 41

ARMOIRE 21 x 38

LINGERIE CHEST 14 x 20

BOOKCASE 11 x 34

HALL CONSOLE 12 x 42

13 x 52
13 x 48
13 x 44
13 x 36

TWIN 9 x 42

DOUBLE 9 x 58

KING OR 2 TWIN 9 x 83

STORAGE HEADBOARDS

BUNCHING BOOKCASES 18 x 38

These templates can be used for charting chests, dressers, serving carts, buffets, china cabinets, credenzas, consoles, hutches, tea carts, bars, stereo cabinets, hope chests, window chests, secretaries, and many other pieces of furniture.

Fabric Basics

Fabrics, like people, have distinct personalities—
some refined, some easygoing, some the life of the party. Brocade and damask convey classic elegance; gingham connotes country. Some fabrics—nubby chenilles or crisp stripes—get along with virtually any style. Take samples of carpet, wallcovering, paint, and other fabrics along when you fabric shop. Take fabric samples home to see how light changes their look. Buy durable decorating fabrics, not garment fabrics; decorating fabrics are typically 54 inches wide. Order all fabric for a project at once.

SOME TERMS TO KNOW

- **BROCADE,** with a raised pattern resembling embroidery, is used in fine, formal upholstery.
- **CHENILLE,** with thick needle-punched designs, is suitable for casual upholstery.
- **CHINTZ,** a plain-weave glazed or unglazed cotton, often has a traditional mood and floral motifs.
- **DAMASK** comes in various fibers and weights and features textural contrast between satiny and dull. It makes durable formal draperies and upholstery but goes casual in loose-fitting slipcovers.
- **MATELASSÉ** has a double weave and an embossed look; use it for elegant bedcovers and throughout the home.
- **MOIRÉ,** with a shimmery finish resembling watermarks or wood grain, sets a traditional mood.
- **PLISSÉ** looks like overscale seersucker with wide puckered stripes; it can feel casual but suits traditional rooms too.
- **TOILE DE JOUY,** a tightly woven fabric with a pictorial print on a neutral ground, shows off best on large seating, walls, and flat drapery panels. It can look formal or casual.
- **STRIÉ,** a good casual and formal mixer, has subtly varied warp-thread colors and irregular streaks.
- **TAFFETA** is a crisp, plain-weave fabric that works well for more formal window treatments because it retains shape with little support.
- **TAPESTRY,** with thick weaves and pictorial designs, suits simple upholstery and flat window panels.
- **TWILL** is tightly woven with a diagonal ridge; two types, denim and herringbone, are ideal for casual upholstery.
- **VELVET** creates a mood of formal elegance with lush cut pile that shimmers in the light.

LEFT: It's the fabrics that give this window and settee their upbeat personalities. The oversize plaid brings new life to the traditional setting. Crisp leaf prints soften the seating and balance the bold curtains. The pillows wear a touch of vibrant pink and yellow to echo the plaid. OPPOSITE: Flowing portieres, or door curtains, create an air of intrigue and intimacy because they afford only a glimpse of the living room beyond. The curtains' floral fabric echoes the red hues in the upholstered seating beside the fireplace.

Choose the Right Fibers

Different areas of your home get different types of use, so consult this handy guide to determine which fabrics are smart choices for your space and lifestyle. For example, you may want to veto linen for a sofa in a high-traffic family room or silk in an everyday dining spot. Instead, upholster the sofa in a sturdy cotton blend that will stand up to stains, spills, and hard wear; cover dining chairs in a durable nylon fabric. Once you've finished this short course on fibers, you'll be ready to head for fabric shops, furniture stores, drapery and upholstery workrooms, or an interior designer's studio.

RIGHT: Sturdy cottons make long-wearing seating and drapery fabrics. Because it takes color well, cotton can bring deep, crisp color to a room. A classic blue and white plaid trims windows and reappears as a mat for whimsical framed sculptures of children's clothing. Yellow walls and a large-scale yellow floral print give the room sunny ambience, even on cloudy days.

THE NATURALS

	COMMENTS	ADVANTAGES	DISADVANTAGES	CARE/COST
COTTON	Creases easily; absorbent; breathes well; easily treated; highly flammable; fair resilience and elasticity.	Strong fiber; takes color well; blends well with other fibers; versatile.	Wrinkles easily; affected by mildew and sunlight; shrinks and stretches unless treated; yellows.	Machine-washable; must be ironed. Inexpensive.
WOOL	Very elastic and resilient; good absorbency; does not burn easily.	Strong fiber; insulates; takes color well; handles and drapes easily.	Attracts moths unless treated; needs careful cleaning; weakened by sun; shrinks unless treated.	Must be dry-cleaned. Moderately expensive.
LINEN	Low resilience and elasticity; natural luster; burns easily; absorbent.	Very strong fiber; nice texture; somewhat resistant to sun and mildew.	Wrinkles easily; inconsistent in quality; somewhat stiff; shrinks unless treated.	Needs special cleaning to preserve appearance; colors may run; must be ironed. Expensive.
SILK	Lustrous; elastic; resilient; good absorbency; does not burn easily.	Strong fiber; drapes beautifully; resists mildew; colors have jewel-like tone.	Weakened by sun; water spots show unless treated; colors may run or change with age.	Dry-clean unless label indicates it can be hand-washed. Very expensive.

THE SYNTHETICS

	COMMENTS	ADVANTAGES	DISADVANTAGES	CARE/COST
RAYON	Creases easily; versatile; high absorbency and moderate elasticity; not flammable.	Drapes well; blends well with other fibers; takes color well; can be made to look like natural fibers.	Weak fiber; shrinks and stretches unless treated; weakened by sun; needs special care.	Dry-clean unless label indicates it can be hand-washed; must be ironed. Usually inexpensive.
ACETATE	Moderately good resilience and elasticity; fair absorbency; burns readily and melts.	Appears lustrous and silklike; drapes well; resistant to mildew; somewhat wrinkle-free.	Weak fiber; weakened by sun; colors fade from atmospheric fumes.	Dry-clean unless label indicates it can be hand-washed; use a cool iron. Moderately inexpensive.
ACRYLIC	Low absorbency; good resilience and elasticity; does not burn easily.	Wool-like in texture; resists mildew, moths, and sun; holds color well; fairly strong fiber.	Tends to pill; stretches somewhat; not as durable as some fibers, especially when it's wet.	Hand-wash unless labeled otherwise; hang to dry. Moderately expensive.
POLYESTER	Very good resilience and elasticity; not absorbent.	Strong fiber; resists wrinkles, moths, and mildew; blends well; doesn't stretch or shrink.	Slick to nubby textures; difficult to dye; sun exposure causes gradual loss of strength; melts in high heat.	Most items can be machine-washed and dried. Moderate cost.
NYLON	Very good resiliency and elasticity; low absorbency; melts under high heat.	Very strong; can be sponge-cleaned; blends well; lustrous; resists abrasion.	Tends to look glassy; fades and weakens from being exposed to sun.	Most items can be machine-washed and -dried. Moderate cost.
OLEFIN	Low absorbency; lightweight with good bulk; somewhat resilient and elastic; not flammable.	Strong; takes color well; good insulator; resistant to stains, sun, and mildew; resists abrasion.	Best as blend or lining due to appearance. Do not iron; can melt in high heat.	Machine wash; dry at low heat. Moderate cost.

Window Sketchbook

Browse through this sketchbook, and you'll find ideas for a variety of window and door treatments.

SINGLE WINDOWS

If you're dressing a single window (see illustrations 1–5), consider its size first. Does the window look small compared with the furnishings or the room itself? Add fullness with gathered tiebacks (4) or flowing curtains (1, 5). If its scale matches other elements, treat it simply with a shade or a top treatment (2, 3). Increase its visual size by mounting the curtain rod beyond the frame top and sides so that panels stack back over walls.

MULTIPLE/SPLIT WINDOWS

A series of identical windows (6–10) invites the light and outdoor view inside. These windows also offer numerous decorating options. First decide whether you want to treat each window separately or the series as one window. Taking a look at your room's style may give you a clue as to which approach is best. In a clean-lined contemporary setting, the geometric look of a bank of windows can be an asset. To get the full architectural impact, use a top treatment only or inside-mount identical curtain panels (6). Do you need more privacy, light control, or energy efficiency? Shades, blinds, and shutters (7, 8) mounted inside each window's molding perform those tasks and offer a tailored look. If you prefer a softer, traditional look, fabric options abound. Flowing, to-the-floor draperies (9) lend timeless elegance to spaces. Crown draperies with a sculpted cornice (10) to add height and formality, or use a cornice alone for architectural interest. For a lighter look, half-curtains can add French-cafe charm, plus privacy and sunshine; in a pared-down setting, simple side curtains add color and pattern. The all-for-one treatment applies to split windows, too, whether you treat them to shades, shutters, or swags and cascades pulled to the outer edges (11).

Window Sketchbook continued on page 422

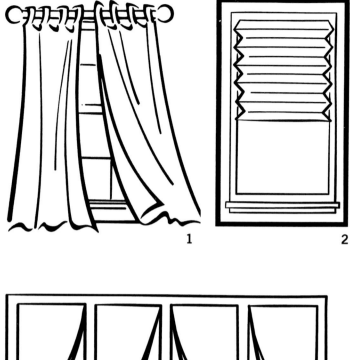

1

2

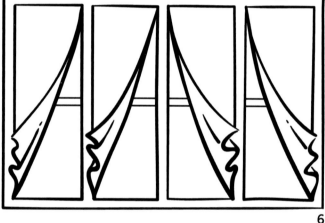

6

9

3

4

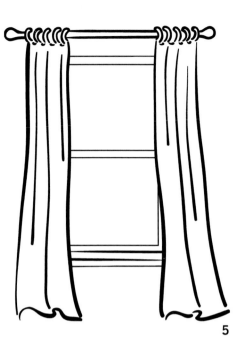

5

7

8

10

11

CORNER WINDOWS

Mirror-image dressings (1–5) allow you to treat corner windows separately but achieve the effect of a single design. Be sure draperies or vertical blinds draw to the outside, and blinds raise and lower without clashing. In small spaces, avoid fabrics with busy patterns and contrasting colors; instead match treatments to wall color to blend them into the background and expand the room.

BAY AND BOW WINDOWS

Like corner windows, the windows within a bay or bow may demand separate but equal treatment (6–10). Like matched series, there are many ways to treat bays. To keep things clean, stick with trim shades or blinds (6), or add a window seat and shutters (7). Outline those tailored treatments with fabric, such as a sweeping swag or a scalloped valance for eye-pleasing softness and color (9). Do you want to fabricate a formal look? Install framing draperies across the front of the window alcove (10), or for an airier look, add sheer panels that slide on cable wire (8). For a curving bow window, consider hanging curtains on a flexible rod that sweeps around the bow.

SLIDING DOORS

Treatments for sliding glass doors must allow free operation and access while also enhancing the doors' appearance and providing privacy and light control. Blinds, shades, draperies, panels that slide to one side, split panels that meet in the middle, or stationary curtain panels flanking the door are options (11–15). Mount treatments so they draw completely beyond the walkway. To control light and privacy, use individual blinds or shades; for more finesse, add a top treatment (12) or (not shown) layer draperies over blinds.

HIGH WINDOWS

The goal in treating high windows is to visually lower them with long treatments and/or by placing a piece of furniture beneath them. If you place a piece of furniture under the window, choose a fitted covering, such as shutters, shades, or blinds (16–18), that will stay out of the way. If your room is full of horizontal elements—beds, chests, and bureaus— add visual interest with a vertical, to-the-floor treatment (19, 20). To make windows appear larger, install a row of fixed shutters below the windows and operable shutters on the panes (17).

Window Sketchbook continued on page 424

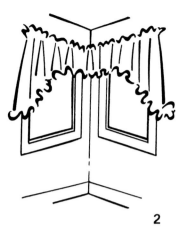

1

2

6

7

11

12

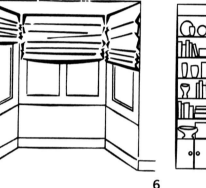

16

17

3

4

5

8

9

10

13

14

15

18

19

20

CASEMENT WINDOWS

Standard casement windows open in or out and can be treated like single windows. However, the ideal covering should mount to the outside so that it falls over the window's cranking mechanism. Swinging crane rods (1) or fixed curtain rods (3) offer good solutions, as do top/down and bottom/up fabric shades topped with a valance (2). If you choose tiebacks, dress each window in a drapery panel that draws to the outer edge of each window where tieback hardware is installed. For inward-swinging casement windows, the treatment shouldn't interfere with window operation. Inset curtains or blinds on each window (5) or inside-mount a roller shade and paint "architecture" with stenciling or freehand designs on the wall around the frame (4).

FRENCH DOORS

French doors combine the problems of outfitting inward-swinging casement windows with those of covering sliding glass doors. The solutions divide into two groups: Either affix your treatment to each door panel, or opt for a treatment that clears the doors by drawing completely to the side or top. For a look that won't interfere with the architecture, mount blinds or shades on each door (6–8). If your decorating style calls for a softer touch, consider shirred lace or fabric panels or door-mounted tiebacks. Traditional drapery treatments are viable options (9, 10). Simply make sure the rod extends well beyond the frame so draperies can be drawn out of the way of the doors.

TRANSOMS, SIDELIGHTS, SKYLIGHTS

The trick to treating windows with sculptural curves and unusual shapes is to flow with the curve or bend with the angle of the opening without sacrificing light or privacy. For windows topped with stationary transom-style panes (11, 12), leave the upper windows bare, or treat the transom panes and lower windows as one with the rod installed at the ceiling line. For doors with sidelights (13), treat the two as one whether you use curtains, sheers, blinds, or shades. Palladian-inspired half-round windows (14) are most spectacular when they're minimally dressed. For skylights, filter sunlight with stationary sheer panels (15) or remote-controlled motorized shades.

1

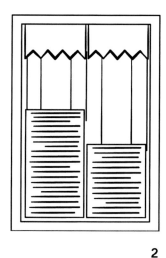

2

6

7

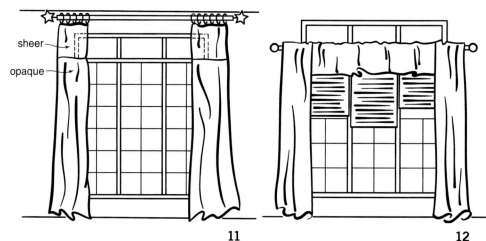

sheer

opaque

11

12

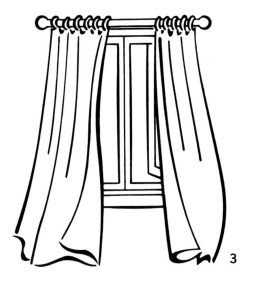

3

4

5

8

9

10

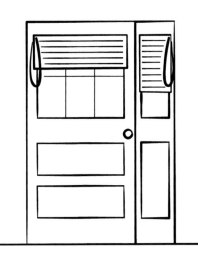

13

14

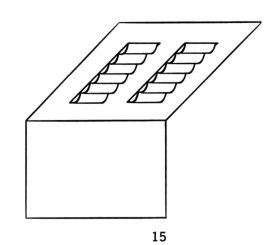

15

FlooringFacts

Selecting the right floor covering to beautifully underscore your room's style

means looking beyond that gorgeous color, bold pattern, or rich wood grain. Will the flooring stand up to heavy traffic? Does it fit your room's style and your comfort demands? For example, hardwood or hard surfaces are better for relieving allergies and maintaining indoor air quality, and vinyls and laminates help you save money. Shop around, and you'll see that you can find a floor covering to fit nearly every job description—and, yes, you can have that gorgeous color, bold pattern, or rich wood you love too. To make the right match, check out our flooring chart.

CARPET AND RUG CONSTRUCTION

	CHARACTERISTICS	ADVANTAGES	DISADVANTAGES	CARE/COST
COTTON	Soft fiber often used for informal area or scatter rugs.	Easily dyed.	Limited durability.	Cleans very well; some rugs machine-washable. Usually inexpensive.
WOOL	Deep, warm, rich look; excellent resiliency and abrasion resistance; has a warm and natural feel.	Excellent durability; flame-resistant; crush-resistant; dyes well in a wide range of colors.	Can be damaged by alkaline detergents; needs moth-proofing; not best medium for bright colors.	Resists soil; not cleaned as easily as many synthetic fibers. Expensive.
COIR, JUTE, AND SISAL	Used for informal matting; available in colors (mainly earth tones); can be stenciled or painted.	Offers textural contrast and a variety of patterns.	Fair-to-poor durability and resistance to wear and soil; not as soft underfoot as conventional carpet.	Offers little resistance to soil; not easily cleaned. Usually inexpensive.
ACRYLIC	Of the synthetic fibers, closest to wool; nonallergenic; resists mildew, moths, and insects; comes in a range of colors.	Crush-resistant; springy; fade-resistant; generates minimal static.	May form pills, or beadlike balls of fiber, on face of carpet; not as resilient, as durable, or as stain-resistant as wool or nylon.	Cleans very well; smooth fibers resist soil. Moderate price.
NYLON	Wide choice of colors; excellent color retention; soft and resilient.	Strongest synthetic fiber; resists abrasion, mildew, and moths; nonallergenic; continuous filament fibers minimize pilling and shedding.	Static-prone unless treated; cut-filament loop carpet may pill.	Good cleanability; stain-resistant treatments offer effective stain protection. Moderate price.
POLYESTER	Similar to wool in look and feel; good color and texture selection and color retention; resists moths, mildew; nonallergenic.	Very durable, resilient; abrasion- and static-resistant; sheds moisture; available in a wide range of colors.	Does not wear as well as wool or nylon; some pilling and shedding; susceptible to oil-base stains.	Good cleanability, enhanced by stain-resistant treatments. Less expensive than nylon or wool carpet.
OLEFIN	Primarily loop and randomly sheared textures; nonabsorbent; resists abrasion, pilling, and shedding.	Fibers can withstand moisture; use indoors or outdoors; very durable in level-loop styles.	Lower grades may crush and flatten.	Excellent cleanability, especially with stain-resistant treatments; resists static, acids, chemicals. Moderate price.

RESILIENT AND HARD SURFACE

	CHARACTERISTICS	ADVANTAGES	DISADVANTAGES	CLEANABILITY
ASPHALT TILE	Porous; resists alkalies; low cost.	OK on cement floor; can be below grade.	Noisy; dents easily; needs waxing.	Damaged by grease and harsh cleaners.
CORK TILE	Handsome, sealed surface.	Warm; comfortable, and quiet underfoot.	Not for heavy traffic.	Easy upkeep; must be sealed for durability.
RUBBER TILE	Handsome, clear colors.	Excellent resilience; quiet; durable.	Expensive; slippery when wet; must be above grade.	Resists dents and stains; damaged by strong detergents and grease.
VINYL COMPOSITION	Resists alkalies; easy to install; low cost.	Durable; colorful.	Not very quiet or resilient.	Embossed surfaces trap dirt; clean with heavy-duty detergents.
CUSHIONED SHEET VINYL	Wide range of colors, patterns, surface finishes, and prices.	Superior resilience; quiet; comfortable; stain-resistant.	Expensive; lower-cost grades susceptible to nicks and dents.	Easy upkeep; no-wax or never-wax feature available
SHEET VINYL	Wide range of colors, patterns, and surface finishes available.	Good resilience.	Less expensive grades susceptible to nicks and dents.	Easily maintained; some with no-wax feature.
SOLID VINYL TILE	Often simulates natural materials.	Easy to install; durable.	Only fair resilience.	Stain-resistant; easy to clean and maintain.
WOOD	Natural or painted; wide range of patterns possible.	Good resilience; hardwoods very durable.	Softwoods less durable than hardwood counterparts.	Should be sealed with a penetrating oil sealer (with wax protector) or waterproof polyurethane; manufactured floors usually are presealed.
BRICK, SLATE, QUARRY TILE	Natural look; variety of exciting shapes.	Durable; beautiful.	No resilience.	Slate and quarry tile may need sealer; good stain resistance.
STONE (GRANITE, LIMESTONE, ETC.)	Offers a natural look.	Durable; beautiful.	No resilience.	Some types absorb stains easily.
CERAMIC TILE	Colorful; many shapes and designs.	Beautiful; stain- and fade-resistant.	No resilience; cold underfoot; noisy under hard-soled shoes.	Clean with soap and water only.
MARBLE	Costly; formal.	Beautiful.	Hard underfoot; noisy under hard-soled shoes; stains easily.	Needs waxing; stains are difficult to remove.
TERRAZZO	Smooth, shiny finish; variety of multicolor effects.	Durable; stain- and moisture-resistant.	Comes in limited designs; permanent installation.	Easily cleaned.
CONCRETE	Design flexibility; wide range of colors and patterns.	Mimics other materials, including stone and tile, at lower cost.	Porous; seal so stains don't penetrate.	Easily cleaned.
LAMINATES	Wide range of colors and patterns; wood and stone looks available.	Scratch- and stain-resistant.	Some types prone to water damage unless sealed; some need underlayment to deaden sound.	Easily maintained; avoid wet mopping.

Decorating Taste Test: What's Your Style?

Decorating at its best is a self-portrait. Your rooms reflect your individuality through the colors, furnishings, and accessories you choose. Created in the spirit of fun, the Decorating Taste Test is designed to help you explore your personal style. Choose your answers honestly. If none of the answers is exactly you, select the one closest to your taste. When you've finished, transfer your answers to the scoring columns on the next page; then analyze the results to find what your answers reveal about your decorating personality. (For more fun, have your partner take the test too and then compare answers.)

1. **In your dream-house dreams, you picture yourself settled happily into:**
a. A Victorian "painted lady" with a carriage house and garden, all lovingly restored
b. An architect-designed log home wrapped in window walls and woods and lake views
c. A gallery-style loft with skylights and skyline views in a renovated warehouse

2. **Browsing through the neighborhood bookstore, you spot one title you can't resist adding to your decorating library:**
a. Romantic Style
b. Second Home: Finding Your Place in the Fun
c. Bauhaus for Today

3. **You've inherited an antique pine farm table for the dining room. For seating, you:**
a. Search for chairs of the same vintage
b. Paint mismatched chairs cottage-style white
c. Pull up post-modern metal chairs

4. **You never miss your favorite TV "home" show:**
a. This Old House
b. Trading Spaces
c. Extreme Homes

5. **Out of three invitations, you choose to attend:**
a. An estate sale at an 1896 mansion
b. A street fair featuring local artisans
c. A lecture on Japanese pottery

6. **The colors you love to live with come from:**
a. The jewel box
b. The flower garden
c. The beach

7. **For you, the perfect reading chair would be:**
a. An antique Chippendale wing chair, upholstered in toile de Jouy
b. A down-filled chair-and-a-half and ottoman, upholstered in chenille
c. A steel-and-leather Le Corbusier chaise with a pashmina throw

8. **On a "do as you please" weekend, you:**
a. Work on genealogy on the Internet
b. Dive into that long list of do-it-yourself projects around the house
c. Grab your camera and shoot some arty black and white images for framing

9. **Your sofa needs fluffing up, so you choose:**
a. Matching accent pillows for each end
b. A large pillow at one end and two or three smaller ones in mixed fabrics at the other
c. One or two exquisite handcrafted pillows

10. **For a special dinner party, you dress the table to the nines with:**
a. Grandmother's Limoges china, antique crystal, and a big bouquet of cabbage roses
b. Mismatched handcrafted pottery, stainless flatware, and wildflowers in a basket
c. Square white plates, colorful chopsticks, and gerbera daisies in a metal pitcher

11. **Your living room seating has been begging for slipcovers, so you choose:**
a. Damask for the sofa, velvet for chairs
b. Cotton duck for the sofa, denim for chairs
c. Natural linen over all

12. **If you could find a special piece of art for that needy spot over the mantel, it would be:**
a. A gilt-framed, period English landscape
b. A folk-art painting of children
c. An African kuba cloth framed in black

13. **You're off on that long-awaited vacation to:**
a. Tour the homes of Colonial Williamsburg
b. Cruise the Mississippi River on a houseboat
c. Visit the Napa Valley for a wine-tasting tour

14. **When the Antiques Roadshow rolls into town, the treasure you bring for appraisal is:**
a. Your Grandmother's Imari plate
b. The crazy quilt you found at a garage sale
c. Your childhood cache of Star Wars figures

15. **For your living room windows, you choose:**
a. An English floral swag-and-jabot treatment
b. Roman shades in natural linen
c. The view, so you leave windows undressed

16. **The person, past or present, you'd love to invite to your next dinner party is:**
a. English gardener Gertrude Jekyll
b. Actor Tom Hanks
c. Architect Frank Lloyd Wright

17. **If you bought a new bed, it would be:**
a. A carved mahogany four-poster
b. A pine frame and garden-gate headboard
c. An upholstered platform bed

18. **On weekends, you're likely to wear:**
a. Khakis and a cashmere sweater
b. Jeans and a buffalo-check shirt
c. Jeans and a white silk shirt

19. **The best gift your home ever received is:**
a. Antique candlesticks you wired into lamps
b. A wicker trunk you use as a coffee table
c. Iron finials you display as sculpture

20. **To reflect your personality and interests, what mood do you want your home to convey?**
a. Gracious ease with timeless furnishings—nothing stuffy, but tradition is important
b. Comfort first with relaxed furnishings and natural textures in an un-self-conscious mix
c. A sophisticated love of design with restrained schemes and varied-vintage classics—editing is your forte because you dislike clutter.

Scoring

After you've circled "a," "b," or "c" for each question, transfer your answers to the appropriate columns below. Then total each column at the bottom. The column with the highest score indicates the decorating mood that suits you best.

COLUMN 1	COLUMN 2	COLUMN 3
1. a	1. b	1. c
2. a	2. b	2. c
3. a	3. b	3. c
4. a	4. b	4. c
5. a	5. b	5. c
6. a	6. b	6. c
7. a	7. b	7. c
8. a	8. b	8. c
9. a	9. b	9. c
10. a	10. b	10. c
11. a	11. b	11. c
12. a	12. b	12. c
13. a	13. b	13. c
14. a	14. b	14. c
15. a	15. b	15. c
16. a	16. b	16. c
17. a	17. b	17. c
18. a	18. b	18. c
19. a	19. b	19. c
20. a	20. b	20. c
TOTAL	TOTAL	TOTAL

Analyzing the Results

Now have fun using your answers to decide which of three main decorating moods best suits your tastes—classic, casual, clean and simple, or a mix. No matter what decorating style you prefer—romantic, cottage, 18th century, Art Deco, modern—it can fit into any of these basic categories. For instance, graceful Chippendale chairs can go formal or minimalist, depending on your room's mood.

CLEARLY CLASSIC If most of your answers were in Column 1, you like formality, and your home may be a gracious melding of timeless, classic furnishings in symmetrical groupings. In this broad category, you may choose from period French, 18th-century Chippendale, or Queen Anne furnishings, as well as Oriental and formal modern pieces. You mix antiques, quality reproductions, and lovingly collected accessories. Colors are often rich and mellow.

CASUAL COMFORT If the majority of your answers were in Column 2, you like a casual decorating style. You choose furnishings with relaxed comfort in mind, and you prefer unfussy seating with carefree fabrics in earthy or neutral colors. Seating is arranged in informal groupings for easy conversation. Your favorite things include lighthearted and whimsical accessories. Your home's only demand: Put your feet up and enjoy.

CLEAN AND SIMPLE If most of your answers were in Column 3, you like a sophisticated, elegantly simple look inspired by your interests in art and design. You carefully edit furnishings and accessories, choosing each element, whether modern or traditional, for its distinctive lines and integrity of form. Even color is often kept to a minimum, with hues drawn from the neutrals—especially black, white, and gray—often punched up with a brilliant accent color, such as red.

PERSONALITY MIX If your answers are spread over all three categories, you're confident about your personal style and want to combine the best from several design periods and styles. Chances are that your answers lean, at least slightly, toward one of the main categories. The key is to understand and heed your main attitude toward furnishing your home so you can combine disparate elements into a harmonious whole. For instance, if you lean toward simplicity but also love the classics, you might team Chippendale dining chairs with a sleek glass-top dining table for the best of both styles.

Your fun challenge is to create beautiful, comfortable rooms that draw on the best resource of all—your personality.

TO FIND OUT MORE ONLINE, VISIT US @ www.bhg.com/bkhousehome

Index